Equality BY STATUTE

Equality BY STATUTE

LEGAL CONTROLS
OVER GROUP DISCRIMINATION

by Morroe Berger

WITH A FOREWORD BY
ROBERT M. MacIVER

New York 1952

COLUMBIA UNIVERSITY PRESS

Published in Great Britain, Canada, and India
by Geoffrey Cumberlege, Oxford University Press
London, Toronto, and Bombay

Manufactured in the United States of America

IN MEMORY OF MY FATHER
AND MY BROTHER

FOREWORD

by Robert M. MacIver

FOR the first time, in this country, the question of what law can and cannot do, should and should not attempt to do, toward the reduction or abolition of intergroup discrimination has become a matter of practical importance. The reason is that in this country, for the first time, a substantial movement of public opinion has developed against such discriminatory attitudes. We shall not ask why this movement has taken place. The fact suffices for the argument. State after state, responsive to the movement, has been passing laws to give it further impetus. Law adds the sanction of enforcement to a general rule. Law is meaningless, or rather it is not law, unless it has the power, and makes some kind of use of the power, to punish the violator of the rule it enacts.

What is the impact of these new laws? The commissions entrusted with their implementation have been wary of bringing violators before the courts. They have preferred on the whole to use methods of persuasion and education, with direct enforcement as a reserve power to back their authority. How far have they succeeded? How far can they be expected to succeed? In this book Morroe Berger reviews the evidences with clarity and cogency. He offers a valuable conspectus of the judicial and legal components of a movement that, in ways many of our people hardly dream of, is of primary significance for the well-being of this country and for its place in world history.

In addition he addresses himself to the background issue, the relation of new laws to old traditions, broadly the relation of laws to morals and to social attitudes. A good deal of the resistance to antidiscrimination laws rests its case on assumptions concerning this relationship. Here I shall add a few words in support of Mr. Berger's position.

No law should require men to change their attitudes, but most laws require something that is contrary to the attitudes of some group of men, whether large or small. No law should punish men for their beliefs or attempt to suppress these beliefs, but many laws are necessary or desirable that require behavior contrary to what some men approve or believe to be the right course. The whole sphere of opinion must be held inviolate by law, if the primary condition of democracy is to be fulfilled. But it does not follow that the behavior prompted by opinion or belief should not be regulated for the public good. The distinction is elementary. In a democracy we do not punish a man because he is opposed to income taxes, or to free school education, or to vaccination, or to minimum wages, but the laws of a democracy insist that he obey the laws that make provisions for these things.

On the same principle there should be no laws against ethnic or racial prejudice. A man should never be subject to legal penalties because he is anti any thing, anti any group, anti any faith, anti any form of government. If he is foolish enough to detest any people as such or to think he belongs to the master race, and if we cannot teach him the foolishness of his folly, then let him stew in it, so long as he does not seek to injure in overt ways those against whom his prejudice is directed. We may not let our "righteousness" interfere with the liberty of any opinion, for that is the beginning of the road to totalitarianism itself. Righteous indignation can be the most insidious enemy of democracy.

So let him think what he will, and if besides he refuses to associate socially with the groups he regards as his inferiors, let him narrow the boundaries of his world and make his folly the limit of his experience. In his private relationships he can discriminate as he pleases. But when he runs a factory or a hotel it is different, for now his activity is invested with a public interest. In his business he cannot treat his employees as he pleases. He cannot pay them what wages he pleases or work them as many hours as he pleases or under what conditions he pleases. The same considerations of public welfare can properly limit his right to discriminate as he pleases when hiring his employees, to reject members of groups against which he is prejudiced, if he rejects them not on grounds of qualification but instead to gratify his bias. Here too important considerations of public welfare are involved—and they reach up to the very highest interests of the state, for precisely this kind of discrimination, especially against the members of the "colored" peoples, is a major factor in defeating the world influence and the world leadership that this country is now called upon to assume.

If we clearly understood the flagrant evils, domestic and international, that antigroup discrimination inflicts upon us, we would no longer look with suspicion on the new laws and the new court decisions that seek to diminish it. It is in a way curious that people who support a considerable amount of moralistic legislation that is contrary to the mores and a direct violation of the private life should cry out against this equitable legislation that is in line with the changing mores, violates no one's private affairs, and does no more than assert the cause of fair play and fair dealings among the groups that together constitute the nation to which we owe a common loyalty and common service.

ACKNOWLEDGMENTS

I am indebted to several persons, organizations, and publishers for help in writing this book. My main debt is to Robert M. MacIver, not only for his guidance at every stage of its preparation, or for his introduction, but also for his encouragement and wise counsel over many years on many matters. I want to thank Mr. Osmond K. Fraenkel, and Professors Robert L. Hale and Noel T. Dowling of Columbia University, who offered valuable advice on Chapters Two and Three. To Mr. Will Maslow and Mr. Roderick Stephens I am indebted for the opportunity to learn their views and to consult their data on the subject of Chapter Four. My main obligation concerning that chapter is to Commissioner Caroline K. Simon and Mr. Milton Rosenberg, of the New York State Commission Against Discrimination. The labor of preparing the manuscript for the press was considerably eased by Miss Anne Wiener and Miss Audrey Meltzer.

Thanks are due to the American Jewish Committee, especially Mr. Edwin J. Lukas, the director of its Civil Rights Department, for making publication possible.

The *Columbia Law Review* and the *Cornell Law Quarterly* have kindly permitted the use of material, in Chapters Three and Four respectively, which first appeared in those journals.

Mr. Charles W. Collins has kindly granted permission to quote from his book, *The Fourteenth Amendment and the States*, published by Little, Brown and Company in 1912.

Finally, I want to thank the following publishers for permission to quote from books they have published:

Columbia University Press: *Studies in Southern History and Politics* (1914).

Cornell University Press: *Federal Protection of Civil Rights*

(1947), by Robert K. Carr; and *Safeguarding Civil Liberty Today* (1945).

Franklin and Marshall College: *The Task of Law* (1944), by Roscoe Pound.

Harcourt, Brace and Company: *The Negro Ghetto* (1948), by Robert C. Weaver.

Harper and Brothers: *Patterns of Segregation* (1943), by Charles S. Johnson; *The Communication of Ideas* (1948), ed. by Lyman Bryson; *An American Dilemma* (1944), by Gunnar Myrdal, with the collaboration of Arnold Rose and Richard Sterner; *Discrimination and National Welfare* (1949), ed. by Robert M. MacIver.

Kegan Paul, Trench and Trubner (London): *The Theory of Legislation* (1931), by Jeremy Bentham.

The Johns Hopkins University Press: *The Adoption of the Fourteenth Amendment* (1908), by Horace E. Flack.

The Macmillan Company: *The Web of Government* (1947) and *The More Perfect Union* (1948), by Robert M. MacIver; *Lectures on the Relation between Law and Public Opinion in England during the Nineteenth Century* (1914), by A. V. Dicey.

Princeton University Press: *Gauging Public Opinion* (1944), by Hadley Cantril.

Viking Press: *A Man Called White* (1948), by Walter White.

Yale University Press: *The Twilight of the Supreme Court* (1934), by Edward S. Corwin; *A Union Officer in the Reconstruction* (1948), by John W. de Forest; *Social Control Through Law* (1942), by Roscoe Pound.

M. B.

February, 1952

CONTENTS

Equality BY STATUTE

INTRODUCTION

"WHERE assurance of good conduct in . . . fields of public concern has not been forthcoming from citizen groups," observed President Truman's Commission on Higher Education in 1947, "the passage of laws to enforce good conduct has been the corrective method of a democratic society."

But can the passage of laws really enforce good conduct if the laws are not popularly supported—as, in fact, has often been the case in Western society and in the United States? Morris R. Cohen once made a remark that must always be considered simultaneously with this observation of the President's Commission. "That in a democracy the law is the will of the people," he said, "is a statement not of a fact but of an aspiration." Laws can be enacted in response to the demands of a small minority, or without the knowledge of the majority; and much law is created by courts and administrative agencies, not merely by representative legislatures.

Americans seem to want laws expressing high ideals, but they seem also to want the convenience of ignoring or violating many of them with impunity. Our Federal Constitution and statutes clearly require a general equality of treatment for all individuals, but our conduct just as clearly denies this condition to many millions, citizens and noncitizens, in all regions. In recent years, Americans have shown some concern over the difference between the broad legal standard on the one hand and particular legal measures and discriminatory practices on the other. This interest in civil rights has taken an especially legal turn: those who want to improve group relations show a new reliance upon law as a means of social control.

Such reliance, in the specific forms it has taken, and by the groups which manifest it, is something relatively new in this country. In the past, two notions affecting minority groups have been dominant. First, it has been held that each man should be judged as an individual, that he should be limited by nothing except his own capabilities and inclinations, and by the restraints that apply equally to all of us regardless of color, religion, or national origin. At the same time we have been skeptical of government in most realms, believing in as few governmental restraints as possible. Before the first of these two values could be effectively promoted by law, it was necessary that the second be considerably modified. This modification occurred slowly after World War I and more rapidly during the 1930s. When the conditions of continuous crisis and international prominence focused the attention of Americans upon intergroup relations, the nation was prepared to apply the machinery of government to a problem that was felt to be one affecting the whole community, not merely the disadvantaged groups within it. Given this revived interest in civil rights, it is understandable that it has relied upon law and government more directly and profoundly than during previous periods of similar interest.

Law, we have learned, can work both ways. It can sustain discrimination, as it does throughout the South and in some states in the North, or it can sustain equal rights, as it has been doing more and more in the last decade or so. Many opponents of laws against discrimination argue that such behavior, based upon private attitudes and tastes, cannot be altered by law. Yet they themselves usually support laws which require discrimination. To accept their position (and that of many well-meaning persons who misunderstand law) would be to say that where a law is backed by the community it is unnecessary, and where a law is opposed by the community it is futile. This view, implied more often than stated, simply ignores the real problem of the effective limits of legal controls in specific situations. Those who deny the efficacy of law in group relations must, to be consistent, favor the repeal of the vast network of legislation which now imposes and supports discriminatory patterns through the requirement of segregation. If all such laws in the South were to be immediately removed, no one, of course, would expect that there would be free relations between Negroes and whites. There are, after all, no laws requiring the exclusion of Jews from many places which effectively exclude them, and Negroes encounter discrimination even where the law forbids it. But the elimination of discriminatory legislation would at least pull out another of the props that support a system of relations which violates the Federal Constitution and even the stated values of the violators themselves.

The opponents of group equality know the influence of law: they use it to defend their own values and would deny its power to defend opposite values. Despite the attempt to spread confusion on the role of law, it is nevertheless clear where the law, as a whole, stands. It stands, in this country, against discrimination, enforced segregation, and any other kind of inequality in word or fact. This makes the opponents of equal opportunity rebels against the law, and impels them to devise schemes to circumvent its clear intent. The defenders of equality are the defenders of law, and this is usually a source of genuine superiority in moral position; it is increasingly becoming a source of superiority in political and legal position as well.

In recent years this legal position has been greatly strengthened on both the state and federal levels. While there has been no new major civil rights legislation by Congress, the executive and judicial branches of the federal government have made substantial contributions to the improvement of minority status, minority welfare, and intergroup relations. Legislation, meanwhile, has been the chief legal means of the states to accomplish the same ends.

I have attempted in the following chapters to describe and evaluate some of these developments from the Reconstruction period to the most recent years, both on federal and on state levels. In the final chapter I have attempted to formulate some general principles on the relation between law and custom, public opinion and the mores, and to evaluate the efficacy of law as a means of controlling prejudice and discrimination.

CHAPTER ONE

Civil Rights Today and During the
Reconstruction Era

THERE have been two widely separated periods during which the American people and their government have been profoundly concerned with group relations. The first wave of interest came in the wake of the Civil War, the second began in the mid-1930s and continues to the present day. Both periods show great reliance upon the apparatus of government, federal and state, to make good the promise of democracy and equality of opportunity. But in the recent and current period attempts have been made to deal specifically with problems left over from the earlier era of accomplishment.

Just after the Civil War "group relations" meant almost exclusively the relations between Negroes and whites, and governmental machinery was put to the task of making the Negro a full citizen in all respects and in somewhat wholesale fashion. In our own day we are dealing with the reforms not completed and with those which were undone in the years following the Reconstruction. Current concern with group relations, further, deals not only with Negroes, but also with religious minorities and with Americans of foreign birth or parentage. In addition, current efforts to improve group relations do not usually lead to broad civil rights measures designed to protect minorities in all areas of life; rather, they are specific, separate drives in various areas, such as employment, education, housing, and voting.

Perhaps the most significant difference between these two

periods of interest in civil rights derives from the fact that just prior to the recent period the concept of the proper role of government underwent a fairly rapid change—a change in a direction already noticeable before the 1930s. The acceleration under the New Deal gave the federal government more direct power in economic affairs, which was reflected clearly in the welfare and status of minority groups, especially Negroes. In this chapter we shall discuss the two periods of interest in civil rights and group relations, as well as the effects of the New Deal and the changing role of government upon these aspects of American life.

CIVIL RIGHTS DURING THE RECONSTRUCTION

As we shall see in greater detail in Chapter Two, Congress at the end of the Civil War enacted five laws and successfully proposed three constitutional amendments to strengthen the freedom of the recently liberated Negroes. The Thirteenth Amendment (1865) abolished slavery. The Civil Rights Act of 1866, intended to combat the Black Codes, guaranteed Negroes "full and equal benefit of all laws and proceedings for the security of person and property." To remove all doubt as to the constitutionality of this law, Congress soon submitted to the states the Fourteenth Amendment (finally ratified in 1868), which forbids the states to make or enforce laws limiting certain rights of United States citizens and of other persons. In 1867 Congress outlawed peonage. Three years later the Fifteenth Amendment took effect, protecting the Negro's right to vote. In 1870, too, Congress reenacted the Civil Rights Act of 1866. The following year Congress passed a law protecting all persons in the exercise of their rights under the Federal Constitution. In 1875 Congress enacted a comprehensive law to guarantee all persons equal accommodations in public places and means of transportation.

By these acts and amendments Congress sought to raise the

Negro to full status as an American citizen. Chapter Two will show how this intention was thwarted by Supreme Court decisions; in addition, political developments in the entire country as well as economic affairs which distracted the nation from the "Negro problem" rendered most of this program futile at least during the immediate period of its inception.

The states, too, were interested in civil rights in this period. Most of the state legislation between 1865 and 1883 was enacted in the South, where Negro and white Republicans controlled the governments.[1] Some notion of the effect of the federal laws to advance Negro rights is revealed in the data, compiled by William Watson Davis, on their enforcement during the period 1870–97, especially in the South.[2] During those years the federal courts throughout the country handled about 7,500 criminal cases under the federal "force acts." Of these, about 5,100 were heard in thirteen Southern states. Of the national total, about 1,400 cases, or nearly 20 percent, led to convictions; in the South there was about the same proportion of convictions. Over two thirds of the cases in the South came in the years 1871–75, after which there was a substantial drop. Because most of the prosecutions occurred in the South, the cost of maintaining the federal courts there accounted for about half of the total annual expenditure by the Department of Justice in all thirty-seven states. During the five most active years, 96 percent of all such cases were in the Southern states. The Southern federal courts handled 263 cases in 1871, 832 in 1872, 1,271 in 1873, 954 in 1874 and 221 in 1875. After that the number of Southern cases fell below 200 per year. In 1878, the year following the withdrawal of federal troops from the last of the Southern states in which they were stationed, those states had only twenty-five criminal cases under the federal civil rights laws. In the entire period 1870–97, the four states with the largest number of prosecutions were South Carolina (1,519); Mississippi (1,172); North Carolina (623); and Tennessee (509).

According to Davis, there were "three fatal defects" in the enforcement of this legislation in the South after indictments had been obtained. First, the prosecution had to prove "conspiracy" and "intent" to deny the rights of persons under the Constitution. Federal judges insisted upon reasonable testimony. Besides, the whites more and more predominated on juries, and white judges were lenient toward other whites prosecuted under the testimony of Negroes. "Race prejudice," Davis concludes, "thus checked the rigid application of the law." Second, the twenty-four federal district courts in the South could not handle so many cases. Grand juries and marshals indicted and arrested ten times as many offenders as the courts could try at the time. Third, the United States Supreme Court, "through a process of reasoning very similar to that of Democratic legislators, deprived the enforcement legislation of much strength."

The great watershed in this early period of national concern with the status of the nation's largest minority was the Supreme Court decision in the *Civil Rights Cases* in 1883. Previous decisions, as reviewed in Chapter Two, had already limited the federal power in this area, but the opinion in a group of cases in 1883 went even further by invalidating the Civil Rights Act of 1875. The Court held that the Fourteenth Amendment did not empower Congress to deal with "individual invasions of individual rights" and that the exclusion of Negroes from places of public accommodation was not a "badge of servitude" forbidden under the Thirteenth Amendment.

After this decision the Southern states through law supplemented the customary segregation of Negroes and whites. In the North the long-range result was the enactment of state laws similar to the invalidated federal law of 1875. In the year following the Supreme Court decision, four states passed laws of this kind, eight others did so in 1885, and still others in later years.[3]

Within a short time after the beginning of this post-Civil

War interest in civil rights, as we have already seen, the movement began to run into powerful barriers. The white Southern community could not be reconciled to federal attempts to protect the Negroes. The Supreme Court did not prove friendly to the full intent of Congress. The civil rights legislation of the Northern states, following the *Civil Rights Cases* of 1883, led to little change in the status of the vast majority of Negroes living in the South, where new legal disabilities were added to customary subjection of the former slaves. Along with these limitations upon the civil rights program came the gradual undoing of the whole Reconstruction policy. As early as 1870, control of the border states and Georgia returned to the conservative whites. In those states which they still dominated, the reconstructionists did not prevail in the white counties but only in the Negro areas. As they gathered strength and political power, the whites further restricted the Negroes, and the "solid South" came into being. With the Hayes-Tilden Compromise of 1877 the last of the federal troops left the South, which continued to disfranchise the Negro by law and by sheer force.[4]

At the same time Congress itself was weakening its own civil rights acts even before the completion of the program in 1875. "The rearrangement which the acts underwent in the *Revised Statutes* of 1873," former United States Attorney General Francis Biddle has asserted, "effectively concealed the whole scheme for the protection of rights established by the three amendments and five acts by separating their provisions under unrelated chapters of the *Revised Statutes*. The act of 1894 and the codification of 1909 repealed most of the sections protecting the franchise." [5]

Twenty years after the end of the Civil War the civil rights program of the federal government not only was over, but a substantial part of what had been once put into effect had been undone. What is usually referred to as a failure, however, must be considered to have succeeded to an extent generally overlooked in the emphasis upon the unrealized part of the program. The legal measures did have effect. Southern state legislation against the Negro did not, after the passage of the Thirteenth, Fourteenth, and Fifteenth Amendments, accomplish what, to judge by the Black Codes which these amendments invalidated, some powerful sections of the white South wanted. Much of what Southern legislatures could not do constitutionally, of course, they did by subterfuge, and the white community did as a matter of custom, both reinforced by an imposing legal system of segregation and discrimination. Yet the federal and state laws did act as a deterrent to even greater disabilities, and laid the basis for the substantial gains Negroes and other groups were able to make in the decades following the Reconstruction. There is, nevertheless, no question but that the legal measures fell far short of accomplishing their stated purposes.

Five facts help explain this failure. First, the Congressional civil rights program failed in the Supreme Court partly because it cut across the issue of the federal-state balance. The Northern victory in the Civil War did not signify the total subjection of the states to the central government. Second, the interest in civil rights was not sustained over a long period of time, and the legal changes were not reinforced by other institutional changes in work, housing, recreation, and so on. The new laws were the very first breach in a strongly entrenched system. Besides, the powerful and constant opposition of the substantial white minority in the South won out over the shifting and less adamant majority throughout the nation. In contrast to this determined minority, whose main concern was the "Negro problem," the rest of the nation found other matters of interest, such as the growth of manufacture and commerce, the labor-capital disputes, and civil service reform. The majority did not focus its interest on a single matter and was obviously unwilling to go the whole extent against the Southern whites in order to implement the civil rights program in its every detail. Third, the program itself was so broad, and contained so many elements requiring special means of enforcement and varying lengths of time for their solidification in the community, that it could hardly succeed in its entirety. It aimed at the virtually immediate advancement of former slaves to the full measure of citizenship and its social and interpersonal concomitants. Such a program cannot be achieved by legal enactments in a short period of time, though it can be successfully initiated by legislation. Pushing out in all directions, the federal government could advance but little in any one of them; concentration upon a few basic situations amenable to control through law might have promoted minority group interests more intensively and enduringly. Fourth, the civil rights statutes in the Northern states did not enjoy vigorous enforcement. Most of them, unlike the current laws in the same areas of group relations, required the wronged individual to start the legal machinery functioning. Provisions of this kind are not conducive to enforcement of the rights protected in the law. Where, however, the government itself, acting for the community, initiates proceedings, as in recent state laws, enforcement is more effective. Fifth, the federal and state governments neglected much that they could accomplish administratively, without special legislation, in government employment and in the armed forces.

Most of these shortcomings have been considerably reduced in the current period of concern with group relations. Most dramatic are the new type of state laws—exemplified in the New York State Law Against Discrimination which will be discussed fully in Chapter Four—and the extent of the federal government's accomplishments without civil rights legislation. In the decades between the two waves of interest in minorities the federal and state governments have greatly increased in power; they now act in areas in which they were formerly without authority, with the result that they can protect minorities not only by legislation but also by direct fair treatment of a kind we shall now review.

THE GOVERNMENT AND MINORITY RIGHTS

It is not surprising that this renewed concern with inter-group relations should center around the functions of state and federal governments, for during the early 1930s the United States experienced a profound change in the popular conception of the role of government in the life of the community. Just as the nation lost faith in the theory of a self-regulating private economy and supported programs of state regulation of affairs previously considered private, so it had ceased to believe in the voluntary adjustment of minority grievances and turned to government for action on civil rights.

In modern times, and in greater and greater degree, the state is the main agency of social control. This was true in the United States a hundred years ago, and the full development of the trend became clear, in the twentieth century, with the advent of the New Deal in 1933.[6]

Negroes and Orientals (especially persons of Japanese descent) have been perhaps the most seriously injured groups in the United States, and we may therefore consider their advances as indicative of the general climate of group relations in recent years. It will be seen that virtually all these advances, since 1930, have resulted from governmental policy and action —with some exceptions that will be noted. The Negroes' gains, especially, have occurred in those realms where the federal government has been able to impose certain conditions and requirements. These advances themselves, however, presuppose some degree of community support or, at least, toleration of the protective activities of government. The climate of American opinion has become such that official enforcement of minority rights is not merely permitted but is even demanded. Into many important areas of group relations where prejudice, though traditional, has been weakening, government at all levels has been able to push antidiscriminatory action.

Expansion of Functions of Government

The New Deal under President Franklin D. Roosevelt, especially in its early years, penetrated into virtually every American community, rural and urban, small and large, through its many aid programs. Perhaps for the first time in American life the government was something that people responded to favorably, a help rather than an obstacle to be avoided or overcome. The New Deal's activities, many of them concerned with the working classes and the indigent, inevitably reached the Negro, who for the first time in generations found himself the object of governmental solicitude. Though it cannot be shown that President Roosevelt had the Negro especially in mind when he developed his aid programs, it is clear that his administration on the whole meant to carry out this program without regard to the color or creed of the beneficiaries. There was discrimination and unfairness in the administration of federal economic aid in the South, but such conduct was in violation of Washington policy, and responsibility for it lay with the local officials.

It was a strange alliance that kept Southern Democrats in the New Deal for so many years. The South was simply too much in need of federal funds to afford its politicians the luxury of opposing the New Deal's general program. So long as President Roosevelt made no overt moves to challenge the basic racial values of the South, its representatives were willing to vote for New Deal measures. That President Roosevelt knew well the terms of this bargain is shown by his remarks to Walter White, secretary of the National Association for the Advancement of Colored People, in 1935: "The Southerners by reason of the seniority rule in Congress are chairmen or occupy strategic places on most of the Senate and House committees. If I come out for the anti-lynching bill now, they will block every bill I ask Congress to pass to keep America from collapsing. I just can't take that risk." [7]

During the years of the New Deal and World War II the

vast majority of Negroes lived in the District of Columbia and the following sixteen states: Delaware, Maryland, Virginia, West Virginia, North Carolina, South Carolina, Georgia, Florida, Kentucky, Tennessee, Alabama, Mississippi, Arkansas, Louisiana, Oklahoma, Texas. In 1930 these states included 79 percent of all Negroes in the United States, and in 1940 they included 77 percent of the total Negro population.[8] The governments of most of these states were undergoing changes similar to those of the federal government and the rest of the state governments in this period. Largely through federal influence, the South by 1938 was participating in the public assistance program of the federal Social Security Act and had enacted unemployment compensation laws as well as legislation on housing, soil conservation, and planning. After the early New Deal years the South intensified its welfare programs.[9]

At the same time, as Howard Odum has pointed out,[10] the nation in the 1930s rediscovered the South as a separate "problem" area after almost two decades during which there appeared to be little special interest in the South. In the depression and New Deal eras, studies of Southern resources and Southern economy labeled that area as the nation's "Number One economic problem," while politically the South became synonymous with conservatism. Following this attention upon the South came the influence of World War II, when the "American dream," of which more Americans became aware during the national crisis, was shown to be far from realization in the entire country, but especially and startlingly so in the South. Under the impact of depression and war, then, the nation turned again to an examination of its own limitations, and Americans from all regions, the South included, looked upon that group of states as most in need of adjustment to the ideals of democracy.

Industrialization and Urbanization in the South

The South, meanwhile, during and after the New Deal, was experiencing certain economic changes which have brought it more into line with the rest of the United States. From 1900 to 1940, for example, the South did not gain proportionately so much in total population as the United States, but it did gain proportionately more in urban population and in the number of gainful workers. In the decade 1930 to 1940, in the country as a whole the number of wage earners fell by 11 percent, while in the South it increased by 3 percent. In the three decades ending in 1930 the number of workers in the nation's mechanical and manufacturing industries nearly doubled, but the number of such workers in the South doubled and then increased by almost one half again.[11]

The increasing industrialization of the South becomes apparent in another set of data. In 1929, 15 percent of all the manufacturing workers in the United States were in Southern states; by 1939 this proportion had risen to 17 percent. Before World War II the South had a little more than a million and a half workers in manufacturing. At the peak of the war boom in November, 1943, this number had increased by about 70 percent. In August, 1946, the South still had about two and a quarter million workers in manufacturing, an increase of 40 percent above the prewar figure.[12]

Urbanization has accompanied the industrialization of the South. The urban population of the United States as a whole remained virtually stationary from 1930 to 1940, increasing by only 0.3 percent, to reach 56.5 percent of the total population. The urban population in the South Atlantic states, meanwhile, increased from 36.1 to 38.8 percent; in the East South Central states, from 28.1 to 29.4 percent; and in the West South Central states from 36.4 to 39.8 percent.[13] Another way of measuring urbanization has been presented by Warren S. Thompson and P. K. Whelpton. They divided all counties into urban and rural, an urban county being defined as one containing a city of 10,000 or more persons in 1930, or one within ten miles of a city of 100,000; a rural county was one not classified as urban. Only about half of the urban counties in the United States as a whole increased their population by 7 percent or more in the decade 1930–40, but more than three fourths of the urban counties in the South Atlantic states, and about two thirds of those in the East South Central states, experienced a like increase. (We omit from consideration the four West South Central states, since they include Arkansas, Oklahoma, and Texas, which had abnormal population changes owing to the developments in the "dust bowl.") Within each Southern area, too, the urban counties gained more than the rural. In the South Atlantic states 78 percent of the urban counties gained at least 7 percent, while only 41 percent of the rural counties made that gain. In the East South Central states 67 percent of the urban and only 48 percent of the rural counties gained 7 percent or more. In the West South Central states, too, this differential still held, with 49 percent of the urban and only 35 percent of the rural counties gaining 7 percent or more in their population.[14]

Increasing urbanization and industrialization, though they may result in greater racial tension for a while, have a tendency to reduce minority discrimination in the long run. The anonymity and impersonality of urban life make large numbers of people indifferent to the propaganda of bigots. Political liberalism and trade unionism, both of which work in the direction of greater minority rights, are urban rather than rural phenomena. Finally, in urban areas a minority is able to exert political influence as a concentrated pressure group with a bloc of votes that is attractive to all political parties. In an industrial, urban area the racial tension is likely to lead to large-scale violence, as in the Detroit and New York riots in recent years. These outbreaks, often the result of interracial contact under conditions of poor and insufficient housing or of employment rivalry, do not mean that discrimination is rising. The absence of overt tension between majority and minority is not necessarily a sign of good group relations, for such relations require more and more intergroup contacts on a basis of equality, and it is almost inevitable that the increased contacts will lead also to increased tension and violence. But in urban areas the *setting* for reasonably good group relations exists. Especially for the Negro, inferiority has been an accompaniment of the rural, feudal economy of the South and of its legacy.

In the last two decades, then, considerable changes have occurred in this economic and social legacy, many of them stemming from the South's relations with the federal government. The economic aid extended under the New Deal was not the kind to arouse much Southern opposition on the ground that Negroes might benefit from it. The South is usually agreeable to plans to improve Negro health and housing, for example, so long as the bulk of the funds for these purposes does not come from the state treasuries but from private organizations or from Washington. Relief and work relief, aid to farm owners and laborers, and federal housing were the main types of federal aid which reached the Negroes directly, both in the South and North.

The Negro in the Federal Relief Program

The data on federal relief during the 1930s show that Negroes constituted a higher proportion of relief recipients than they did of the total population. This fact suggests, of course, that Negroes suffered more acutely from the results of the depression, but it suggests also that the relief program was administered with more respect for the need of the recipients than for their color. While payments probably did not meet all the needs of Negroes and other minorities, neither did the program meet all the needs of the rest of the American people. Equality in the need for and in the distribution of charity is, of course, not the kind of justice for which underprivileged minorities have felt the greatest respect. Yet the relatively fair way in which the federal government granted relief was something new in the experience of America's minorities.

At its height in February, 1934, the federal relief and works programs benefited about 8,000,000 households, including about 28,000,000 persons. By August, 1937, these totals had declined to 4,500,000 households and 14,000,000 persons. The "recession" beginning in that year led to an increase, and in October, 1938, there were 7,000,000 households and 21,000,-000 persons benefiting. In September, 1940, just before the United States entered upon the national defense program, the number of beneficiaries had again fallen to 5,000,000 households and 14,000,000 persons.[15]

Several studies by the Works Progress Administration indicated that Negroes received relief in a proportion higher than their proportion of the total population. In May, 1934, it was found that Negro households constituted 18.9 percent of all relief households in 79 cities, while the 1930 census showed that Negro households were but 7.6 percent of all urban households. In each of 46 Northern and Southern cities where Negro households were at least 5 percent of the total relief households, the proportion of Negro households on relief was greater than the proportion of all Negro households in the city. In 18 Southern cities and 12 Northern cities Negro households were on relief respectively in about twice and three times their proportion of the population of those cities.[16]

In point of money spent and of the number of persons benefiting, the Works Progress Administration was the largest federal relief or works program under the New Deal. In February, 1939, Negro workers constituted 14 percent of all W.P.A. workers. In April, 1941, they were 16 percent of the total, and their proportion rose to 18 percent in February, 1942, and to 20 percent in October, 1942.[17] The growing proportion of Negro W.P.A. workers from 1939 through 1942 reflected the entrance of increasing numbers of white workers

into jobs created by the war, and the Negroes' difficulty in
obtaining such employment.

The Negro in the Federal Farm Program

The New Deal farm program was carried out by the Agricultural Adjustment Administration. Though primarily an
economic program, the A.A.A. has had significant political
and social effects upon Negro-white relations in the South.
Under the terms of the statute, owners, tenants, and share-
croppers on cotton lands must vote on the continuation of the
crop restriction program. Myrdal describes the results:

Negroes have participated in unrestricted numbers in these annual elections (since 1938) and have voted in perhaps even greater
proportion than whites. They vote at the same polling places as
whites and at the same time. There is little physical opposition
from the whites because the majority favor crop control, and
they know that Negroes will vote in favor of it; they are told that
if Negroes are prevented from voting, the election will be illegal.
They also know that any irregularity would be observed by
federal administrators and vigorously prosecuted in federal courts.
Although the unrestricted voting by Negroes in the A.A.A. refer-
enda does not give them any political power, it, nevertheless, may
be of great significance. It accustoms whites to the presence of
Negroes at polling places and perhaps makes them think beyond
the myth of black domination and consider the real issues involved
in Negro voting. It provides the South with an example of elections based on significant issues and with less corruption than usual.
It also gives the Negro a chance to vote and perhaps to discover
the nature of the political process.[18]

One of the special studies made for the Carnegie Corporation project on the Negro, directed by Myrdal, obtained
data from the Agricultural Adjustment Administration which
showed that in at least one country in each of the states of
Alabama, Arkansas, Florida, Georgia, Louisiana, Mississippi,
Oklahoma, South Carolina, and Texas, the total vote in the
referendum of December, 1938, exceeded the number of white

farmers in the county, indicating some degree of Negro participation.[19]

Another important part of the New Deal farm program was carried out by the Farm Security Administration, whose main province was the standard loan program under which loans were made to improve farming methods, to enable an operator to get out of debt, or for the necessaries of life. In 1935 Negroes constituted 12.6 percent of all farm operators, and during the years 1936–39, they obtained 12.5 percent of all loans made by the F.S.A. Measured in terms of need, however, the share received by the Negroes was not equitable. While one out of five needy white families was helped by the program, only one of nine needy Negro families was helped. In 1939, loans to Negroes in sixteen Southern and border states averaged $606, compared to $659 for whites, but in five Southern states loans to Negroes averaged higher than loans to whites. In relation to net worth at the time of the loan, Negro borrowers obtained bigger loans than whites. Most Negro borrowers were able to raise their status to that of full or part owners or of tenants. The average net income of Southern Negro borrowers rose 62 percent from the year before a loan was made to the 1939 crop year.[20]

The Negro in the Federal Housing Program

Under the New Deal, Negro housing improved considerably. Robert C. Weaver has observed that public housing under the Public Works Administration and the United States Housing Authority reserved for the Negro a fair share of the new homes. Both agencies, he adds, operated in a generally nondiscriminatory spirit.[21] In the period 1933–37, Richard Sterner reports,[22] the P.W.A. built 21,319 dwelling units in forty-nine projects in thirty-six cities. Fourteen of these projects were reserved for Negroes, and another seventeen were for joint Negro-white occupancy. Negroes were provided with 7,507 dwelling units, more than a third of the total. Almost half of these units reserved for Negroes were in the South. From 1937 to July 31, 1941, the U.S.H.A. sponsored the construction of 176,000 dwelling units, of which 53,000, or about 30 percent, were for Negroes.

During World War II, says Weaver, "the extent of Negro participation in public war housing was appreciable, and, if not in accord with relative need, it did approach that need in many areas." In July, 1945, nearly 100,000 units were occupied by or planned for Negroes. This number was about 16 percent of all the public war housing units built or planned, and most of them were in the North. The extent to which Negroes depended upon the federal government for new homes is shown by the fact that while 56 percent of all war housing for whites was accomplished by private agencies, only 14 percent of all war housing for Negroes was built under private auspices.[23]

Negro War and Postwar Employment

During World War II the Negroes made substantial gains in the direction of equal opportunity, even though there were many examples of increased tension and of overt clashes.[24]

Although free Negroes in the period before the Civil War were often skilled artisans, the emancipated Negroes were barred from entering the better-paid and more pleasant kinds of work which they were either qualified to do or for which they could have been trained. It was generally during a crisis that Negroes found it possible to obtain jobs from which they had been excluded; thus in the nineteenth century they entered the meat-packing, iron and steel, and other heavy industries as strike breakers, and the shortage of unskilled labor in World War I enabled them to make further gains in these industries and in the newer fields of mass production.[25] It was likewise a labor crisis which was the occasion for the Negro's employment gains in World War II, but the labor shortage was not enough this time—the added impetus of government action was needed. The Committee on Fair Employment Practice, in its final report, listed three influences leading to the elimination of job discrimination: first, the employers' need for workers; second, the employers' patriotism; and third, the employers' dislike of being exposed as violators of the government's rules on employment procedures. The report significantly adds: "The practice [of discrimination], however, seldom disappeared spontaneously. The intervention of a third party, with authority to act if necessary, was required to start the process in motion." [26]

A wartime survey by the federal government concludes: "The greatest gain in employment opportunity has come from the opening up of jobs to Negroes as semiskilled and skilled workers, principally in factories." Among Negro males, for example, the number employed as skilled craftsmen and foremen doubled from 1940 to 1944, while the number of farm laborers decreased by about 300,000. Negro women, too, left the farms and domestic service to take factory jobs. The number employed on farms fell by 30 percent in this period, while the number of Negro women employed as skilled workers, foremen, and factory workers increased fourfold. [27]

Because of the high level of industrial activity, these gains by Negroes have been substantially maintained in the years following the end of the war production program in 1945. Another government study concludes that "reconversion of industry to peacetime activities brought no major downgrading in the occupational composition of the Negro workers." Thus in 1940 seven out of ten employed Negroes were in farming, domestic service and nonagricultural labor. In 1944, only five out of ten were employed in these jobs, and in 1947 this proportion was still the same. Among the Negro nonagricultural workers, 19.5 percent held industrial jobs in 1940. By 1944 the proportion of Negro industrial jobholders had risen to 31.2 percent, and in April, 1947, the proportion had dropped slightly to 30.2 percent. Negro clerical and sales workers in 1940 comprised only 2.3 percent of all Negro non-agricultural workers, and by 1944 these workers were 3.9 percent of the total Negro nonagricultural employees; they continued to gain in the postwar years, and in April, 1947, they comprised 4.9 percent of the total. The proportion of Negro women working as domestic servants in 1940 was 72.1 percent of all Negro women holding nonagricultural jobs. By 1944 this proportion had fallen to 49.1 percent, and it continued to fall, standing at 47.9 percent in 1947. That Negroes generally moved out of agricultural employment during World War II is shown by the fact that in 1940 34 percent of all employed Negroes worked on farms, while in 1944 only 21 percent did, and in 1947 only 17 percent were still employed in agriculture.[28]

Not only do Negroes suffer from discrimination by employers, but they are also unfairly treated by some labor unions, mainly the older craft organizations. A government study [29] showed that in 1936 twenty-two American Federation of Labor and unaffiliated unions excluded Negroes entirely, segregated them into separate locals, or barred them from holding office. In 1944 Herbert Northrup [30] was able to add one union to the list. But in 1944 and 1945 Negroes won Supreme Court cases [31] which led to modification of discriminatory practices by unions. From 1945 to the end of 1948 nine unions made discriminatory constitutional clauses inoperative in New York in order to comply with the state's Law Against Discrimination, and eight additional unions eliminated such clauses entirely.[32] The most significant gains Negroes have made in the labor unions have been in those affiliated with the Congress of Industrial Organizations. While there is some discrimination in the locals of C.I.O. unions, no national excludes Negroes from membership or segregates Negro members into separate locals.

Negro Voting

In a review of Supreme Court rulings on minority rights since 1937 we shall see that the Negro's right to vote in the Southern Democratic primary elections has been given greater and greater federal protection. Legally, no state may bar Negroes from the Democratic primary, but while it is likely that some Negroes participate in it in every Southern state, the discrimination against them is still widespread in many counties in each state. In August, 1948, for the first time since the Reconstruction period in South Carolina, a substantial number of Negroes voted in the Democratic primary. Negro leaders estimated that about 30,000 Negroes voted, out of a total of about 300,000 throughout the state.[33] In April, 1948, the chairman of the state Democratic party invited those Negroes who were qualified to vote in the Columbia city election the following month to participate in the party primary and help nominate two city council candidates.[34]

The Southern Regional Council in 1948 sponsored a study of Negro voting in the South which showed that from 1940 to 1947 the number of qualified Negro voters in twelve Southern states had increased threefold, to reach more than 600,000. This was still only 12 percent of the total number of Negroes of voting age in these states in 1947, but it compares favorably with the 2 percent qualified in 1940. The report states by way of summary: "Certainly during the last eight years [since 1940] the Negro has advanced in the exercise of the right of franchise at a much faster rate than at any other time in the past half century."[35] The National Association for the Advancement of Colored People estimated that 3,000,000 Negroes voted in 1948, compared with one million in 1944.[36]

The Negro in the Armed Forces

The inception of the war program in the United States might have provided a genuine opportunity to find out what a democratic, intelligent racial policy could accomplish. Timidity and prejudice combined to minimize that opportunity.[37] The Army, largest of the armed services, announced at the outset of the draft that Negroes would be accepted in proportion to their number in the total population. But Negroes were not so proportionately assigned their tasks in the Army, for they were concentrated in the service troops and were in general segregated. There were many incidents of unwise policy at the top level of command and bitter prejudice at lower levels. Some advances, nevertheless, were made. Negroes in the officer candidate schools were not segregated. Many more combat arms were open to Negroes than ever before, and they were given a measure of equality, though small, which was at least greater than in earlier years. On a small experimental basis, Negro infantry platoons were placed in the same companies and regiments with whites. Most of these gains have endured into the postwar period, and there have been additional gains since these.

On July 26, 1948, President Truman directed, in an executive order, "that there shall be equality of treatment and opportunity for all persons in the armed services without regard to race, color, religion or national origin." [38] In the same order the President appointed a Committee on Equality of Treatment and Opportunity in the Armed Services "to examine into the rules, procedures and practices of the armed services in order to determine in what respect such rules, procedures and practices may be altered or improved with a view to carrying out the policy of this order."

The Committee in May, 1950, summarized the progress of the Navy, Air Force, and Army. It reported that in the Navy all assignments, ratings, and schools were open to enlisted men without regard to race or color. "Negroes in general service are completely integrated with whites in basic training, technical schools, on the job, in messes and sleeping quarters, ashore and afloat." At the end of 1945 only 5 percent of the Negroes in the Navy were in general service and 95 percent were in the messman's branch; in 1950, however, 43 percent were in general service and only 57 percent in the messman's branch.[39]

The Air Force had by 1950 abolished most of the Negro segregated units. It had 1,301 mixed Negro-white units, which included about three quarters of all the 25,000 Negroes in the service; its fifty-nine Negro units included the remaining Negroes in the service. All Air Force jobs and schools were open to qualified persons without regard to race, and Negroes who served in mixed units were completely integrated with whites in living conditions as well. In the Army, however, there were fewer advances. The Army had by 1950 abolished Negro enlistment quotas and opened all jobs and schools without racial restrictions. Although Negroes serving in mixed units were fully integrated with the other soldiers on the job, in the barracks and messes, the elimination of segregation had not progressed so far as in the Navy and Air Force.[40]

Persons of Japanese Descent Since 1945

Persons of Japanese descent in the United States, though constituting a minority of only about 120,000, suffered severe discrimination by the government and by private individuals during the war, especially on the West Coast. Their exclusion from that area and their detention and subsequent resettlement is described in Chapter Three. In 1942 "loyal" persons of Japanese descent began to leave the government camps to live again in free American communities. They encountered a great deal of discrimination, but unfavorable attitudes waned as the Nisei war record became widely known. A War Relocation Authority study emphasized that acceptance of Nisei in the East and Midwest was better than "mere tolerance." The study added: "It may also be noted that during the retrenchment period immediately following the end of hostilities the fear of widespread unemployment among Nisei did not materialize, few being affected by reconversion of heavy industry." [41] Despite occasional examples of prejudiced treatment of returning veterans, Americans of Japanese descent fared much better at the hands of individuals than at the hands of the federal government—a reversal of the usual pattern of minority discrimination. Some state governments showed a new attitude. Utah and Oregon, for example, repealed their alien land laws.[42]

The record of the federal government is not entirely negative. In 1948, for example, Congress put aliens ineligible for citizenship (the Japanese immigrants) on the same basis as other aliens with respect to applications for a stay of deportation proceedings.[43] Previously the Attorney General of the United States could not suspend the deportation of those Japanese aliens who had become deportable after Pearl Harbor. Early in 1948 a federal judge held that the wartime renunciation of American citizenship by 2,300 American-born persons of Japanese descent was made under duress and hence void.[44] In another case a similar decision was upheld by the United States Circuit Court of Appeals in 1949, following which the Attorney General's office announced that the government would accept this ruling and apply it to about 4,000 other persons in a similar situation.[45] On June 1, 1948, meanwhile, Congress had ended its total ban on the naturalization of Japanese and other Orientals by permitting veterans to become naturalized citizens regardless of race.[46]

The Interest in Group Relations Since the 1930s

The developments in minority status and welfare which we have just reviewed both reflected and stimulated further concern with group relations during the last fifteen years or so, both in the community and on the part of governments at all levels.

Community interest has been manifested not only in the numerous favorable civil rights laws but also in the recent motion pictures dealing with discrimination and prejudice, the many books and articles in the mass circulation magazines on intergroup relations, and the establishment of municipal agencies in many cities to improve relations among their various groups.[47] Government, we have seen, acquired new functions and was able, in executing its tasks, to impose a greater measure of equal opportunity. Federal employment, in which minorities have usually found fairer treatment than in private employment, increased enormously. The national and local governments went into the housing industry and could thereby assure minorities both jobs and homes on a more equitable basis than they previously enjoyed. Social security, rural and urban relief, loans to farmers and home owners, federal emergency work programs—all these enabled minorities to secure relatively fair treatment. Government, bound to carry out its job without discriminating on the basis of color, religion, or national origin, inevitably gave minority groups a greater share of their due as its operations reached new fields.

Yet the federal and state governments took more direct steps, too, in attempting to improve group relations. The prolonged depression and the war which followed it had focused attention upon many fundamental political and economic problems for which a democracy, if it was to remain one and to secure its future, must find temporary or basic solutions. Nazi and fascist sponsorship had put racism in a bad light; opposition to such extremism was a favorable setting for the advancement of minorities in America.

Civil Rights in the United States Congress

From 1937 to the end of 1950 the United States Congress enacted no major law intended to advance minority rights or to improve group relations. This statement, however, conceals a great and increasing interest in the subject during this period. The 75th Congress (1937–38) introduced only ten bills of this kind; the 76th Congress (1939–40), fourteen bills; the 77th Congress (1941–42), thirty-five bills; the 78th Congress (1943–44), thirty-four; the 79th Congress (1945–46), forty-one; the 80th Congress (1947–48), fifty-one; and the

81st Congress (1949–50), seventy-two.[48] These figures include only favorable bills introduced; it is likely that the number of bills unfavorable to minorities decreased during this period.

The Civil Rights Section of the Department of Justice

Early in 1939 Attorney General Frank Murphy (later, until his death in 1949, Associate Justice of the United States Supreme Court) created a unit in the Department of Justice to study the Constitution and federal laws on civil rights, to make recommendations, and to prosecute violations of existing statutes.[49] As we shall see in Chapter Three, some of the cases handled by this unit (later called the Civil Rights Section, or C.R.S.) led to the clarification of both Constitutional and statutory law.[50] According to wartime Attorney General Francis Biddle, few of the complaints the C.R.S. received related to the violation of federal rights created by recent statutes. Rather, he remarked, the "great body of complaints is concerned with exactly the same problems with which Congress sought to deal when it first enacted the civil rights statutes; that is, the general protection of the right to vote and of the other civil rights of the Negro." [51] Robert K. Carr, who has carefully studied the work of the C.R.S., concludes that its "great achievement" has been the demonstration of the "new role of government" as a sword for the protection of civil rights, not merely a shield. "No similar administrative agency in our history," he says, "has developed a more significant program of governmental activity on such a limited basis of improvisation and experimentation. Certainly no other agency, within a period of less than a decade, has forced a greater change in our constitutional philosophy." [52]

The Federal Committee on Fair Employment Practice

The growing shortage of labor during the war and the timely application of pressure by Negro organizations led President Roosevelt to issue a directive, in 1941, creating a federal Committee on Fair Employment Practice. This response to the concern for civil rights later became a rallying point for the groups that defended the principle behind the F.E.P.C. and campaigned for legislation to establish a permanent agency to enforce the right to employment without regard to color, religion, or national origin.[53] The wartime F.E.P.C. led an uncertain life from year to year, badgered by a fairly large group of hostile Southerners in Congress and supported vigorously by a few legislators only.[54] Nevertheless, the agency's record shows some substantial gains in the elimination of employment discrimination in the federal government and in some private firms and industries.[55] More important for our purposes in this discussion, the F.E.P.C. was made the object of a political battle during which objectives were clarified and diverse organizations brought together for common action. The F.E.P.C., to its friends, was the proof that governmental controls, even of the tenuous sort granted to F.E.P.C., could materially reduce employment bias. The experience during the war spurred many persons and groups to campaign for laws to enforce fair employment practices both nationally and in the states, and this lively activity has kept the whole program before the various legislatures and the public.

Presidential Investigatory Commissions

Unlike President Roosevelt, whose deeds on behalf of minority groups were primarily in the economic realm, President Harry S. Truman has forcefully campaigned for the protection and advancement of civil rights by the appointment of investigatory bodies, the presentation of a coordinated legislative program, and the issuing of executive orders on group relations in the federal government service.

Toward the end of 1946 President Truman appointed a Committee on Civil Rights to "make recommendations with respect to the adoption or establishment, by legislation or otherwise, of more adequate and effective means and procedures for the protection of the civil rights of the people of the United States." [56] About a year later the Committee presented a report noted for its thoroughness and forthright statements. Nearly every one of its thirty-odd recommendations called for immediate federal or state legislation. One of its broad suggestions was the "elimination of segregation, based on race, color, creed, or national origin, from American life." [57]

Several months before he created the Committee on Civil Rights, President Truman had appointed a Commission on Higher Education, which made public its report a few weeks after the appearance of the former's. Devoting a chapter of one of its six volumes to discrimination, the Commission presented its findings on inequality of opportunity because of color, religion, and national origin. It, too, took a forthright stand against discriminatory practices, not hesitating to condemn segregation. "This Commission concludes," it reported, "that there will be no fundamental correction of the total condition until segregation legislation is repealed." [58] A minority of four members opposed this recommendation.[59] Rejecting the notion that "voluntary action will be adequate," the Commission urged "that educators support in their respective States the passage of carefully drawn legislation designed to make equally applicable in all institutions of higher learning the removal of arbitrary discriminatory practices in the carrying out of admissions policies." [60]

Both of these reports gained wide circulation, especially that of the President's Committee on Civil Rights. In a message to Congress endorsing the Committee's recommendations, President Truman, on February 2, 1948, urged the enactment of a federal fair employment practice law, the outlawing of the poll tax and of lynching, the strengthening of existing civil rights legislation, a law to enforce fairness in elections, an end to racial obstacles to citizenship, and the creation of a permanent commission on civil rights, of a similar joint Congressional committee, and of a civil rights division in the Department of

Justice. Of special significance was his request that Congress prohibit not merely discrimination but segregation as well in interstate transportation facilities.[61] In addressing a joint meeting of Congress in special session in the summer of 1948, the President again asked for the enactment of this program.[62]

At about the same time President Truman issued an executive order directing elimination of racial and religious discrimination in federal employment and establishing a fair employment board in the Civil Service Commission.[63] In another executive order on the same day he ordered "equality of treatment of all persons in the Armed Services without regard to race, color, religion or national origin." [64] We have already discussed the steps taken to implement this directive.

State Legislation

While the federal government has enacted few laws favoring minority groups or improving group relations, the state governments have expressed their interest in civil rights mainly through legislation rather than administrative or judicial action.

From the formation of the Union until October, 1948, the states have enacted at least 217 antidiscrimination and antibias laws.[65] The importance of the present decade is revealed in the fact that 57 of these 217 statutes, or 26 percent, were passed during the years 1940–48. In 1949, when forty-two state legislatures were in session, the trend continued.[66] Bills that would eliminate employment discrimination were introduced in twenty-three states. A total of thirty-six state legislatures received well over one hundred bills to eliminate discrimination or segregation, or to improve group relations not only in employment but also in places of public accommodation, in the professions, and in education, health, housing, insurance and loans, marriage, the armed forces, and voting. Some bills dealt with group defamation, the rights and status of aliens and foreign-born, and mob violence. Among the states whose legislatures had these bills before them were Alabama, Arizona,

Arkansas, Delaware, Florida, Georgia, Kansas, Maryland, Missouri, New Mexico, South Carolina, Tennessee, Texas, Virginia, and West Virginia. Of the more than a hundred bills introduced, forty-one became law in twenty-two states.

SUMMARY: THE TWO PERIODS

We have sketched the civil rights program of the Reconstruction, the changing status and welfare of Negroes and other minorities during the last two decades, and the civil rights program of the present period.

The emphasis during the nineteenth century was upon broad legislation, but this was not accompanied by institutional changes of an economic, political, and social nature. These laws protecting minorities had to be set in motion by individuals. Today civil rights are advanced by the government in a different way. Between the two periods there have come (one series of events on top of another) America's severest economic depression, the New Deal, a second world war, and the threat of a third. Under the constant, forceful impact of these developments, the American conception of the role of government changed, and attitudes toward racial and religious minorities have become more favorable. As a result, the civil rights of these minorities are, in our day, protected more directly by the state. All levels of the government do things that affect us more intimately than before, and in these activities government is increasingly providing its services without discrimination. On the federal level, governmental protection and advancement of civil rights has used administrative and executive powers; the relatively independent judicial power, as we shall see in a later chapter, has likewise been applied against discrimination. State governments have relied upon new legislation as well as upon administrative and executive power. This legislation is of a new type—it asserts that discrimination harms not merely the victim but the community as well, and consequently makes a state agency responsible for reducing the incidence of discriminatory practices. The state acts for the individual—as it did not under the older federal laws—in a situation deemed a peril to the entire community.

CHAPTER TWO

The Supreme Court, 1868–1937:
Buttressing the Caste Order

SINCE the late 1930s there has been a considerable enlargement of the federal power, especially in the economic realm. Congress and the Executive have created new functions and have extended their reach into the affairs of the community, while the Supreme Court has refrained from exercising the limiting powers it used so frequently from about 1920 to 1937. In the area of civil and minority rights, however, the Court has enlarged its function as a restraint upon the state and federal legislatures. If property was raised to a preferred position by the courts since 1890, in the last decade or so it has been civil rights that has enjoyed this elevated status. Thus the Court is now playing a different role in group relations from that of its predecessors.

With the emancipation of the Negro slaves, the ratification of the Fourteenth Amendment in 1868, and the heavy immigration from Europe and the Orient beginning around 1880, the problem of intergroup relations in the United States inevitably reached the Supreme Court on many occasions. How did the successive courts handle the issues before them? What role did they play in the adjustment of group to group, in the efforts of minorities to achieve the full measure of their rights under the American system of government? An assessment of the Supreme Court's role in group relations from 1868 to 1937 must be understood in its proper perspective. The Court has a broad freedom, of course, to select among various doctrines and precedents, yet this freedom is not unlimited, for the Constitution marks out the lane within which judicial review moves. By interpretation the Courts may narrow and widen the lane, but its center is still delineated by the Constitution.

The Supreme Court, too, bears a certain relation to public opinion, a relation that it is difficult to define precisely. Aside from the problems of ascertaining and describing the "state of public opinion," one must also consider that in this country there is usually a whole range of "public opinion" on leading political issues. In addition, it can be argued that the Court not only reflects but frequently influences the beliefs we hold. It nevertheless seems clear that in the Reconstruction period and later the Supreme Court, in considering cases involving group relations, reflected the views of those segments of the population that were not anxious to advance minority rights. It is equally clear that the Court since about 1937 has not only reflected the views of those segments of the population that want to improve group relations by advancing minority rights, but that it also has influenced American thinking in the same direction. Though the present court is still cautious in this area, its decisions no longer have the effect of buttressing the caste system with respect to Negroes.

THE FOURTEENTH AMENDMENT

At the end of the Civil War, Congress, determined to strengthen the freedom of the liberated Negroes, enacted five laws and proposed three Constitutional Amendments which the states accepted.[1] The Thirteenth Amendment (1865) abolished slavery and involuntary servitude, "except as a punishment for crime whereof the party shall have been duly convicted." The Civil Rights Act of 1866 aimed to combat the Black Codes, a body of laws enacted by Southern states for the purpose of returning Negroes to some degree of servitude by restricting their freedom to travel and work. This act gave sweeping protection to the Negroes' rights as citizens, guaranteeing them "full and equal benefit of all laws and proceedings for the security of person and property, as is enjoyed by white citizens," regardless of any other law or custom which might exist anywhere in the United States. Other provisions of the act sought to insure its rigid enforcement by requiring federal rather than state procedures wherever possible, and punishing private persons or officials who obstructed its execution. Because the constitutionality of this law was brought into question, Congress soon submitted to the states the Fourteenth Amendment (finally ratified in 1868), which provides that: "No State shall make or enforce any law which shall abridge the privileges or immunities of citizens of the United States, nor shall any State deprive any person of life, liberty, or property without due process of law, nor deny to any person within its jurisdiction the equal protection of the laws."

Meanwhile, in 1867, Congress outlawed peonage. Three years later the Fifteenth Amendment took effect, providing that: "The right of the citizens of the United States to vote shall not be denied or abridged by the United States or by any State on account of race, color, or previous condition of servitude." In the same year, 1870, Congress reenacted the Civil Rights Act of 1866, emphasizing federal protection of the right to vote now guaranteed in the Fifteenth Amendment. In 1871 Congress passed another law to implement the rights established by the Fourteenth Amendment, intended this time primarily to protect all persons in the exercise of their "rights, privileges, or immunities secured by the Constitution of the United States." In 1875 Congress passed still another civil rights act, providing that "all persons within the jurisdiction of the United States shall be entitled to the full and equal enjoyment of the accommodations, advantages, facilities, and privileges of inns, public conveyances on land or water, theatres, and other places of public amusement; subject only to the conditions and limitations established by law, and applicable alike to citizens of every race and color, regardless of any previous condition of servitude."

By these acts and amendments Congress announced federal jurisdiction over many classes of rights of all persons as well as United States citizens. In order to establish its authority more firmly, the legislature included in the three amendments the following enforcement clause: "The Congress shall have power to enforce by appropriate legislation the provisions of this article." The Fourteenth Amendment, designed to protect a broader class of rights than either the Thirteenth or the Fifteenth, has been the subject of most disputes over discrimination against minorities.

The Rights of United States Citizens: "Privileges and Immunities" Clause

Even before 1875, the year in which the last of these statutes was passed, the Supreme Court had begun to limit the protection they and the three amendments seemed to offer minorities. The first case to reach the Court under the Fourteenth Amendment, in 1873, did not involve minority rights, but the majority opinion in the *Slaughter House Cases* [2] had grave meaning for minorities. The main issue to be decided was whether or not a New Orleans act of 1869, setting up a private company as the only one authorized to operate a slaughter house in the city, violated the Fourteenth Amendment by depriving one thousand other United States citizens of their federal privilege to engage in the same business. The slaughter house operators who had been put out of business by the New Orleans law insisted that the Amendment protected not only the freed slaves but all persons as well. Against these claims Justice Miller, for a bare majority of one, made two significant points. First, he said, the "pervading purpose" of the Thirteenth and Fourteenth Amendments was "the freedom of the slave race, the security and firm establishment of that freedom, and the protection of the newly-made freeman and citizen from the oppressions of those who had formerly exercised unlimited dominion over him." [3] It appeared at this juncture that the Court was going to reserve these two Amendments for the exclusive protection of the Negro, but Justice Miller went on to restrict their application even further. In the second significant statement he described two types of citizenship, federal and state. The slaughter house operators, it appeared, had rested their claims upon the erroneous assumption that these two types are identical. Justice Miller pointed out that the first sentence of the Fourteenth Amendment mentions both federal and state citizenship, while the privileges and immunities clause in the next sentence mentions only federal citizenship; in this fact he found ample warrant to conclude that the Amendment placed under the protection of the federal government only the privileges and immunities of federal citizenship, and that those of state citizenship are still protected, as before the ratification of the Amendment, by the states. [4] The privileges or immunities of what we traditionally call civil rights, therefore, were not placed under federal protection, the majority held.

For the minority of four, Justice Field argued that the position of the majority makes the Fourteenth Amendment useless if it merely gives federal protection to what were always federal rights, since the states could never abridge them in the first place. By virtue of the Fourteenth Amendment, the minority asserted, "A citizen of a State is now only a citizen of the United States residing in that State. The fundamental rights, privileges, and immunities which belong to him as a free man and a free citizen, now belong to him as a citizen of the United States, and are not dependent upon his citizenship of any State." [5]

This majority judgment regarding the meaning of the privileges and immunities of federal citizenship has survived nearly eighty years of often tempestuous Supreme Court history. [6] From time to time the Court has listed some of these privileges and immunities, but it has never been willing to define them fully, preferring to leave itself as many choices as possible for the future. By the following year, in 1874, the entire Court had accepted the interpretation set forth by Justice Miller in the *Slaughter House Cases.* A Missouri resident, fully qualified to vote in all respects but one, tested the validity of that state's constitutional provision excluding women from voting.[7] Pointing out that the Fourteenth Amendment added no rights to those that citizens already had, but that it merely enforced existing rights, Justice Waite held for a unanimous Court that suffrage is not one of the privileges and immunities of federal citizenship protected by that Amendment.[8] Nor could the Court find anything in the Fifteenth Amendment to prevent Missouri from refusing to permit the plaintiff to vote, since that Amendment mentions only abridgment "on account of race, color, or previous condition of servitude." [9]

In 1876 the Court once more refused to recognize as federal privileges and immunities certain rights which it insisted remained under state protection regardless of the Fourteenth Amendment. In *United States v. Cruikshank* [10] the issue was whether or not certain charges against a group of defendants constituted federal offenses. Some Louisiana citizens had been indicted on thirty-two counts under Section 6 of the Civil Rights Act of 1870, which provides a maximum fine of $5,000 and a maximum prison term of ten years for two or more persons who "shall band or conspire together . . . to injure, oppress, threaten, or intimidate any citizen with intent to prevent or hinder his free exercise and enjoyment of any right or privilege granted or secured to him by the Constitution or laws of the United States." [11] Among the charges were the following: intent to prevent citizens from freely exercising their right to peaceful assembly, to bear arms lawfully, to be secured the full and equal protection of the laws, and to vote; and intent to deprive citizens of their lives and liberty without due process of law. Other counts charged the defendants with intent to deprive persons of their privileges and immunities as citizens of the United States and Louisiana merely because they were Negroes. Chief Justice Waite, speaking for the entire Court (Justice Clifford concurring) held that the crimes ascribed to the defendants were not federal offenses but offenses against the state of Louisiana. The right of peaceful assembly, he stated, is a federal right only when the assembly is for a purpose connected with the powers or duties of the federal government. The right to bear arms lawfully, to life and liberty, to the free exercise of all rights with full and equal protection of the laws and to vote freely, are all rights that are protected by the states. With respect to the four counts charging deprivation of rights because of race, the Court held that the indictment could not be sustained because it vaguely referred to all rights instead of specific ones, as well as because it lacked a description of charges such that the accused could reasonably defend themselves and such that a court could decide whether the facts supported the charges.[12]

Shortly before it decided the *Cruikshank* case, the Court was presented with one under the Fifteenth Amendment. In *United States v. Reese* [13] Chief Justice Waite held for the majority (Justice Hunt dissenting) that Sections 3 and 4 of the Civil Rights Act of 1870 were so broad that they were not within the Congressional power under the Fifteenth Amendment. That Amendment, it was held, permits Congress to punish officials who hinder Negroes in the exercise of their right to vote solely on account of "race, color, or previous condition of servitude," while Sections 3 and 4 of the 1870 statute punished wrongful acts in general and interference with this right of Negroes through "force, bribery, threats, intimidation, or other unlawful means." Thus, said the Court, Congress exceeded the limits of its power under the Amendment.

For decades after these decisions the Supreme Court refused to find new privileges and immunities of United States citizenship; this clause remained useless in the federal protection of the rights of minorities. In 1935 the Court suddenly rediscovered the clause, not in a minority-rights case but in one defending a business interest. For the first time in its long history the Court, in *Colgate v. Harvey*,[14] invalidated a state law on the ground that it denied the "privileges or immunities" of federal citizenship. Justice Sutherland, for a six-to-three majority, ruled that a Vermont statute taxing interest received from money loaned outside that state while exempting interest from loans within its borders was a classification "based upon a difference having no substantial or fair relation to the object of the act—which, so far as this question is concerned, simply is to secure revenue." [15] In a vigorous dissent for himself and Justices Brandeis and Cardozo, Justice Stone upheld the constitutionality of the Vermont law, and pointed out: "Feeble indeed is an attack on a statute as denying equal protection which can gain any support from the almost forgotten privileges and immunities clause of the Fourteenth Amendment." [16] Justice Stone then cited forty-four cases in which state laws were unsuccessfully challenged on the ground that they violated this clause.[17]

A few years later the Court had another opportunity to decide the fate of this clause. In *Hague v. C.I.O.*[18] five justices upheld the right of certain individuals and the C.I.O. peacefully to conduct meetings and distribute literature on the streets and in the public parks of Jersey City; two Justices dissented, and two did not participate. Justices Roberts and Black insisted upon the applicability of the privileges and immunities clause, but Justices Stone and Reed preferred instead to rely upon the due process clause of the Fourteenth Amendment. Chief Justice Hughes, making the same determination of the case as these four members of the Court, held that the privileges and immunities clause was not applicable only because the record did not show that the aim of the respondents was to discuss a national issue. Justice Stone argued that the Court had without exception rested freedom of speech and assembly upon the due process rather than upon the privileges and immunities clause. If the Court were to hold that the latter clause made the federal government the guarantor of the fundamental personal and property rights which before the Fourteenth Amendment were the attributes of state citizenship, said Justice Stone, the independence of local government would be jeopardized.[19]

The following year the Court again made the privileges and immunities clause virtually inoperative. In *Madden v. Kentucky* [20] it was claimed that a state law violated this clause by taxing bank deposits in Kentucky only ten cents on each one hundred dollars, while it taxed bank deposits in other states fifty cents on the same amount. This time, however, the Court, by seven to two, held through Justice Reed that the Kentucky tax was not an unconstitutional classification, and that "the right to carry out an incident to a trade, business or calling such as the deposit of money in banks is not a privilege of national citizenship." [21] It then flatly overruled its decision in the *Colgate* case, thus putting the privileges and immunities clause back where it was before its revival in 1935.

The States Protect Minorities:
The "Due Process" Clause

The "due process" clause of the Fourteenth Amendment has had a controversial history. Originally applied to procedure, due process meant a fair hearing by a properly constituted authority in criminal and civil cases. As late as 1877, in *Munn v. Illinois*,[22] the Court refused to accept the argument that due process, as guaranteed by the Fifth and Fourteenth Amendments, meant that a state could not establish a maximum charge for the services performed by a private company when deemed related to the public interest. Under the impact of a growing industrial capitalism, however, the Court yielded to the interpretation of due process as restraining the substance as well as the procedure of federal and state laws. It was in 1890, in a railroad case, that the Court first invalidated legislation because it was held to be unreasonable.[23] After that year, as the states increasingly attempted to regulate economic affairs, more cases than ever were based upon the Fourteenth Amendment, all but a few pointing to the due process and equal protection clauses. From 1868 to 1878 only three cases were decided under the Amendment, and none in 1878–79. During the next decade there were forty-six. But between 1896 and 1905, after the change in interpretation made in 1890, 297 cases invoked the Fourteenth Amendment in the Supreme Court. "What was the cause of this inundation?" asks Edward S. Corwin. "In the main it is to be found in the Court's ratification of the idea, following a period of vacillation, that the term *liberty* of the 'due process' clause was intended to annex the principles of *laissez faire* capitalism to the Constitution and put them beyond reach of State legislative power." [24]

While expanding the due process clause to check state legislation which it considered to be an "unreasonable" invasion of property rights, the Supreme Court was also restricting the federal government's power under this clause to protect the rights of accused persons against state infringements. In 1884 the Court held, in the important case of *Hurtado v. California*,[25] that a state constitutional provision permitting prosecution by either information or indictment did not violate the due process clause in the Fifth or Fourteenth Amendments of the Constitution of the United States. Justice Harlan dissented strongly, insisting that the due process clause of the Fourteenth Amendment was intended "to impose upon the States the same restrictions, in respect of proceedings involving life, liberty and property, which had been imposed upon the general government" by the Bill of Rights.[26] In 1900, in *Maxwell v. Dow*,[27] the Court held that the Fourteenth Amendment did not secure all persons in the United States against state infringement of the rights listed in the first eight amendments to the Federal Constitution. Justice Harlan dissented again. The specific rights in the case before the Court were two: the right (as in the *Hurtado* case) of an accused person to be tried in a state court on the basis of an indictment rather than information, and his right to be tried by a jury of twelve rather than eight members. Neither of these rights, said the majority, was an essential feature of due process of law. In 1908, the Court again held, in *Twining v. New Jersey*,[28] with Justice Harlan again dissenting, that the Bill of Rights restrained only the federal government, but not the states. Here the specific issue was the right of an accused person to refuse to incriminate himself by testifying at his trial. This right, too, the Court decided, was not "fundamental in due process of law, nor an essential part of it." [29]

Not until 1925 did the Supreme Court check this trend in a civil rights case. In 1897, however, it had held that the Fifth Amendment's clause prohibiting the federal government from taking private property for public use "without just compensation" also restrained the states through the due process clause of the Fourteenth Amendment.[30] By this ruling the property interests of a railroad were defended against the city of Chicago. It took more than another quarter-century for the Court to apply this reasoning to civil rights. In the *Gitlow* case [31] in 1925 the Court said in passing that it accepted the doctrine that "freedom of speech and of the press—which are protected by the First Amendment from abridgement by Congress— are among the fundamental personal rights and 'liberties' protected by the due process clause of the Fourteenth Amendment from impairment by the States." [32] This, however, was dictum. But in 1927 the Court held that the Kansas criminal-syndicalism act, as applied in the case before it, was "an arbitrary and unreasonable exercise of the police power of the State, unwarrantably infringing the liberty of the defendent in violation of the due process clause of the Fourteenth Amendment." [33] In 1931 the Court confirmed this interpretation by invalidating a Minnesota statute on the same ground.[34] Under this interpretation the Court has in recent years been using the due process clause to protect civil liberty, whereas earlier courts had used it to protect property.

Group Discrimination by Law:
"The Equal Protection of the Laws"

The Fourteenth Amendment contains a third clause of great significance for minorities, that forbidding a state to "deny any person within its jurisdiction the equal protection of the laws." A series of decisions beginning in 1877 limited the value of this clause for minority groups, especially Negroes, by permitting some types of classifications which have had the effect of limiting their rights. The equal protection clause has not restrained the states from requiring segregated, and generally inferior, facilities for Negroes.

The *Civil Rights Cases* of 1883 [35] led to one of the most important opinions with respect to the equal protection clause. On the authority of the Civil Rights Act of 1875 the federal government sought to convict persons who denied to Negroes the accommodations of an inn or hotel, admission to a theatre, and a seat in the ladies' car of a railroad train. The Court, by eight to one, through Justice Bradley invalidated the statute on several grounds. First, it was not within the Congressional power under the Fourteenth Amendment to deal with "individual invasions of individual rights," since that Amendment restrained the states, not private persons. Second, the Act went too far to be authorized by the Thirteenth Amendment. A Negro's inability to enter an inn, a public carrier, or a place of amusement because an individual operator refused to admit him, the Court held, is not a badge of slavery. Thus the Court ruled that the Fourteenth Amendment gave Congress the power to prohibit discrimination, but only if practiced by a state, not by individuals; the Thirteenth Amendment, according to this opinion, does permit Congress to restrain the actions of individuals, but it does not cover the particular actions which the Civil Rights Act of 1875 sought to prohibit. In these cases the minorities issue was caught up in the separate issue of the limits of federal power. The Court hesitated to go so far as Congress went in the expansion of national power during the Reconstruction period.

The decision in the *Civil Rights Cases* still prevails, though not unchallenged. Its reasoning was forcibly disputed in a famous dissent by Justice Harlan. "I cannot resist the conclusion," he said, "that the substance and spirit of the recent amendments of the Constitution have been sacrificed by a subtle and ingenious verbal criticism." [36] In reply to the majority view that the Fourteenth Amendment was a restraint only upon the states, he insisted that it grants full United States citizenship to a former slave group, and empowers Congress, by the last clause, to enforce "by appropriate legislation" all the other provisions of the Amendment; Congress might thus not only prohibit the states from certain acts, but might also directly restrain private persons who violate the civil rights of others. To support this position Justice Harlan pointed to an early case, *Prigg v. Pennsylvania*,[37] in which the Court upheld a Congressional act punishing persons who obstructed an owner or his agent in seizing an escaped slave. This law of 1793 was said to be based on Article IV, Section 2 of the Constitution, which provides: "No person held to service or labor in one State, under the laws thereof, escaping into another, shall, in consequence of any law or regulation therein, be discharged from such service or labor, but shall be delivered up on claim to the party to whom such service or labor might be due." The Court ruled that the Constitutional provision was self-enforcing, that if Congress could establish the owner's right to the return of his slave, Congress could enforce this right. "The fundamental principle," said Justice Story for a unanimous Court, "applicable to all cases of this sort, would seem to be, that where the end is required, the means are given; and where the duty is enjoined, the ability to perform it is contemplated to exist on the part of the functionaries to whom it is entrusted." [38] Relying on this opinion, Justice Harlan observed in his *Civil Rights Cases* dissent: "I insist that the national legislature may, without transcending the limits of the Constitution, do for human liberty and the fundamental rights of American citizenship, what it did, with the sanction of this court, for the protection of slavery and the rights of the masters of fugitive slaves." [39] The *Prigg* case, despite Justice Harlan's cogent argument, nevertheless rests on different grounds than the *Civil Rights Cases*. The earlier case rests on the fully warranted ground that the Constitution gave a slaveowner a claim to recover an escaped slave, but Justice Harlan's opinion rests on the much less solid ground that the United States citizenship carries with it a right not to be discriminated against by private persons.

Justice Harlan pursued his own objective relentlessly. In reply to the majority view that the discriminatory actions prohibited by the Civil Rights Act of 1875 were not a "badge of servitude," he argued that these actions were inimical to the freedom granted the Negro in the Thirteenth Amendment. He seemed to accept the government's contention that the discriminations which the statute sought to eliminate, though practiced without legal prescription and only by private individuals, were so widespread as to constitute an institutional or customary disability that was truly a "badge of servitude." [40] Justice Harlan also cited the *Cruikshank* case [41] dictum that while the right of suffrage is not itself an attribute of federal citizenship, the Fifteenth Amendment made it a federal right for a citizen to be protected, in his right to vote, from abridgment because of race or color or previous condition of servitude. The same reasoning, he asserted, should apply to the Civil Rights Act of 1875: the state is the fount of civil rights in general, but the right to be protected against their abridgment because of race or color is guaranteed by the United States government.[42]

The result of the majority opinion in the *Civil Rights Cases* was that the federal government could not punish individuals who excluded or segregated Negroes. By the combination of a previous and a later decision the Supreme Court ruled that the states, too, could not prohibit segregation on interstate public carriers. The first of these cases was *Hall v. de Cuir*,[43] in 1877, involving a Louisiana statute of 1869 which forbade carriers in that state to segregate passengers according to race or color. A Negro woman boarded a ship at New Orleans for Hermitage, in the same state, and was refused space in a cabin reserved for white travelers. The Supreme Court, reversing the highest court in Louisiana, held the law unconstitutional as an attempt by one state to regulate the conditions of inter-state commerce. Though the statute prescribed that segregation was prohibited only while the carrier was in the state of Louisiana, the Court held that it affected the operator's "conduct to some extent in the management of his business throughout his entire voyage," and was hence unconstitutional. "If the public good requires such legislation," said the Court, referring to antidiscrimination laws, "it must come from Congress and not from the States." [44] We have just seen, however, in the *Civil Rights Cases* of 1883, that an attempt by Congress to punish segregation on the part of common carriers was declared to be likewise unconstitutional. The Court in 1877 had ruled that only Congress could prevent segregation on public conveyances, but in 1883 invalidated a federal law designed to do just that. (There were three justices, Waite, Field, and Bradley, who were members of the Court during both cases and decided with the majority each time.) In 1877 the Court ruled on the basis of the commerce clause, but in 1883 it ignored that clause, under which the federal government's authority to eliminate segregation on interstate carriers might conceivably have been upheld.

In 1890 the Supreme Court added the final touch to these inconsistencies in a case [45] involving a Mississippi law which required separate accommodations on railroads for Negroes and whites. The issue here was the same as in the *Hall* case of 1877: does the state law regulate interstate commerce? But now, where the law required rather than prohibited segregation, the Court upheld its constitutionality. Attempting to distinguish this case from the *Hall* case, Justice Brewer for the majority pointed out that in the earlier one the Louisiana Supreme Court had held that the law applied to interstate carriers while in that state, whereas in the present case the Mississippi Supreme Court held that the law applied only to commerce within the state. The Court, said Justice Brewer, felt constrained to accept the construction placed upon the law by the state's highest tribunal. And since what affects "only commerce within the State is no invasion of the powers given to Congress by the commerce clause," he concluded, the Mississippi law was not unconstitutional.[46]

Justice Harlan, again dissenting (this time joined by Justice Bradley), saw no such distinction between the two cases. "In its application to passengers on vessels engaged in interstate commerce," he said, "the Louisiana enactment forbade the separation of the white and black races while such vessels were within the limits of that State. The Mississippi statute, in its application to passengers on railroad trains employed in interstate commerce, requires such separation of races, while those trains are within that State. I am unable to perceive how the former is a regulation of interstate commerce, and the other is not."[47] By ruling as it did in these two cases, then, the Court urged that a Louisiana law *prohibiting* segregation on carriers while in Louisiana was unconstitutional, whereas a Mississippi law *requiring* segregation on carriers while in Mississippi was constitutional.

In the very year that the Court upheld this Mississippi statute, 1890, Louisiana passed a similar law requiring separate but equal accommodations for Negroes and whites on railroads carrying passengers within the state. Plessy, a Louisiana citizen of one-eighth Negro descent, refused to leave a coach reserved for whites; he was ejected and subsequently imprisoned. In the Supreme Court [48] he claimed that the law under which he was convicted violated the Thirteenth Amendment, but the majority, with one justice not participating and Justice Harlan again dissenting, held that the statute "implies merely a legal distinction between the white and colored races," and did not tend to "reestablish a state of involuntary servitude." [49] The Court also rejected the argument that the statute violated the Fourteenth Amendment. Though the object of that Amendment, said Justice Brown for the Court, was to enforce the equality of the races before the law, "in the nature of things it could not have been intended to abolish distinctions based upon color, or to enforce social, as distinguished from political equality, or a commingling of the two races upon terms unsatisfactory to either." [50] Such a distinction, it was added, does not imply the inferiority of one of the races; if inferiority is inferred from it, "it is not by reason of anything found in the act, but solely because the colored race chooses to put that construction upon it." [51] Asserting that "legislation is powerless to eradicate racial instincts," the Court concluded: "If one race be inferior to the other socially, the Constitution of the United States cannot put them upon the same plane." [52]

In its argument that law cannot enforce a "commingling of the two races," the Court was ignoring one fundamental fact —that the state of Louisiana was not merely *permitting* the races to remain apart, but was *requiring* their separation by law. Legislation, said the majority, could not bring social equality, but it upheld legislation prescribing social inequality. Justice Harlan stated prophetically: "In my opinion, the judgment this day rendered will, in time, prove to be quite as pernicious as the decision made by this tribunal in the *Dred Scott case*." [53]

Having decided that state laws requiring segregation of Negroes from whites do not violate any clause in the Fourteenth

Amendment, the Supreme Court began to insist upon the "separate but equal" rule in the cases which followed *Plessy v. Ferguson.* One of the objectives of Negro organizations has been to secure the equal facilities to which the Court has said they are entitled. This has been a hard struggle, for Negroes cannot afford to appeal to the courts every time they are provided inferior facilities, and the courts have no arrangements for undertaking investigations of the separate but equal facilities they prescribe. The result is that Negroes have been treated as less than the equals of whites in spite of the Fourteenth Amendment and federal and state laws intended to guarantee them the "equal protection of the laws."

The Supreme Court has usually been firm in its insistence upon the separate but equal rule in certain areas of Negrowhite relations. In reversing one part of a lower court's decision in 1914, the Court held that an Oklahoma law of 1907 was a violation of the Fourteenth Amendment because, while requiring separate but equal railroad coaches and waiting rooms for Negroes and whites, it permitted the railroads to run sleeping, dining, and chair cars for the exclusive use of either group.[54] Justice Hughes, in his opinion for a unanimous Court, rejected the reasoning behind the law that there might not be enough Negroes seeking such accommodations to warrant the cost of providing them. He stated: "It makes the constitutional right depend upon the number of persons who may be discriminated against, whereas the essence of the constitutional right is that it is a personal one." [55]

A few years later, in *Buchanan v. Warley* [56] in 1917, the Court ruled that no state or local government may pass a law limiting a person's right to occupy, buy, and sell property merely because of his color. One result of this decision was that persons who wished to prevent minority group members from occupying certain land made private agreements for that purpose. In 1926 the constitutionality of such private restrictive covenants was challenged in *Corrigan v. Buckley*,[57] but the Supreme Court unanimously ruled that such private contracts did not violate the Fifth Amendment, which restrains only the federal government; or the Thirteenth Amendment, which deals only with involuntary servitude; or the Fourteenth Amendment, which restrains only the states. The Court ignored the argument that the enforcement of restrictive covenants by state courts constituted "state action" enjoined by the Fourteenth Amendment, and dismissed the case for lack of jurisdiction over the other claims advanced.[58]

The attainment of equal facilities in education has been a major objective of Negro organizations especially since 1908, when the Supreme Court held that a Kentucky statute requiring that all schools give instruction to Negroes and whites separately was not a violation of the Fourteenth Amendment.[59] A tabulation of cases [60] from 1865 through 1934 involving the separate school for Negroes reveals some interesting facts. The validity of educational segregation was challenged in state courts of last resort thirty-seven times, and each time the constitutionality of the separate school was upheld. Though unable to undermine the legal basis of segregation in the schools, Negroes succeeded in twenty-four cases, without a single setback, in preventing segregation in the absence of a state law on the subject. They brought suit twenty-eight times to compel the providing of equal facilities in the separate schools, but won only nine of these cases. In the nineteen lost cases the principle of equal facilities was recognized, but the courts held that the existence of inequality was not properly shown.

That the Supreme Court doctrine of separate but equal facilities for Negroes has failed in the educational field is shown by data prepared by the United States Office of Education. As of 1950, the following twenty-one states as well as the District of Columbia either required or expressly permitted segregation in the schools: Alabama, Arizona, Arkansas, Delaware, Florida, Georgia, Kansas, Kentucky, Louisiana, Maryland, Mississippi, Missouri, New Mexico, North Carolina,

Oklahoma, South Carolina, Tennessee, Texas, Virginia, West Virginia, Wyoming.[61] According to data collected by the Office of Education, most of these states have provided far from equal facilities for Negroes if one judges by the current expense per white and Negro pupil in average daily attendance. Seventeen states and the District of Columbia together spent an average of $104.66 per white pupil in average daily attendance in 1946, and only $57.57 per Negro pupil. The data for 1948–49 are not complete but they show a similar discrepancy. The figures for each state and the District of Columbia follow.[62]

TABLE 1

Expense per White and Negro Pupil in Segregated Schools in Seventeen States and in the District of Columbia

(Figures are for 1946, except those marked with an asterisk, which are for 1948–49)

	White	Negro		White	Negro
Alabama	$120.50 *	$ 81.83 *	North Caro-		
Arkansas	111.15 *	62.22 *	lina	131.85 *	115.02 *
Delaware	188.35 *	131.67 *	Oklahoma	166.31 *	175.32 *
Florida	134.76	61.75	South Caro-		
Georgia	82.57	31.14	lina	148.48 *	69.65 *
Kentucky	90.05	98.35	Tennessee	80.30	55.44
Louisiana	136.12	43.81	Texas	123.14	91.22
Maryland	130.40	110.66	Virginia	104.29	53.15
Mississippi	122.74 *	26.81 *	West Virginia	100.63	111.47
Missouri	$137.68	$133.35	District of Co-		
			lumbia	281.41 *	210.42 *

The Supreme Court has protected the rights of minorities against the attempts of certain states to place them at a disadvantage in economic pursuits. In an early case in 1886, *Yick Wo v. Hopkins*,[63] the Court unanimously invalidated as a violation of the Fourteenth Amendment a San Francisco ordinance which, authorizing a board of supervisors to grant and withhold licenses for the operation of laundries, was obviously aimed at driving Chinese laundry owners out of business.

In 1915 an Arizona statute was invalidated under the same Amendment in *Truax v. Raich*.[64] The law, passed in 1914, ordered that in all establishments with five or more workers 80 percent of them must be citizens of the United States. In compliance with the law a restaurant owner told his Austrian cook he would have to leave the job. The Supreme Court held the law to be an unreasonable classification: "It requires no argument to show that the right to work for a living in the common occupations of the community is of the very essence of the personal freedom and opportunity that it was the purpose of the [Fourteenth] Amendment to secure." [65]

Three Supreme Court decisions issued on the same day in 1879 protected Negroes and other minorities from unfair discrimination in the selection of juries. In the first case, *Strauder v. West Virginia*,[66] the Court invalidated a state law, which excluded Negroes from juries, on the ground that it violated the equal protection clause of the Fourteenth Amendment. This decision protected both the Negro's right to serve on juries, and the Negro defendant's right to be tried by a jury selected without exclusion of any person merely because of race or color.[67] In the second case, *Virginia v. Rives*,[68] the Court held that a Negro defendant does not have the right to be tried by a jury on which some Negroes serve, but that he does have the right to be tried by a jury from which Negroes have not been excluded on the ground of their race or color. "A mixed jury in a particular case," said Justice Strong for the entire Court, "is not essential to the equal protection of the laws." [69] In the last of the three cases, *Ex parte Virginia*,[70] the Court upheld that section of the Civil Rights Act of 1875 which prohibited the exclusion of any citizen from a jury "on account of race, color or previous condition of servitude." This Act, it ruled, was an appropriate implementation of the Fourteenth Amendment. Thus the Court again protected the right of Negroes to exemption from exclusion from juries simply on racial grounds.

The Supreme Court's record on the voting rights of minorities is a mixed one. Before taking up the cases involving the Fourteenth Amendment, the subject of this section, brief mention may be made of an important case under the Fifteenth.[71] In 1915 the Court declared unconstitutional an amendment to the Oklahoma constitution which provided that no one might vote unless he could read or write any section of the state constitution, but which then provided that the following classes of citizens could vote even if they failed the literacy test: those who were entitled to vote on or before January 1, 1866, or who lived in a foreign country before that date, or lineal descendants of such persons. This amendment, the famous "grandfather clause," thus required that Negroes pass a literacy test to vote but that other groups need not pass it to vote. While holding that the states might legitimately set up the literacy requirement, the unanimous Court (one justice not participating) pointed out that in this case the literacy requirement was so intimately connected with the unreasonable test of one's status or one's forebears' status before January 1, 1866, that both provisions must be struck down.[72]

Another widely used method in the South to keep the Negro from voting is the "white primary." Negro organizations have conducted a running battle to gain for Negroes the right to vote in the primary elections of the Democratic party, the only election in the South in which there is a genuine contest around significant issues. The South has exhibited, here as in no other area of civil rights, that its leading holders of political power do not recognize the spirit of the law of the land when it goes counter to the basis and condition of their supremacy. No sooner has the Supreme Court outlawed one way of excluding Negroes from the Democratic primaries than Southern legislatures and executives, usually backed by their judiciaries, have found another way to accomplish the same end.

It was in 1927 that the Court first struck a blow at the white primary. In *Nixon v. Herndon* [73] the Court invalidated a Texas statute forbidding the Negro to vote in the Democratic primary, on the ground that it violated the Fourteenth Amendment. Five years later the Court, in a five-to-four decision,[74] defeated a Texas attempt to continue the illegal exclusion by making it appear that it was no longer the state that was denying the right in question. A statute had been passed which empowered the executive committee of the Democratic party to prescribe the qualifications for membership in it. Justice Cardozo ruled for the narrow majority that the existence of the Texas law meant that it was the state which continued to deny Negroes the right to a voice in the primary. But he clearly revealed the next step for Texas Democrats when he asserted that the inherent power to run the party lay not in the executive committee but in the state convention. This decision was given on May 2, 1932. Three weeks later the state convention of the Democratic party voted to exclude nonwhites. In 1935 this action was contested in the Supreme Court; in *Grovey v. Townsend* [75] the Court unanimously held that the exclusion by the Texas Democratic party did not violate any part of the Fourteenth Amendment.

Section 51, Title 18 of the United States Code is a law that has had many designations since its enactment in 1870.[76] It protects the federally secured rights and privileges of citizens and persons against conspiracies of two or more persons. An early decision in 1884 [77] held Section 51 (then known as Section 5508, Revised Statutes) an appropriate attempt by Congress to protect the right of citizens to vote freely for federal offices, a right guaranteed under Article I, Section 4 of the Constitution. In 1915 the Court again upheld the authority of the United States government to punish persons who conspired to injure voters in the free exercise of their right to vote in a Congressional election.[78] Two years later, however, the Court restricted the application of this federal statute (known at that time as Section 19, Criminal Code of 1909), holding that it could not apply to a primary election even though it was for a national office.[79] The protection of a citizen's right in the primary, Justice Clarke said for a unanimous Court, was a function of the state governments. In 1918 the Court ruled that this federal statute did not protect citizens against conspiracies to bribe voters.[80]

Mention of a case [81] involving the Thirteenth Amendment concludes our review of the Supreme Court's work until about 1937. In *Clyatt v. U.S.* the Court permitted the accused a new trial, but it laid down a general proscription of peonage, which it defined as "a status or condition of compulsory service, based upon the indebtedness of the peon to the master." [82]

Whose Fourteenth Amendment?

This review of Supreme Court decisions on minority rights has shown that the Court has limited the protection afforded by the constitutional amendments and statutes which followed the Civil War. The Fourteenth Amendment was considered a bulwark against discrimination, but its three famous clauses, protecting the "privileges or immunities" of United States citizens and guaranteeing all persons "due process of law" and "the equal protection of the laws" against abridgment by the states, were so narrowly construed as to make them far weaker supports than they seemed at first. As we have already noted, this Amendment gave more protection to industrial capital than to minorities. From 1868 to 1911, Collins found,[83] the Supreme Court handed down 604 decisions in cases involving the Fourteenth Amendment, but only twenty-eight of them affected Negro rights. Of these twenty-eight, Collins added, twenty-two were decided against the Negro interest.[84] "It is not the negro," he concluded, "but accumulated and organized capital, which now [1912] looks to the Fourteenth Amendment for protection from State activity." [85] Big Business continued to find protection in the Fourteenth Amendment. From 1920 to the end of 1936 the Supreme Court in 132 cases held a state law unconstitutional because it violated that Amendment, and about two thirds of these decisions prevented the states from dealing with important economic problems in the way they saw fit.[86]

At the same time that the Court was limiting the protection which the Fourteenth Amendment could afford minorities, it was broadening that Amendment's applicability to business by including corporations within the meaning of "persons" as used in the due process and equal protection clauses of the first section. In the *Slaughter House Cases* in 1873 Justice Miller had said of the equal protection clause: "We doubt very much whether any action of a State not directed by way of discrimination against the negroes as a class, or on account of their race, will ever be held to come within the purview of this provision." [87] This was not good prophecy, for the Court later gave corporations effective support in their attempts to prevent the states from regulating their activities too closely. Despite this support for corporations in the economic realm, the Court, in the *Berea College* case,[88] refused to uphold a corporation in the field of education against state control. Berea College, giving unsegregated instruction to Negroes and whites, was accused of violating a Kentucky statute of 1904 forbidding such teaching by persons or corporations. The Supreme Court chose not to pass upon the constitutional questions presented to it, but upheld the conviction of Berea College on the ground that, as a corporation, it was subject to state control; hence Kentucky could properly withhold from the institution the right to give unsegregated instruction to Negroes and whites.[89] Thus it did Berea College no good to point to its corporate status and the Fourteenth Amendment in defense of its activity, though corporations were frequently able to halt state regulation on the same ground.

There has been much debate over what Congress intended by the Fourteenth Amendment and what the American people took it to mean. In his detailed account of its origin and passage, Flack has claimed that the intent of Congress was:

"1. To make the Bill of Rights (the first eight Amendments) binding upon, or applicable to, the States.

"2. To give validity to the Civil Rights Bill [of 1866].

"3. To declare who were citizens of the United States." [90]

Contrary to the Supreme Court's interpretation as we have reviewed it, Flack also found that the Amendment was meant to give Congress "the power to determine what were the privileges and immunities of citizens, thereby being enabled to secure equal privileges and immunities in hotels, theaters, schools, etc." [91] And Flack has concluded that, "according to the purpose and intention of the Amendment as disclosed in the debates in Congress and in the several state Legislatures and in other ways, Congress had the constitutional power to enact direct legislation to secure the rights of citizens against violation by individuals as well as by States." [92]

THE SUPREME COURT'S ROLE IN GROUP DISCRIMINATION

This review of the Supreme Court's handling of issues involved in group discrimination between 1868 and 1937 shows that the Court was most consistent in the protection of Negroes' rights to a fair trial, to exemption from forced labor, to equal but separate public facilities, to enter any business or occupation, and to make contracts. These are rights the exercise of which is least likely to bring Negroes into close personal association with whites on a level of equality. Where the exercise of Negro rights might result in equal intergroup association, e.g., in use of the same public facilities, the Court was reluctant to uphold Negro claims. Thus the Court's role was to support laws which enforced the separation of the Negro and white castes and to strike down laws which allowed or encouraged intercaste contact that implied their social equality.

It is necessary at this point to make clear in what sense the word "caste" is used in this discussion. We mean by caste a group of persons so sharply marked off from other groups in point of status or prestige and "style of life" that movement from one group to another is rare and virtually impossible except where a member of one group can feign the attributes of another. There is no way to move up the caste ladder in a manner acceptable to the persons a climber will meet, except to conceal previous membership in the caste below. The use of the concept of caste follows that of Weber,[93] MacIver [94] and Myrdal.[95] As MacIver has put it, "Caste rests always on differences already decided at birth, and these differences cannot be undone by native quality or achievement, by the acquisition of wealth, or by any other means." [96]

The most marked caste differences occur where there are easily discerned ethnic differences, as in the case of Negro-white relations in this country.[97] Ethnic differences, as Weber has remarked,[98] may mean merely that each group avoids contact with the other and considers itself superior. But when such differences become the basis for a hierarchy in which one group is generally considered superior to the other, then there is a caste order of the most rigid kind.

Such is the nature of Negro-white relations in the United States. The caste order of the classic type is generally believed to be that of the Hindus. The American castes, however, as Weber also remarks,[99] do not have the Hindu castes' religious orientation, a quality which strengthens the Oriental structure of caste. Since the beginning of the eighteenth century, when Negro slaves in America were permitted or encouraged to become Christians, the caste order here has lacked this religious prop. In the absence of this particular kind of non-rational justification for the inferior position of the Negro, and in view of the equalitarian and democratic ideology which became popular in the American republic, a "rational" kind of justification was sought in order to defend the treatment accorded the Negroes as either slaves or freemen. Thus there developed the theory of the inherent or "racial" inferiority of the Negro, which still prevails among many white Americans today. Lacking strength in pure religion or magic and facing America's democratic ideology, the caste system has cultivated "scientific" and "rational" justifications based upon alleged biological differences between the castes. Myrdal has shown [100] that the most important beliefs whites hold about Negroes are intended as "rational" justifications of the treatment accorded the latter:

"Practically every type of white-Negro relation, every type of discrimination behavior, every type of interracial policy, raises its own peculiar demands for justification. And practically every special Negro characteristic, actual or only presumed, opens the possibility of meeting one or more of these special demands."

There is a variety of evidence that in carrying out the function just described, the Court was responding to the pattern of conduct and belief in that section of the American community which was not willing to admit the Negro to full citizenship and its implications. There is considerable resemblance between the rank order of decreasing discrimination against Negroes as given by Myrdal and the rank order of successful litigation by Negroes in the Supreme Court.

According to Myrdal [101] discrimination is shown against the Negro in various activities, listed in order of decreasing intensity as follows:

1. Intermarriage and sexual relations involving white women.

2. Other personal relations, e.g., eating, dancing, bathing, and general social intercourse.

3. Use of public facilities, e.g., schools, churches, means of transportation.

4. Political rights, i.e., suffrage.

5. Discrimination in courts of law and by police and other public officials.

6. Economic activities such as landownership, employment, obtaining credit, public relief.

The same general rank order prevails when the Supreme Court decisions on Negro cases are classified by the kind of right claimed by that minority. Waite summarizes all the Negro cases reaching the Supreme Court since the Emancipation.[102] A classification of his data from 1868 through 1936 shows the following results:

1. Negroes won only two of fourteen cases in which they claimed the right to use the same facilities as whites in common carriers, public places, and schools or housing. They brought to the Supreme Court no case in which they claimed the right to intermarriage. These types of rights correspond to the first three types of discrimination listed by Myrdal.

2. Negroes won only six of sixteen cases in which they sought federal protection of their right to vote, or of other rights which they claimed were attributes of federal citizenship. This is the fourth type of discrimination in Myrdal's list.

3. Negroes won twelve of twenty-one cases in which they sought to obtain a fair trial in criminal cases. In five of the nine cases decided unfavorably to the Negro, the Court fully recognized the constitutional rights of the minority, but did not grant the litigant's specific request. This corresponds to the fifth type of discrimination in Myrdal's list.

4. Negroes won all three cases in which they sought federal protection from peonage. This classification most closely resembles the sixth type of discrimination in Myrdal's list. There were two cases, however, which, while not directly involving Negroes, did affect their economic rights. Both were decided in such a way as to protect the minorities. The Supreme Court also invalidated a local government's attempt to restrict the rights of minorities to occupy, buy, or sell land, but refused to outlaw private covenants for the same purpose.

There is further evidence of this correspondence between

Myrdal's list and legal forms of discrimination. In a study of legislation since the Civil War, Franklin Johnson found that the legal disabilities of the Negro likewise corresponded to the actual practice of discrimination as described by Myrdal:

"Statutes in restriction of the colored race may be ranked in accordance with the tendency toward their adoption. The law against intermarriage is not only usually the first to appear chronologically, but is also the most widespread. Next comes separation in education, following that, separation in transportation, and thereafter miscellaneous minor provisions." [103]

The rumors about Negroes, collected and classified by Odum,[104] which spread through the white South from July, 1942, to July, 1943, show a roughly similar rank order. All the rumors reflected the fears of whites that the Negroes were making a concerted attempt to upset traditional "white supremacy" by actions not in consonance with their lower caste position. The most upsetting class of rumors was that which included the stories of Negro men either telling other Negroes and whites that they would soon be "taking care" of the white women, or stories of Negroes actually attempting to become intimate with white women. Other rumors told of Negro domestic workers who refused to work for white women and boasted of the day, soon to come, when the roles would be reversed. Still others told of Negroes who insisted upon equal treatment in buses, trains, stores, and restaurants. In this catalogue of Southern white hysteria the focus was always upon some reported Negro effort to upset the caste order in the realm of personal relations with whites.

It is not surprising, of course, to find this correspondence in rank order of discrimination practiced against Negroes, in laws enacted by legislatures, and in Supreme Court opinions. The nature of minority discrimination is in part dependent upon what the law allows, and what the law allows depends in part upon the customary pattern of discrimination in the community. Neither law nor custom alone has imposed upon Negroes their low caste status. The law itself grants Negroes sufficient equality in some realms to raise them above this status, but in practice these legal guarantees have been too weak to protect them from customary disabilities. Yet the large number of discriminatory statutes indicates that law is itself a strong (perhaps the strongest) means by which discrimination is imposed and supported. It is clear, for example, that in the Black Codes eight Southern states attempted to maintain by law the pattern of Negro-white relations disturbed by the Emancipation and the Confederate defeat. The same use of legal means to impose Negro inferiority is revealed in the report of a contemporary observer, John William de Forest, a Union Army officer who served as an agent of the Freedmen's Bureau in Greenville, S.C.,

whites and blacks resulted
yros in the mystery of free
to be unable to understand
of slavery, or that it could
ious binding and obligating
acts which were brought to
f ludicrous provisions. Ne-
if they were not respectful
ch offense; they must admit
consent of the landowner;
d not keep too many dogs;
vithout leave.[105]

urt's role differs somewhat
art has struck down racial
e "economic" realm, while
long as equal facilities have
a division is not an unfail-
opinions on Negro rights
of other minorities are too
he Court before 1937, for
es against private covenants

restricting their economic right to occupy, buy, or sell land. Nor did it give much protection to Negroes in their political right to vote. Actually, the "economic" right referred to was connected with the "social" right, which Negroes claimed, to reside near whites, and the "political" right to vote in the South means that Negroes must have the "social" right to join the same political party as whites. The right to vote, too, is, properly considered, much more than merely "political," for if Negroes were no more restricted at the polls than whites, their influence in the community would increase enormously and enable them to use this "political" right to obtain other "economic" and "social" rights.

The very special character of the Negroes' "political" right of suffrage is further shown in the attitudes of the white Southern press, from which a collection of editorials, letters, and articles was published in 1940.[107] The editor states in an introduction that thirty-six newspapers were read, and that the book presents about a fourth of all the items extracted on the question of Negro suffrage. "In making the selection," he continues, "I have attempted to indicate roughly the proportionate interest devoted to the topics by the respective papers and the tone of those articles." The compilation includes at least three editorials, originally printed in 1935, 1938, and 1939, which list the rights to which Southern whites believe Negroes are entitled. These rights cover such diverse matters as the Negroes' "cultural aspirations" and "economic hopes;" better health, pay, housing, education, playgrounds, sidewalks, and streets; rest rooms on bus lines; and "equal justice, equal opportunity." Significantly omitted from all three lists was the Negroes' right to vote, either in the primary or in the general elections. The compilation also showed about three editorials against Negro participation in the Southern Democratic primaries to one editorial in favor of such participation. Clearly, some leading groups of Southern whites fear the effect Negro suffrage may have upon their own unity against the Negro.

Negroes have naturally tended to bring to the Court those cases which they think they can win. On its side, the Court was willing to find in favor of the Negro right before it in those areas where public opinion was not intransigent, that is, where the recognition of the right would not mean increased Negro-white contact on a basis of equality about which the white community had clear, strong feelings. Consequently, the Court has been most willing to uphold Negro rights which do not involve Negroes' association with whites. The Court, also, has been least willing to uphold the claims of Negroes to those rights which may bring them into close personal association with whites on a basis of equality, e.g., to intermarriage and to the sharing of facilities in the schools, common carriers, and public places. The one exception to this rule, we have just seen, is the right to vote.

The foregoing analysis points to the Supreme Court's function or role, up to a decade or so ago, in what Myrdal has called the "caste struggle" between the colored and white population in the United States. The Court generally upheld laws which enforced the separation of the two "castes," and struck down laws which permitted or facilitated contact between them on a level of equality.

The Supreme Court's role in the American caste order may be clarified by first briefly summarizing and illustrating the role in this respect of law in general. The federal and state governments have swung between two legal poles, one favorable and one unfavorable to the Negro. This ambiguity has been the result of two impulses, the one to uphold caste, and the other to uphold the official American equalitarian and democratic ideology. Where there have been laws against group discrimination (as there are in many states in both the North and South), until the last few years they have seldom been enforced. Such laws perform the function of enabling us to maintain a high abstract standard of conduct without requiring us to implement the rights guaranteed in the statutes. Where the law has required group discrimination, as throughout the South, its function has been to buttress the caste order when custom no longer sufficed to maintain traditional patterns of Negro-white relations. One of the best examples of this function of law in the United States was the attempt of Southern states, after the Civil War, to maintain the old Negro-white relations by law when the Emancipation and the Confederate defeat were disturbing long-standing custom. As Charles S. Johnson says, eight states "passed the famous Black Codes in a deliberate attempt to define the expected behavior of Negroes so as to coincide as nearly as possible with that which characterized the Old South." [108]

On the other hand, America's equalitarian ideology and its traditional emphasis upon economic freedom permit Negroes and other minority groups to crack the caste line at some points. Weber has stated [109] that one's economic position, especially in our day, is an important element in the determination of one's status, position, or caste, since the ability to maintain any "style of life" depends upon one's wealth. Though the economic opportunities of Negroes have been considerably restricted, many members of the group have succeeded in making enough money to enter the market place for the goods and services which only whites could usually afford. And they have found sellers. But such intermingling with whites threatens the caste order; hence two results follow. First, the Negro's economic position is not permitted to affect his caste position as much as it ordinarily might. Law has functioned to prevent this common American social climbing through wealth—the Negro has been kept from contact with the upper caste in those kinds of social intercourse which imply equality by their intimacy. Here the Supreme Court, as we have said, has until about 1937 buttressed laws which enforce separation and weakened those tending to facilitate the meeting of the two groups on equal grounds. Second, the legislatures and the Supreme Court, mindful of America's equalitarian tradition, have established the "separate but equal" doctrine, which asserts that:

"A statute which implies merely a legal distinction between the white and colored races—a distinction which is founded in the color of the two races, and which must always exist so long as white men are distinguished from the other race by color— has no tendency to destroy the legal equality of the two races, or reestablish a state of involuntary servitude." [110]

It is against the background of the Court's past role in discrimination against Negroes that we now consider the Court's position during the past decade on discrimination against minority groups in general.

CHAPTER THREE

The Supreme Court, 1937–1950:
Undermining the Caste Order

THE philosophy and practice of government in the United States, as we have already seen, changed considerably during the 1930s. Among the leading changes was a shift in the Supreme Court toward greater protection of civil liberties and the civil rights of minority groups.

The Supreme Court's redirection of emphasis corresponded to advances in the status and welfare of minority groups, and in turn strengthened these gains. "Courts," writes R. M. MacIver, "are not themselves primary agents of social change. They register, often laggingly, the changes that move in the community." [1] During the later 1930s the Court followed a different policy from that which guided its predecessors; it now gave to civil rights the same preferred position which earlier Courts had given to property rights. In both cases the Court has singled out some principle of the Constitution for special treatment. This is truly the making of policy. Such fundamental innovations have been infrequent in a body which, despite ever-changing personnel from generation to generation, has been usually oriented to the past in carrying out its role in the government of the United States. Even when it breaks with the past the Court points to precedent, to the very tradition of breaking precedents. Speaking for the majority in a significant civil rights case in 1944, Justice Reed asserted: "In reaching this conclusion we are not unmindful of the desirability of continuity of decision in constitutional questions. However, when convinced of former error, this Court has never felt constrained to follow precedent." [2]

One of the most venerable fictions about judicial review insists that when presented with a constitutional issue the Court merely compares the statute to the fundamental charter of our government, and then declares the law either valid or invalid. This view was enshrined in a majority opinion in 1936,[3] but it no longer commands the respect it once did. It is now generally recognized, on and off the Court, that judicial law-making is inevitable, and that it is far better for judges to be aware of the principles upon which they make law than to do so unsystematically and upon shifting, unexamined premises. Such recognition is implied in Hughes's famous remark, made before he had served as associate justice and later chief justice of the Supreme Court: "We are under a Constitution, but the Constitution is what the judges say it is." [4] The variety of precedents at its disposal has given the Court considerable freedom in the selection of the policies it has wanted to advance at the expense of alternatives it has not found attractive. In the 1920s, for example, the Court blocked legislation on child labor, minimum wages for women, farm problems, and utility valuation. In the decade after the Civil War five major statutes and three constitutional amendments sought to give the newly freed Negroes all the rights and privileges enjoyed by white citizens; but in the following generation the Supreme Court in case after case restricted the application of these statutes and amendments.

THE NEW DEPARTURE IN JUDICIAL REVIEW

The Supreme Court since about 1937, we have said, has emphasized protection of civil rights. It is the application of its restraining powers to this area instead of to property rights which distinguishes the present Court from those before it, rather than a distinction in fundamental approach to the power of judicial review itself. In the realm of economic regulation the present Court allows the federal and state governments considerably greater freedom than they have ever enjoyed, but in the realm of civil rights the Court is less willing to permit such freedom to these governments.

In 1940, Justice Black had stated for the entire Court the philosophy to which it adheres: "No higher duty, no more solemn responsibility, rests upon this Court, than that of translating into living law and maintaining this constitutional shield deliberately planned and inscribed for the benefit of every human being subject to our Constitution—of whatever race, creed or persuasion." [5]

One of the earliest statements of this policy of solicitude for civil rights came from Justice Stone in his majority opinion in the *Carolene Products* case in 1938. Justice Stone pointed out that when a legislature prohibits an Act as dangerous, it is assumed that there are facts to support that judgment; such a statute is not to be held unconstitutional unless the facts show that it does not rest upon "some rational basis within the knowledge and experience of the legislators." Then in a note Justice Stone added with respect to this "presumption of constitutionality" where the subject of the statute is a civil right: "There may be narrower scope for operation of the presumption of constitutionality when legislation appears on its face to be within a specific prohibition of the Constitution, such as those of the first ten amendments, which are deemed equally specific when held to be embraced within the Fourteenth." [6]

Though Justice Stone in this opinion did not find it necessary for the Court to determine just then whether legislation restricting the right to political dissent from the majority view, or legislation directed at religious, national, or racial minorities, ought to be "subjected to more exacting judicial scrutiny" than most other types of legislation, the Court in later years took this very position and asserted that such statutes do "call for a correspondingly more searching inquiry."

The decisions of the Court in the last decade fall into three categories according to the particular group most affected. First are the opinions in which the Court expanded the protection afforded to all minorities, but especially the Negroes, under the Fourteenth Amendment. Second are those in which the Court upheld the right of Congress to limit the liberty of persons (citizens and noncitizens) of Japanese descent. Third are those, involving the Jehovah's Witnesses sect, in which the Court enlarged political and religious freedom while protecting the rights of this religious minority.

THE FOURTEENTH AMENDMENT

We shall now examine the way in which the Court has since 1937 reinterpreted the privileges and immunities, due process, and equal protection clauses of the Fourteenth Amendment to increase their protective value to minority groups.

Revival of the Privileges and Immunities Clause

Soon after the ratification of the Fourteenth Amendment in 1868, the Supreme Court made the privileges and immunities clause virtually inoperative. In 1939 [7] Justice Stone could point to at least fifty cases in which a state law was challenged as a violation of this clause; but in only one case,[8] was a state law invalidated on this ground, and this opinion was expressly overruled in a similar case [9] five years later. The usefulness of this clause, nevertheless, has continued to impress certain members of the Court even though it has not yet been revived.

In 1941 four justices held that a state law violated the privileges and immunities clause. In the *Edwards* case [10] an indigent Texan was brought to California by his wife's brother, in violation of a California law. The issue before the Court was whether the statute, forbidding the bringing or transportation into the state of persons known to be indigent, was within California's police power. The Court unanimously held that it was not, but the justices split five to four on the grounds for this conclusion. Justice Byrnes for the majority of five denied California the power to enact such a statute on the ground that "it imposes an unconstitutional burden upon interstate commerce." [11] This ground evoked considerable opposition from the remaining four justices. Justice Douglas, in an opinion in which Justices Black and Murphy concurred, asserted that "the right of persons to move freely from State to State occupies a more protected position in our constitutional system than does the movement of cattle, fruit, steel and coal across state lines." [12] Justice Jackson pointed out: "To hold that the measure of his [an indigent person's] rights is the commerce clause is likely to result eventually either in distorting the commercial law or in denaturing human rights." [13] Justices Douglas, Black, Murphy, and Jackson all preferred to rest their decision in this case on the ground that the California law violated the privileges and immunities clause of the Fourteenth Amendment. Had these four justices been joined by one, that clause would have come to life once again.

The prospective revival of the clause received a setback in 1944, however, when the Court held,[14] seven to two, that the right to become a candidate for a state office is an attribute of state citizenship, and hence not protected by the privileges and immunities clause, which refers to federal citizenship. The two dissenters showed no inclination to dispute the majority on this particular point.

Justices Stone and Frankfurter were especially intransigent in opposing the revival of the privileges and immunities clause. In his opinion in *Hague v. C.I.O.*, the former stated that to enlarge the scope of the clause "more than is needful to protect relationships between the citizen and the national government" or to use the clause to protect personal and property rights traditionally protected by the states, would result in jeopardizing the independence of local government.[15] And Justice Frankfurter stated in 1947: "I put to one side the Privileges or Immunities Clause of that Amendment. For the mischievous uses to which that clause would lend itself if its scope were not confined to that given it by all but one of the decisions beginning with the Slaughter-House Case . . . see the deviation in Colgate v. Harvey." [16]

These fears do not seem to be entirely warranted. The privileges and immunities clause, as Edwin Borchard argues,[17] could be given its originally intended meaning as protecting the Bill of Rights against encroachment by the state, but not by private individuals, and still not jeopardize the integrity of local government. Actually, however, as we shall see in a moment, the Court has already included most of these civil rights under the due process clause of the Fourteenth Amendment, making it less imperative today to rely upon the privileges and immunities clause.

Expansion and Contraction of the Due Process Clause

The due process clause of the Fourteenth Amendment was originally applied only as a restraint against improper procedure.[18] In the late nineteenth century the clause came to be used also to invalidate legislation on economic matters which, in the opinion of the Court, was "unreasonable." [19] One of the most significant developments in judicial review during the last decade has been the Supreme Court's reluctance to decide what is reasonable or unreasonable, wise or unwise, in the economic realm. Thus the Court in 1940, upholding a Texas commission's establishment of oil quotas, asserted that in such disputes "courts must not substitute their notions of expediency and fairness for those which have guided the agencies to whom the formulation and execution of policy have been entrusted." [20]

In 1925 the Supreme Court began to bring the freedoms of the Bill of Rights under the protection of the due process clause of the Fourteenth Amendment. This practice continued during the next decade, until the Court has by now declared that a considerable number, though not all, of these rights restrain the states as well as the federal government.[21] The majority of the Court, being unwilling to transfer all liberties from state to federal protection, has rejected a number of pleas based upon the due process clause. In one case in 1942, a six-to-three majority held that while state action which violates certain specific guarantees in the first eight amendments "may, in certain circumstances . . . operate, in a given case, to deprive a litigant of due process of law in violation" of the Fourteenth Amendment, its due process clause "does not incorporate, as such, the specific guarantees found in the Sixth Amendment." [22] The issue then before the Court was whether the right of an accused in all cases to be furnished counsel when he cannot afford it is so fundamental that the Fourteenth Amendment makes this a right in state courts. The majority held that this right is not of such a fundamental character. The three dissenters, Justices Black, Murphy, and Douglas, opposed the majority on both issues, insisting that "the Fourteenth Amendment made the Sixth applicable to the states," and that the right to counsel is so fundamental a part of due process that it is included within the rights protected directly by the Fourteenth Amendment.[23]

In *Adamson v. California* [24] the Court in 1947 faced the very same problems, this time with respect to the rights embodied in the Fifth Amendment. Adamson, convicted of murder and sentenced to death, claimed that a California law which permits the court and counsel to comment upon, and the court and jury to take into consideration, an accused person's failure to take the witness stand, was in violation of the Fourteenth Amendment. In the *Betts* case this kind of claim had won the support of three members of the Court, and in the *Adamson* case Justice Rutledge joined the *Betts* case dissenters. This time the four justices stated plainly that the Fourteenth Amendment protects all the guarantees in the first eight amendments against infringement by the states.

One of the most important cases to reach the Supreme Court in this period was *Screws v. United States* [25] in 1945. Sheriff

Screws of Baker County, Georgia, with the aid of a policeman and a special deputy, placed Robert Hall, a Negro, under arrest at his home late at night. The three officers beat Hall severely, and he died a short time later. The federal government prosecuted under Section 52 of Title 18 of the United States Code (originally part of the Civil Rights Act of 1866), which prescribes a maximum fine of $1,000 or a maximum prison term of one year, or both, for any one who, "under color of any law, statute, ordinance, regulation, or custom, willfully subjects or causes to be subjected, any inhabitant of any State, Territory, or District to the deprivation of any rights, privileges, or immunities secured or protected by the Constitution and laws of the United States, or to different punishments, pains, or penalties, on account of such inhabitant being an alien, or by reason of his color, or race, than are prescribed for the punishment of citizens." [26] Six members of the Court held this statute constitutional despite a variety of claims that it was invalid, thus preserving (and reviving) an important protective device for Negroes and other minorities. (Justice Murphy dissented from the majority opinion, subscribed to by five justices, not on the constitutional issue but on their order of a new trial for the convicted officials because of an improper charge to the jury.)

While preserving Section 52 as a protective device for minorities, the Court in the *Screws* case also took an important step in the determination of what constitutes "state action" under the prohibitions of the Fourteenth Amendment. In two of the 1879 jury cases [27] the Supreme Court had ruled that state action included the conduct of any governmental branch of the state, legislative, executive, or judicial. "The constitutional provision, therefore," said the Court in the later of these two cases, "must mean that no agency of the State, or of the officers or agents by whom its powers are exerted, shall deny to any person within its jurisdiction the equal protection of the laws." [28] In the *Screws* case the Court further defined state action by including, against the claims of the officials on trial and the three dissenters, even unauthorized acts performed by representatives of the state. Referring to the phrase "under color of law" in Section 52, Justice Douglas said for the majority: "Acts of officers who undertake to perform their official duties are included whether they hew to the line of their authority or overstep it." [29]

This brief review of the due process clause as interpreted by what we may conveniently call the Roosevelt Court [30] indicates that while this provision of the Fourteenth Amendment is no longer the obstacle it once was to legislation in the economic realm, it has been employed with increasing frequency to protect civil rights.

More "Equal Protection of the Laws"

The equal protection clause of the Fourteenth Amendment was the chief instrument of federal protection of minority rights in the earlier periods of Supreme Court history, and has also been the chief instrument of the present Court. By a changing interpretation of what constitutes equal protection of the laws, the Court is moving toward a point where it can apply this clause in its full strength. Discrimination (and, to some extent, segregation) has been powerfully assaulted by the Court in criminal trials, suffrage, housing, transportation, and higher education.

Juries. It was in 1879 that the Supreme Court first prohibited the states from excluding Negroes from juries solely on the ground of race or color.[31] The Court has continued to protect this right against state infringement, and in 1935, in *Norris v. Alabama*,[32] made it even more effective. Until the settlement of this case it was necessary, in order to prove discrimination, to present direct evidence that the exclusion was on racial grounds alone. In the *Norris* case, however, the Court held that discrimination could be inferred from the continued absence of Negroes from the lists of jurors and from juries.

Chief Justice Hughes stated this doctrine for a unanimous Court (Justice McReynolds not participating):

We think that the evidence that for a generation or longer no negro had been called for service on any jury in Jackson County, that there were negroes qualified for jury service, that according to the practice of the jury commission their names would normally appear on the preliminary list of male citizens of the requisite age but that no names of negroes were placed on the jury roll, and the testimony with respect to the lack of appropriate consideration of the qualifications of negroes, established the discrimination which the Constitution forbids.[33]

The Roosevelt Court has consistently applied this doctrine to the cases brought before it. In upholding the conviction of a Negro sentenced to death for murder, the Louisiana Supreme Court held that although no Negroes were on the grand jury, their absence was not the result of exclusion because of race. But Justice Black, for all the members of the Court, held that while the view of the Louisiana high court was entitled to respect, the Supreme Court must make its own determination of the facts when a man's life is at stake.[34] The Court ordered a new trial on the basis of the following facts: that from 1896 to 1936 not a single Negro had served on a grand jury or petit jury in that particular parish of Louisiana; that Negroes constituted nearly half of the total population of the parish; and that most of the Negroes of the parish could read and write. These facts, said the Court, were sufficient to establish the fact of improper exclusion of Negroes. A year later, in 1940, the Court unanimously ordered a new trial in a Texas case on the same ground.[35] In 1942 the Court again upset a Texas trial, holding that it was not necessary to prove that there was deliberate racial discrimination in the absence of Negroes from grand juries for sixteen years; one had only to show systematic exclusion, said the Court.[36] Three years later the Court had before it a case [37] from the same county in Texas. The county had placed one Negro on a grand jury panel, and this act, said Justice Reed for the six-to-three majority (Justice Rutledge concurring), had satisfied the requirement of equal protection of the laws. Chief Justice Stone and Justice Black dissented without giving a statement, while Justice Murphy dissented on the ground that by limiting the number of Negroes on the panel to one, the jury commissioners had refused "to disregard the factor of color." [38] Again in 1947 the Court applied the doctrine that systematic exclusion is evidence of improper discrimination against Negroes as jurors. In a Mississippi case,[39] Justice Black held for a unanimous Court that indictments and verdicts cannot be sustained when made by juries selected in such a way that for thirty years no Negro had been chosen for service.

Suffrage. In 1935 minority rights suffered a setback when the Supreme Court unanimously ruled in *Grovey v. Townsend* [40] that exclusion of nonwhites from membership by the convention of the Texas Democratic party did not violate the Fourteenth Amendment. This decision prevailed until 1941, when the Court decided the famous *Classic* case.[41] Though not directly involving Negroes or minorities, this case has proved to be of the greatest importance for them.

Election officials of Louisiana were prosecuted by the federal government under Sections 51 and 52 of Title 18 of the United States Code for having altered ninety-seven ballots in a primary election to nominate a candidate for Congress, thus acting under the color of law to deprive qualified voters of their right to have their primary election ballots counted as they cast them. Justice Stone, speaking for the majority of five (Chief Justice Hughes not participating), stated that the issue before the Court was whether this right was one guaranteed by the federal government within the meaning of Sections 51 and 52, and whether the acts of the election officials violated those sections.[42] To both these questions the answer was in the affirmative. For the first time the Court took notice of the fact that in the South the Democratic party primary is the only election in which there is any contest, since the general election uniformly brings victory to that party. "Interference with the right to vote in the Congressional primary . . . for the choice of Democratic candidate for Congress," said Justice Stone, "is thus, as a matter of law and in fact, an interference with the effective choice of the voters at the only stage . . . when such interference could have any practical effect on the ultimate result, the choice of the Congressman to represent the district." [43] Where, as in the South, the primaries are a step in the general elections, Congress has the power, Justice Stone asserted, to regulate primaries for federal offices under Article I, Section 4 of the Constitution. The Court upheld the validity of Sections 51 and 52 as well as their applicability to the acts of the accused. Although the dissenters (Justice Douglas, Black, and Murphy) denied that the acts of the election officials were covered by these two sections, they agreed with the majority that the sections were constitutional, and that Article I of the Constitution gave Congress the power to govern both primary and general elections for federal office.[44] This is to be compared with the situation in 1917 when, in the *Gradwell* case,[45] the Court had unanimously refused to hold that the federal government could govern a primary election, insisting that the rights of a candidate at that stage were derived wholly from the state.

As soon as the *Classic* case decision established federal control over Southern primaries for national offices, the legal department of the National Association for the Advancement of Colored People picked up a case and started it through the judicial mill to advance Negro rights even further. The case, similar to the earlier ones testing the constitutionality of the Texas Democratic party's exclusion of Negroes from the primaries, reached the Supreme Court in 1944 as *Smith v. Allwright*.[46] Smith, a Negro, was refused a ballot in the 1940 Democratic primary in Harris City, Texas. The Supreme Court took the case as an opportunity to resolve the claimed inconsistency between the opinion in *Grovey v. Townsend* and that in the *Classic* case. The issue, said Justice Reed in his opinion for the majority, was whether the Texas Democratic party could exclude Negroes without violating the Fourteenth or Fifteenth Amendment or whether such exclusion constituted the state action which they proscribe.[47] Following the *Classic* case decision, the Court held that the relation of the primary to the general elections "makes clear that state delegation to a party of the power to fix the qualifications of primary elections is delegation of a state function that may make the party's action the action of the State." [48] Was it, then, the majority asked, state action or private action that excluded Negroes from the primary? Answering that it was state action in violation of the Fourteenth and Fifteenth Amendments, the Court pointed to a number of Texas statutes relating the primary election of the Democratic party to the affairs of the state itself. "We think that this statutory system," concluded Justice Reed, ". . . makes the party which is required to follow these legislative directions an agency of the State in so far as it determines the participants in a primary election." [49] And again: "When primaries become a part of the machinery for choosing officials, state and national, as they have here, the same tests to determine the character of discrimination or abridgement should be applied to the primary as are applied to the general election." [50] On the question of the relation between the *Grovey* and *Classic* case opinions, the Court stated flatly: "Grovey v. Townsend is overruled." [51]

Justices Roberts and Stone were the only members of the Court during the *Smith* case who had also taken part in the *Grovey* case. The latter went along with the majority in overruling the earlier opinion, but Justice Roberts bitterly dissented. Arguing for the maintenance of the *Grovey* opinion, which he had delivered for the Court, Justice Roberts indicated that he was particularly disturbed that the Court should now hold that the *Classic* case opinion overruled *Grovey v. Town-*

send, since he himself had voted with the majority in the *Classic* case. The tendency of the present Court to overrule earlier decisions, he pointed out, "involves an assumption that knowledge and wisdom reside in us which was denied to our predecessors." [52]

The decision in *Smith v. Allwright* did not, of course, result in the immediate admission of Negroes into the Democratic party in Southern states. The reaction of an important group in Southern political life was revealed in the remarks by United States Senator Burnet R. Maybank of South Carolina, who told his colleagues in session: "We are going to treat the Negro fairly, but in so doing we do not intend for him to take over our election system or attend our white schools. . . . Regardless of any Supreme Court decisions and any laws that may be passed by Congress, we of the South will maintain our political and social institutions as we believe to be in the best interest of our people." [53]

About the same time, the Governor of South Carolina called the legislature into special session to circumvent the *Smith v. Allwright* opinion. These events are recounted in the decision delivered in 1947 by District Judge Waring in *Elmore v. Rice.*[54] At the meeting of the legislature on April 12, 1944, the Governor's message was read, stating that because of the *Smith* case opinion "it now becomes absolutely necessary that we repeal all laws pertaining to primaries in order to maintain white supremacy in our Democratic Primaries in South Carolina." The legislators proceeded to repeal one hundred and fifty laws, every trace of a statute on the primaries. Georgia adopted the same course (though it later reenacted its primary laws) and other states threatened to follow suit. Two years later, in August of 1946, Elmore, a Negro, was refused a Democratic party primary ballot in Richland County, South Carolina. The issue before the judges of the District Court was whether this action was an unconstitutional violation of Elmore's rights. Judge Waring relied on the *Classic* and *Smith* cases. Rejecting the claim that the Democratic party, in the absence of any laws relating to the primary, was a "private club," he pointed out that "private clubs and business organizations do not vote and elect a President of the United States, and the Senators and members of the House of Representatives of our national congress; and under the law of our land, all citizens are entitled to a voice in such selections." [55] Judge Waring reported that in the very primary from which Elmore was excluded, 290,223 votes were polled for Governor, whereas in the general election the following November only 26,326 votes were cast for that office. Since 1900, he showed, every governor of South Carolina and every member of the General Assembly as well as all the state's representatives in the United States Senate and House of Representatives, were in the Democratic party. In the preceding quarter-century, he added, that party was the only one holding statewide primaries for the nomination of candidates to federal and state offices.[56] The Democratic party of 1947, he held, was not materially different from the Democratic party of 1944, and hence its exclusion of Negroes was still state action in violation of the Fourteenth Amendment. When an appeal [57] to the Circuit Court of Appeals failed, South Carolina applied to the United States Supreme Court for a review of the case, but in April, 1948, the Court refused to hear it.[58]

This series of setbacks, however, did not deter the officers of the South Carolina Democratic party from further efforts to exclude Negroes. After the Supreme Court's refusal to hear the *Elmore* case, the Democratic party convention on May 19, 1948, adopted two sets of rules for voting in the primaries, making it more difficult for Negroes to qualify than for whites. Judge Waring describes this technique as follows: [59] The convention established a rule limiting membership in the "club" to "white Democrats." Another rule provided that "members" might vote in the primaries, and that Negro electors, "in conformity with the Order of Judge J. Waties Waring in the case of Elmore, etc. v. Rice et al.," might also vote if they took the oath required of all those who wanted to vote in the primary. This oath, given in still another rule, required a voter in the primary to state that he "will support the social (religious) and educational separation of races," and that he opposes a federal "F.E.P.C. law." [60]

Judge Waring said of these rules: "It would . . . seem that the action of the convention was a deliberate attempt to evade the apparent consequence of the Elmore case." Then he made clear the obligation of the Democratic party of South Carolina: "It is important that once and for all, the members of this Party be made to understand—and that is the purpose of this opinion—that they will be required to obey and carry out the orders of this court, not only in the technical respects but in the true spirit and meaning of the same." [61]

Federal protection of suffrage rights was also extended in *United States v. Saylor,*[62] decided by the Supreme Court in 1944 about the same time as the decision in *Smith v. Allwright.* This case widened the application of Section 51, punishing conspiracies of two or more persons which hinder any citizen in the exercise of the rights guaranteed him by the United States. The government prosecuted election officials of Harlan County, Kentucky, for having stuffed the ballot box in favor of their own candidate, thus impairing the right of other voters to have their votes counted for the opposing candidate. A six-to-three majority held that Section 51 included within its proscriptions the fraud committed by the indicted officials. Justices Douglas, Black, and Reed vainly insisted that it should be limited to those cases in which voters were actually deprived of the right to vote or to have their own ballots counted. This opinion, taken with that in the *Classic* case, as former Attorney General Biddle stated, restored "the power of the federal government to punish election frauds, which appeared to be lost with the repeal of the Enforcement Act in 1894." [63]

Still another means of preserving the white primary in the

South was used in Alabama. In 1946 the legislature adopted the "Boswell amendment" to the state constitution, requiring that persons who register to vote must be able to "understand and explain" any article in the United States Constitution. Several Negroes brought suit charging the Boswell amendment violated the Federal Constitution because it vested unlimited discretionary powers in the local boards of registrars, applied no reasonable or recognizable standard or test, and was used in such a way that Negroes were required to give lengthy explanations and were then refused registration, whereas whites registered without having to give any explanations at all. A federal district court in 1949 declared this amendment in violation of the Fifteenth Amendment to the United States Constitution, concluding that "its main object was to restrict voting on a basis of race or color." [64] Shortly thereafter the United States Supreme Court affirmed this judgment,[65] thus withdrawing the legal prop from another method for preventing Negroes from voting in a Southern primary election.

As a result of these decisions on suffrage, Negroes are voting in increasing numbers in Southern Democratic primaries and general elections. A report of the Southern Regional Council stated in 1948 that "it would be difficult to point to more than a handful of Southern cities of 25,000 or more in which there is vigorous opposition to Negroes becoming registered voters." [66] The Negroes' judicial victories have divided the white South. In South Carolina, after the Democratic party convention on May 19, 1948, took the action already described, there was considerable opposition throughout the state, and six counties announced that they would defy the state convention by qualifying Negroes and whites on the same basis.[67] The political future of the South is being shaped in these years of change. In the granting of the legal right of Negroes to vote in all phases of Southern elections, the democratic ideology triumphed over the caste ideology. What can the white upper caste do now, if Negroes are able to make their voting power felt in an impressive way? If it continues its attempts at exclusion, then the Negroes are very likely to be impelled to vote solidly, as a bloc. This development would increase the present tension and make the minority even more "dangerous" as a cohesive unit. If, however, the white South accepts the Negro as a voter in the Democratic party, the white-Negro dichotomy will be somewhat blurred, and the Negroes will probably divide at the polls in much the same way that whites do.

Housing. Many members of minority groups, especially Negroes, are in the lowest income brackets in the United States. But this is only one explanation of the fact that housing of the colored minority is generally substandard. Weaver lists these additional obstacles:

Community, neighborhood, and individual opposition to colored neighbors.
Race restrictive housing covenants.
Agreements, practices, and codes of ethics among real estate boards and operators.
FHA acceptance and perpetuation of real estate practice.
Neglect of Negro market by private builders and sources of finance.
Local government's fear that adequate or more housing will encourage Negro migration.
Local political action to restrict Negroes to given areas.
Development of exclusive one-class neighborhoods.[68]

The Roosevelt Court has at least been able to weaken the racial restrictive covenants among individuals, which prohibit the sale or leasing of land and other property to certain minorities. When in 1917 the Court invalidated a Kentucky city ordinance requiring residential segregation,[69] there was a great increase in the number of private agreements made for the same purpose, especially in the Northern cities to which thousands of Negroes had migrated during and after World War I. In 1926 the Court held that such private agreements did not violate the Fifth, Thirteenth, or Fourteenth Amendments.[70] The extent of general coverage of racial covenants is described by Weaver: "That pattern is as follows: desirable housing surrounding centers of Negro concentration is largely covered by racial covenants in many cities; the rest of the surrounding housing is usually closed to Negroes by intense neighborhood hostility, often inspired by the existence of covenants in the better areas; other sections of our cities have become and are becoming race restrictive housing conscious; and in all cities deed restrictions are effective barriers to minorities' entrance into new, desirable subdivisions and the vast majority of new houses." [71] A similar estimate of coverage was made by the Department of Justice in its *amicus curiae* brief in the covenant cases argued before the Supreme Court late in 1947.[72]

The four cases in which this brief was submitted brought to a head a concerted attack upon the validity of judicial enforcement of private restrictive covenants. Two of these cases [73] dealt with covenants in Washington, D.C. A unanimous Court (Justices Reed, Rutledge, and Jackson not participating) held that the District of Columbia courts' enforcement of the agreements is prohibited by the federal Civil Rights Act of 1866, although the agreements themselves are not prohibited. For the two cases outside of the capital,[74] the Court relied upon the settled doctrine that judicial action is state action. Justice Vinson stated for the six participating justices that "the restrictive agreements standing alone cannot be regarded as violative of any rights guaranteed . . . by the Fourteenth Amendment." But, he added, the state courts have enforced the covenants in the cases now up for settlement. "That the action of state courts and of judicial officers in their official capacities is to be regarded as action of the State within the meaning of the Fourteenth Amendment, is a proposition which has long been established by decisions of this Court." [75] By enforcing the restrictive agreements, the state, concluded

Justice Vinson, deprived the minorities of their right to the equal protection of the laws.

In a later and likewise significant case, however, the Court rejected an opportunity to review a New York court decision which disappointed the groups seeking unsegregated housing. The New York State Court of Appeals in 1949 held, by a vote of four to three,[76] that the refusal of the Metropolitan Life Insurance Company to lease to Negroes in its Stuyvesant Town development did not constitute state action prohibited by the Fourteenth Amendment. The unsuccessful Negro applicants had claimed that this refusal was in fact state action because the company built the houses with New York City aid in the form of condemnation of a substandard area, tax exemption for twenty-five years, and the closing of certain streets within the area. In 1950, a United States Supreme Court majority, from which Justices Black and Douglas dissented, refused to review this case.[77]

Transportation. In the past, the Supreme Court had steadfastly refused to invalidate legislation on transportation facilities requiring and enforcing the separation of Negroes and whites. Nevertheless the Court has upheld the rights of minorities to "equal facilities" where they are separate. In 1941 Chief Justice Hughes made a particularly forceful statement for this interpretation of the equal protection clause of the Fourteenth Amendment.[78] Congressman Arthur W. Mitchell, a Chicago Negro, was forced to give up a Pullman seat at Memphis during a journey from Chicago to Hot Springs, Arkansas, on the Chicago, Rock Island, and Pacific Railway, and to ride in a coach reserved for Negroes which did not have a seat of the same quality as his original seat. The Interstate Commerce Commission, to whom the Congressman protested, dismissed the complaint on the ground that there was little demand by Negroes for the accommodations he was denied at Memphis. Justice Hughes reversed this ruling and that of the United States district court supporting it, pointing out for a unanimous

Court that the denial of a personal right cannot be justified by the fact that there are few persons who want to exercise it.

Five years later, in 1946, the Supreme Court, in *Morgan v. Virginia*, for the first time invalidated a state law requiring segregation.[79] A Negro woman boarded a bus in Virginia, bound for Baltimore, Maryland, through Washington, D.C. Told by the driver to take a back seat, she refused and was arrested and later convicted of violating a Virginia statute requiring the segregation of Negroes and whites on common carriers. The Court chose to rest its decision on the commerce clause of Article I rather than on the equal protection clause of the Fourteenth Amendment. Justice Reed stated for the majority (Justice Jackson not participating and Justice Burton dissenting) that Article I, Section 8 of the Constitution gave Congress the power to "regulate commerce . . . among the several states," and that a state law materially affecting interstate commerce might be invalid even in the absence of conflicting Congressional legislation. The Virginia statute, the Court held, was a "burden" upon interstate commerce: "A burden may arise from a state statute which requires interstate passengers to order their movements on the vehicle in accordance with local rather than national requirements."[80] This ruling, of course, left intact the many state laws requiring segregation within the state borders.

In the *Morgan* case just reviewed the Court invalidated a state law requiring segregation in interstate transportation. Three years later the United States Circuit Court of Appeals for the Sixth Circuit invalidated, on the basis of the *Morgan* opinion, a bus company's regulation requiring such segregation.[81] The Court held that not only did the company's action constitute state action prohibited by commerce clause of the Federal Constitution, but that even if there were no state action involved, the company's regulation would be invalidated as a private interference with interstate commerce.

In 1948 the Court settled an interesting minority rights

case [82] involving the commerce clause again. A Michigan company, owning most of the island of Bob-Lo, which is part of Ontario, Canada, operates the area as an amusement park for Detroit residents. The company in 1945 also owned and operated two ships exclusively to transport patrons between Detroit and the island. When it excluded a Negro from one of its ships, the company was convicted of violating Section 146 of the Michigan civil rights act, which provides that all persons are entitled to "full and equal accommodations . . . of . . . public conveyances on land and water." The company claimed it was not subject to the act because it operated ships in foreign commerce, but the Court, through Justice Rutledge (Chief Justice Vinson and Justice Jackson dissenting), held that "the island is economically and socially, though not politically, an . . . adjunct of the city of Detroit," and hence the company was engaged in local commerce.[83]

These two cases illustrate that even where the present Court does not feel itself justified in invoking the equal protection clause it will go far to protect minorities—unlike the Courts in the Reconstruction period and later.

The *Mitchell* case of 1941 was the basis upon which the Supreme Court in 1950 unanimously (Justice Clark not participating) held that a Southern Railway Company regulation violated the antidiscrimination section of the Interstate Commerce Act.[84] In 1942 Elmer W. Henderson, a member of the wartime Committee on Fair Employment Practice was refused service in a dining car because the two rear tables reserved for Negroes were occupied in part by whites. He filed a complaint with the Interstate Commerce Commission, which found that he had been subjected to undue and unreasonable prejudice and disadvantage but that it was a casual incident. A federal district court in 1946, however, held that the railroad's dining car regulations did violate the Interstate Commerce Act. The company then instituted an arrangement under which one table in each dining car was reserved exclusively for Negroes and was separated from the others by a curtain or partition. The Commission ruled that this arrangement did not violate the Act, and a federal district court sustained this ruling. The Supreme Court, however, held that the *Mitchell* case was applicable to this one. The railroad's practice, said Justice Burton, violated the antidiscrimination clause of the Interstate Commerce Act in that a passenger might be refused service because of this arrangement. He added significantly: "The curtains, partitions and signs emphasize the artificiality of a difference in treatment which serves only to call attention to a racial classification of passengers holding identical tickets and using the same public dining facility." [85]

Education. Negro organizations, carrying on their campaign to advance Negro rights, attacked their problems in education in much the same way as they did in travel segregation —by insisting rigidly upon the "equal facilities" to which the courts said they were entitled. In 1938 a Missouri case [86] increased the requirements of the "separate but equal" doctrine. Lloyd Gaines, a Negro, was refused admission to the University of Missouri law school after graduating from Lincoln University, the state's college for Negroes. In accordance with a state law, he was advised to apply to an out-of-state law school, to which Missouri would pay a "reasonable" tuition fee for him. Gaines protested that he was being deprived of "equal facilities," since Missouri maintained a law school for whites but not for Negroes. The Supreme Court, in an opinion by Chief Justice Hughes (Justice McReynolds and Butler dissenting) upheld this claim, reiterating that his right to a law school education in Missouri was a personal one unaffected by the fact that few Negroes chose to exercise it.

Early in 1948 the Supreme Court advanced minority rights still another step. Ada Sipuel, a Negro woman, applied for admission to the law school maintained by the state of Oklahoma. She was denied admission in accordance with a state law requiring the separation of Negroes and whites in the schools.

Her case [87] was argued in the Supreme Court on January 7 and 8, and the Court delivered its decision only four days later, a one-page mimeographed, unsigned statement for all its members. The statement ordered Oklahoma to provide a legal education for the Negro applicant "as soon as it does for applicants of any other group." This was a clear reference to the fact that a new semester would open late that month at the regular Oklahoma law school. By stressing the time element the Court was giving the state only two alternatives— to admit the Negro or to establish a law school for Negroes within a few weeks. It is further apparent from the remarks and questions by the members of the Court that some at least did not think a law school established in less than a month could provide an education equal to that obtainable in the older institution. Justice Jackson, for example, observed that a school with only one student would not provide "much of a law education." [88] Oklahoma officials, nevertheless, managed to put together a law school that opened its doors for Negro registrants on January 26. Miss Sipuel, however, refused to apply there and sought instead a mandamus from the Supreme Court to compel her immediate acceptance by the regular law school. In another unsigned, but not unanimous, opinion the Court held that the state district court "did not depart from our mandate" when it permitted the state to meet the original Supreme Court order by setting up a new law school. [89] The opinion also pointed out that the original plea did not raise the question whether a state could satisfy the equal protection clause by organizing a separate school for Negroes. Justice Rutledge dissented, insisting that the applicant should have been admitted to the existing law school at once. The first of the Court's two rulings in this case was not without effect, for the state universities of Arkansas and Delaware within a few weeks announced that Negroes would be admitted to white classes in courses not given in the college reserved for Negroes. [90]

In June, 1950, faced with two direct challenges to segregation as violating the Federal Constitution, the Supreme Court managed to increase still further the requirements of the separate but equal doctrine without having to decide whether or not that doctrine is itself valid. In *Sweatt v. Painter* the Court narrowed the issue to that of the extent to which the equal protection clause of the Fourteenth Amendment limits the "power of a state to distinguish between students of different races in professional and graduate education in a state university." [91] To comply with an earlier state court ruling, the University of Texas in 1947 opened a law school for Negroes, which the state courts later held provided facilities equal to those for white students in the University of Texas Law School. The Supreme Court, however, reversed these opinions and held that the segregated school for Negroes could not provide them equal facilities, since it was inferior in regard to faculty, the variety of courses offered, and, significantly, in "those qualities which are incapable of objective measurement but which make for greatness in a law school." These qualities, according to Chief Justice Vinson, speaking for a unanimous Court, are reputation of the faculty, school tradition and prestige, and influence of the alumni. The Fourteenth Amendment, the Court concluded, required that the Negro plaintiff be admitted to the University of Texas Law School. [92]

In another case decided on the same day, *McLaurin v. Oklahoma*, the Court further expanded the requirements of the separate but equal doctrine. Pursuant to a federal district court decision, the University of Oklahoma admitted a Negro graduate student but segregated him from the white students. At the time the case was decided by the Supreme Court, this segregation had been mitigated so that the Negro student sat in a special row in classrooms, ate at a special table in the university cafeteria, and used a special table in the library. These restrictions the Court found to violate the Fourteenth Amendment. Set apart from others, said Chief Justice Vinson for a unanimous Court, the Negro student "is handicapped in his pursuit of effective graduate instruction. Such restrictions impair and inhibit his ability to study, engage in discussions and exchange views with other students, and, in general, to learn his profession." Having been admitted to instruction, the Court concluded, he "must receive the same treatment at the hands of the state as students of other races." [93]

Thus, by a progressively stringent interpretation of what constitutes "equal facilities," the Supreme Court has virtually outlawed all forms of segregation in higher education. While the court has not directly discarded the separate but equal doctrine of the *Plessy* case, it is difficult to see how any aspect of segregation in higher education can be sustained now in the light of the opinions in the *Sweatt* and *McLaurin* cases.

In the fall of 1950, only a few months after it had handed down its rulings in the *Sweatt* and *McLaurin* cases, the Supreme Court refused to rehear a Maryland case in which the Southern regional education plan was involved. This plan, adopted in 1948, is an agreement among Southern states to pool their higher educational resources and assign students from all these states to certain segregated schools within the entire region. Following its acceptance of the plan, the University of Maryland refused a Negro woman admission to its school of nursing, and offered to finance her education at Meharry Medical College in Tennessee, a segregated institution for Negroes. She brought suit, and early in 1950 the highest court of Maryland held that, in conformity with earlier United States Supreme Court decisions, the state could not legally assign the plaintiff to an out-of-state school so long as it provided the course of study in a state institution.[94] In October, 1950, the United States Supreme Court denied Maryland's petition for a review of the case,[95] thus in effect upholding the state court's invalidation of one aspect of the regional educational plan as a means of perpetuating segregation and inequality in higher education.

Negro Labor's Rights

Along with its general toleration of legislation designed to strengthen the bargaining position of the working class through trade unions, the Supreme Court in the last decade began to protect the Negro and other minorities against discrimination by labor organizations. In 1944 the Court unanimously held that a union authorized by the federal Railway Labor Act to represent an entire craft, including those not members of the union, may not discriminate in its representation of certain workers simply on the basis of race or color.[96] The Brotherhood of Locomotive Firemen and Engineers, which by its constitution excluded Negroes from membership, was therefore disobeying the statute when it arranged with twenty-one railroads in the South to restrict the employment and advancement of Negro firemen. This decision is to be compared with that in a similar case,[97] involving the Santa Fe Railroad in Kansas City, Kansas, and the Brotherhood of Railway Carmen of America, where the Kansas Supreme Court in 1946 rested its opinion in favor of the Negro employees on the broader ground that the Railway Labor Act had made the union an agency of the government. Hence in discriminating against the Negro carmen, the Brotherhood violated the Fifth Amendment of the United States Constitution.

In 1945 the Supreme Court unanimously upheld the constitutionality of those sections of the New York State civil rights law punishing officers and members of unions which deny membership to any qualified persons because of race, color, or creed, or which withhold equal rights for the same reason.[98] The Railway Mail Association, defending its discriminatory practices, vainly evoked the due process and equal protection clauses of the Fourteenth Amendment.

Before we consider the Supreme Court's treatment of the issues involved in the wartime evacuation and detention of persons of Japanese descent, and in the Jehovah's Witnesses religious and civil rights cases, we may briefly summarize its record on general minority and Negro rights. The present Court has continued to protect the rights of accused persons; advanced the protection of federal civil rights by strengthening Sections 51 and 52 of the United States Code; ended federal toleration of the South's white primaries; made it unlawful for courts to enforce racial restrictive covenants; outlawed segregation in interstate travel; and advanced a step closer to educational equality by a progressively stricter interpretation of what constitutes "equal facilities."

WARTIME EVACUATION OF PERSONS OF JAPANESE DESCENT

In three wartime cases involving persons of Japanese ancestry the Supreme Court's adherence to a policy of discouragement of racial or national discrimination was severely tested. The Court was under great pressure to approve the federal government's program of evacuation and detention, yet most members found it extremely difficult to condone the basis for this program. The result was a mixed record for the Court: approval of some of the wartime acts of the federal government with simultaneous reaffirmation of broader principles rejecting such classification of Americans based upon national or racial origin.

The federal program for the 110,000 persons of Japanese descent on the West Coast was to subject them to a curfew, to exclude them from the West Coast area, and to detain them in special camps until the loyal could be relocated in other parts of the country.[99] The very first local judicial decision [100] on the curfew set the tone of the later Supreme Court cases. An American-born citizen of Japanese ancestry, a resident of Seattle and wife of a citizen of the Philippine Commonwealth, charged that her liberty was improperly abridged by the order establishing a curfew for and restricting the movements of all persons of her national origin. The oral opinion rejecting her claim argued that to accept her contentions might mean the destruction by "an invading army" of the very Constitution and laws of the United States to which she announced her loyalty. To her insistence that she was an American citizen only and not loyal to Japan, the court replied that "in Tokyo they" consider persons like her still to be Japanese subjects from whom they expect military aid. Thus the court justified the restriction of her liberty upon the curious ground that if she were really loyal to the United States she must understand that she had to be treated as disloyal, and upon the further ground of a foreign government's expectations with respect to the conduct of an American citizen.

The first case to reach the Supreme Court, in 1943, was one testing the constitutionality of the curfew order. Though presented with the opportunity to rule on the evacuation order as well, the Court chose to confine itself in *Hirabayashi v. United States* [101] to the order of the military commander establishing the curfew. Did this order, asked the Court, result from an unconstitutional delegation of legislative power by Congress to the Executive, and did it unconstitutionally discriminate between citizens of Japanese ancestry and other citizens, in violation of the Fifth Amendment? [102] The Court unanimously answered both these questions in the negative. Chief Justice Stone argued in his opinion for six members of the Court (Justices Douglas, Murphy, and Rutledge concurred in separate statements) that the Constitution gives to Congress and the Executive branch of the government wide powers in wartime, and the Court must not impose its own view of the way in which this power should be used. When Congress passed the law, in March of 1942, delegating broad powers to the Executive, said the Chief Justice, there was an undeniable danger to war production, and some reasonable doubt as to the loyalty of the Japanese in the United States since they had not yet been assimilated and there was evidence of their attachment to Japan. Holding that the curfew order was not a denial of due process, the Court observed: "We cannot close our eyes to the fact, demonstrated by experience, that in time of war residents having ethnic affiliations with an invading enemy may be a greater source of danger than those of a different ancestry." [103] At the same time Justice Stone pointed out: "Distinctions between citizens solely because of their ancestry are by their very nature odious to a free people whose institutions are founded upon the doctrine of equality." [104]

The Court's reluctance to decide in this way was revealed in the separate concurring opinions, perhaps best in Justice Murphy's statement: "Today is the first time, so far as I am aware, that we have sustained a substantial restriction of the personal liberty of citizens of the United States based upon the accident of race or ancestry. . . . In my opinion this goes to the very brink of constitutional power." [105] Conceding the validity of the curfew at the time of its promulgation, Justice Murphy added that "whether such a restriction is valid today is another matter." [106]

In 1944 the Supreme Court, in the case of *Korematsu v. United States,* [107] was faced with a test of the evacuation program itself. Korematsu protested his conviction in a federal court for remaining in a "military area" in California in violation of Civilian Exclusion Order Number 34 of the Commanding General of the Army's Western Command, which excluded all persons of Japanese ancestry after May 9, 1942. This time three justices, Roberts, Murphy, and Jackson, dissented separately from the majority opinion by Justice Black. On the basis of the *Hirabayashi* case, said the majority, the evacuation order is deemed to be within the war power of Congress and the Executive, for "exclusion from a threatened area, no less than curfew, has a definite and close relationship to the prevention of espionage and sabotage." [108] This time the Court refused to pass upon the detention feature of the federal government's program for persons of Japanese ancestry. Again the Court pointed to the danger of discrimination: "It should be noted, to begin with, that all legal restrictions which curtail the civil rights of a single racial group are immediately suspect. That is not to say that all such restrictions are unconstitutional. It is to say that the courts must subject them to the most rigid scrutiny. Pressing public necessity may sometimes justify the existence of such restrictions; racial antagonisms never can." [109]

Justice Roberts insisted in his dissent that the evacuation plan could be considered only as part of the whole program which deprived citizens of rights merely because of their national origin.[110] Justice Murphy, who had observed that the *Hirabayashi* case opinion went to "the very brink of constitutional power," now charged that the majority decision in this case "falls into the ugly abyss of racism." [111] In a forceful statement Justice Jackson pointed out: "Had Korematsu been one of four—the others being, say, a German alien enemy, an Italian alien enemy, and a citizen of American-born ancestors, convicted of treason but out on parole—only Korematsu's presence would have violated the order [excluding those of Japanese ancestry]. The difference between their innocence and his crime would result, not from anything he did, said, or thought, different than they, but only in that he was born of different racial stock." [112]

In 1944, the Supreme Court had the opportunity finally to pass upon at least part of the detention feature of the whole program for persons of Japanese ancestry, in the case of Mitsuye Endo.[113] An American citizen, Mitsuye Endo, applied for a writ of habeas corpus, claiming she was being held without any charge and against her will. Following the established procedure for relocation of loyal evacuees, she had applied for "leave clearance." This procedure provided that the applicant, if granted leave clearance, could apply for indefinite leave, but that such leave would not be granted if the applicant proposed to go where "community sentiment is unfavorable." Mitsuye Endo was granted leave clearance in August of 1943, but did not apply for indefinite leave, claiming, instead, illegal detention. The issue facing the Court was whether the federal government could detain a citizen of Japanese ancestry if her loyalty was beyond question.

In a unanimous decision (Justice Roberts and Murphy concurring separately), Justice Douglas stated that the government could not legally hold an evacuee of proved loyalty merely to ease his or her relocation to another community. The detention program, he said, derived from an implied (not an explicitly granted) power, and it must therefore be related at all times to the prevention of sabotage and espionage, the purpose of the act upon which the federal program was based. Detention for any other purpose was therefore illegal, the Court concluded, and Mitsuye Endo must be set free.

These cases involving the wartime evacuation of persons of Japanese ancestry were a severe test of the Supreme Court's position on minority rights. On the one hand the Court wished to allow Congress and the Executive to handle the war emergency in their own way; yet, on the other hand, the Court was reluctant to permit racial or national discrimination. This loyalty to principles which happened to conflict led the Court to uphold the main features of the program while making it clear that it was doing so only because of the extreme emergency. And when the freedom of loyal citizens was at stake, as in the last of these cases just reviewed, the Court unhesitatingly defended the rights of the minority.

Once the war was over, the Supreme Court resumed its course of granting increasing federal protection to both aliens and citizens of Japanese descent. In 1948 the Court in the case of *Oyama v. California* [114] eliminated a special kind of discrimination aimed at this minority, but chose to rest its decision on narrow grounds. In 1944 the state of California filed a petition to take over certain parcels of land which Kajiro Oyama had bought in the name of his son Fred, claiming that the purchases were made with intent to violate the Alien Land Law. This law provided that aliens ineligible for American citizenship might not acquire, own, occupy, lease, or transfer agricultural land, and that property acquired in violation of the law would revert to the state.

The Oyamas insisted that this law deprived both the alien parent and the citizen son of their right to the equal protection of the laws. The Court majority (Justices Reed, Burton, and Jackson dissenting, the latter in a separate opinion) through Chief Justice Vinson held that the younger Oyama was denied the equal protection of the laws, but refused to decide whether the elder Oyama was likewise discriminated against unfairly. The majority rested its decision on the ground that the California law contained an illegal presumption that a gift of land to a citizen son by a parent ineligible for citizenship is but a subterfuge for the parent's acquisition of the land, whereas no such presumption is made in the case of a parent who is a citizen or is eligible for citizenship. Fred Oyama, whose property the state of California wanted to take away, was thus discriminated against merely because his father was a Japanese alien.[115]

Four members of the majority (Justice Black in a concurring opinion subscribed to by Justice Douglas, and Justice Murphy in an opinion for himself and Justice Rutledge) insisted that the Court should go further and invalidate the entire California statute as a violation of the equal protection clause of the Fourteenth Amendment. In his dissent Justice Jackson, too, found the majority's reasoning unsatisfactory. However much he disliked the result reached by the California Supreme Court in upholding the state's petition for escheat, he said, he could not see how the majority's position could logically reach an opposite result. He hinted that he would prefer to declare the whole statute a violation of the Fourteenth Amendment. Justice Reed's dissent (joined by Justice Burton) likewise insisted that to reach the result it did, the majority must invalidate the whole California statute, since, he claimed, the presumption as to subterfuge was a quite reasonable measure if California could legally prevent an alien ineligible for citizenship from acquiring or owning land. The majority, said Justice Reed, did not question California's right to pass the law, and hence could not logically object to the presumption.

Had Justices Black, Douglas, Murphy, and Rutledge been joined by one other member of the Court, the statute would have been held unconstitutional on broad, consistent grounds. It is difficult to see why Justice Jackson, whose dissent is much the same as Justice Black's concurring opinion, did not vote with these four.

In another 1948 case coming from California,[116] the Court protected the rights of Japanese aliens in a forthright way. Takahashi came to America from Japan in 1907. From 1915 to 1942 he obtained a commercial fishing license annually. On his return to California in 1945 after his evacuation and detention, Takahashi found he could no longer obtain a license, because a law had been passed in 1943 prohibiting the issuance of a license to any "alien Japanese," and this law was amended in 1945 to bar any "person ineligible to citizenship." The issue facing the Court, said Justice Black for the majority (Justices Reed and Jackson dissenting), was "whether California can, consistently with the Federal Constitution and laws passed pursuant to it, use this federally created racial ineligibility for citizenship as a basis for barring Takahashi from earning his living as a commercial fisherman in the ocean waters off the coast of California." [117] This action of California, said the Court, was an illegal invasion of federal power to regulate the admission, naturalization, and residence of aliens. To California's claim that a "special public interest" required this ban on aliens since the citizens of the state are the collective owners of all fish in the three-mile belt, the Court replied that whatever merit this argument might have, it did not justify the exclusion of aliens from making their living in a way permitted to all others.[118]

These recent decisions, then, would seem to show that the

Supreme Court is willing to protect the rights of aliens and citizens of Japanese (and other types of national) descent, but that it seeks the very narrowest grounds to do so.

RELIGIOUS AND CIVIL RIGHTS: JEHOVAH'S WITNESSES

The treatment by the Supreme Court of the rights of the unpopular religious group, Jehovah's Witnesses, stands in contrast to its rulings on the wartime rights of persons of Japanese ancestry.[119] Far from leading to the limitation of the Witnesses' rights, the war period actually saw their enlargement.

Cases involving local ordinances requiring a permit to solicit money, or distribute literature, or hold a meeting constitute the largest single group involving Jehovah's Witnesses. In 1938 the Supreme Court invalidated a Georgia municipal ordinance forbidding the distribution of literature except by permission of the city manager.[120] The following year the Court struck down four New Jersey local ordinances, one requiring a permit for canvassing to sell or give away circulars, and the others prohibiting such distribution as a public inconvenience because of the resulting littering of the streets.[121] In 1940 the Court upheld a New Hampshire statute requiring a license for parades on public streets, but stipulated that the withholding of the license could be based only on the public interest in the use of the streets.[122] In 1942 the Court upheld municipal laws in Alabama, Arkansas, and Arizona which required a license fee for selling from door to door,[123] but in a rehearing the following year it reversed this decision.[124] In 1943 the Court invalidated a Texas ordinance forbidding the scattering of handbills on which certain books were advertised for sale.[125] During the same year the Court held unconstitutional a Texas municipal ordinance which required a permit from the Mayor, who could grant or withhold it as he deemed proper, before one could sell books from door to door.[126] In 1944 the Court ruled that a Witness did not have to pay an

occupational license fee to sell the sect's literature even though
he depended upon this activity for his livelihood.[127] In 1946
the Court faced another of those cases [128] to which conflicting
principles could be applied. In the town of Chickasaw, Alabama, owned by the Gulf Shipbuilding Corporation, a Witness stood on the sidewalk of the main street and tried to hand
out literature. Warned that she was not allowed to do so without a permit which she could get, the Witness refused to leave
and was arrested for violating an Alabama law forbidding a
person to enter or remain upon another's property without
permission. With Justice Jackson not participating, the majority numbered five, while Justice Reed dissented for himself
and Justices Stone and Burton. For the majority Justice Black
pointed out that neither a state nor a municipality could, under the Supreme Court rulings, entirely bar the distribution
of political or religious literature. The fact that the town of
Chickasaw was privately owned, he asserted, did not materially
alter this restriction upon local governments: "Ownership does
not always mean absolute dominion. The more an owner, for
his advantage, opens up his property for use by the public in
general, the more do his rights become circumscribed by the
statutory and constitutional rights of those who use it." [129]
And again: "Whether a corporation or a municipality owns
or possesses the town the public in either case has an identical
interest in the functioning of the community in such a manner
that the channels of communication remain free." [130]

In three flag salute cases the Supreme Court has gone far
to protect religious faith against compulsion by government.
In 1940 the Court upheld the resolution of a local school
board in Pennsylvania requiring all children to salute the
American flag.[131] Two children of Witnesses, refusing under
their parents' influence to comply with the rule, were excluded
from the school and had to receive instruction privately, for
which the parents had to pay. The majority, while affirming
religious freedom, held that there were limits on the freedom

to follow one's conscience and that the wisdom of the educational policy followed by the school board was for the legislature, not the courts, to determine. Three years later, however, the Court reversed itself and held that a similar resolution, passed by a local school board in West Virginia, violated the First Amendment.[132] At the same time the Court invalidated a Mississippi statute which made it a felony to encourage disloyalty to the government of the United States or Mississippi or to encourage the refusal to salute their flags.[133]

CONCLUSION

Having completed the consideration of the Roosevelt Court's record on the rights of minorities, we may briefly summarize its work and compare it with that of the Courts preceding it. We saw that the Supreme Court from 1868 to about 1937 supported those laws which tended to enforce the separation of Negroes and whites and weakened the operation of those tending to facilitate the meeting of the two groups except in situations clearly maintaining the superiority of the whites. But since about 1937, the Supreme Court has more consistently upheld the civil rights of minorities. Though the present Court is still cautious in this area, its decisions no longer have the effect of buttressing the caste system with respect to Negroes. And the increasing protection of Negro rights is but part of the Court's general concern for the rights of all minority groups. With the temporary and partial wartime exception of persons of Japanese ancestry, then, the present Court has gone substantially farther than its predecessors in the protection of the rights of racial, national, and religious minorities.

CHAPTER FOUR

The New York State Law Against Discrimination: Operation and Administration

THERE are more than two hundred state laws and constitutional provisions in this country which prohibit discrimination of various types on the basis of race, religion, color, or national origin.[1] Even the Southern states have such provisions. Most of these laws, however, have seldom been rigidly enforced anywhere; the Anti-Defamation League found only five civil rights cases in the *Decennial Digest* for 1926–36 and only twenty for 1936–46, of which a third originated in New York.[2] In recent years a new series of statutes has been enacted, aimed specifically at the elimination of discrimination in private employment, and these have been enforced more stringently than most previous antidiscrimination acts. Four states, New York, New Jersey, Connecticut, and Massachusetts, are the pioneers in this new field; other states and municipalities [3] have passed or debated similar proposals. The New York, New Jersey, and Massachusetts acts declare that the opportunity to obtain employment free from discrimination because of race, creed, color, or national origin is a civil right.

BACKGROUND AND PROVISIONS

The New York State "Law Against Discrimination," [4] also known as the Ives-Quinn law, is the first of these more recent statutes in the private employment field. It offers the best opportunity for an appraisal of such legislation since it has been in operation longest, has evoked widespread comment, and is administered by an agency with a budget larger than those of similar agencies in other states.[5]

Long before the passage of this law New York had outlawed discrimination in jury service, in the right to practice law, in admission to public schools, in places of public accommodation, resort or amusement, in insurance rates and benefits, in public employment, in employment in utility companies, in employment in firms fulfilling public works contracts, in admission to tax-exempt nonsectarian educational institutions, and in civil service, public housing, labor unions, public relief, defense industries, and sale or delivery of alcoholic beverages.[6]

In response to increasing evidence of discrimination against members of minority groups who sought jobs in war industries, the Governor in March of 1941 appointed a Committee on Discrimination in Employment as a subcommittee of the New York State Council of Defense (later the War Council). This Committee's task was to study discriminatory practices in war industries and to carry out a program of education and conciliation to eliminate them. It handled over a thousand cases, of which it settled 95 percent by persuasion, conciliation, and hearings before the state's Industrial Commissioner.[7] Though the Committee was created during the "defense" emergency, its functions were broadly conceived. In its last report the Committee pointed out: "The Governor's mandate . . . had stressed the undesirable effects of discrimination in relation to national defense. The primacy of the national defense program in the Committee's task should be recognized. But the solution of urgent problems should contribute toward more extensive and longer run improvement." Judging by its operations during ten months in 1942, the Committee did not wait for complaints to come to its attention. More than half of its 304 investigations of employers' practices in this period were started on its own initiative. About a fourth of its cases origi-

nated with a complaint by a job applicant, about a tenth with
the complaint of a dismissed worker, and another tenth from
"miscellaneous sources." [8]

In accordance with its instructions to recommend appropriate legislation, the Committee prepared two bills which
were introduced into the legislature in March of 1944; the
second of them would have prohibited discrimination in private
employment. The Governor, in a message a few days later,
told the Legislature that while he supported the intent of both
bills, he felt the subject needed more study. Accordingly he
suggested the creation of a special commission; on the following day the Legislature enacted this suggestion into law. In
protest against what they held was an unnecessary delay, eight
members of the Committee resigned. By June, the New York
State Temporary Commission Against Discrimination had begun its work. [9]

The Temporary Commission, composed of eight members
(four Democrats and four Republicans) of the state Legislature and fifteen public members, held open hearings in November and December of 1944, in Albany, Syracuse, Rochester,
Buffalo, and New York City. In January of 1945, the Commission presented its report. It accepted four propositions:
"(1) Discriminations on grounds of race, creed, color and
national origin are too serious a menace to democracy to be
safely neglected; (2) whatever moves are made against them
must seek to win a strong supporting public opinion; (3) while
wise legislation may assist progress, any attempt forthwith to
abolish prejudice by law can do serious harm to the antidiscrimination movement; (4) prejudice is the fruit of ig-
norance and is subject to the healing influences of education
in the broadest sense of the term." [10] The advocacy of this
combination of compulsion, education, and caution has characterized the approach of most official New York agencies
that have touched the problem of employment discrimination.
The Commission's principal suggestions were introduced as

the Ives-Quinn bill, which was enacted by the Assembly on February 28 and by the Senate on March 5. It was signed by the Governor on March 12, and became effective July 1, 1945.[11]

Most civil rights statutes provide that any person who believes that his rights have been violated may bring suit against the violator and obtain damages. This procedure places the burden upon the individual and has not proved effective. The Ives-Quinn law used a different approach, lodging the function of investigation and the power of enforcement in a special administrative agency to which individuals may bring complaints for both investigation and settlement. This procedure appears to be the best for the enforcement of civil rights statutes.

The New York "Law Against Discrimination" registers, in Section 125, the Legislature's finding and declaration that discrimination of any kind on the basis of race, creed, color or national origin is "a matter of state concern," and that it "menaces the institutions and foundation of a free democratic state." It creates a state agency "with power to eliminate and prevent discrimination in employment because of race, creed, color or national origin, either by employers, labor organizations, employment agencies or other persons." Section 126 asserts that the "opportunity to obtain employment without discrimination" is a civil right. In using the word "creed" the legislators meant only religious belief. Assemblyman Ives told the Legislature: "For the sake of the record, in case any court may sometime want to know what the legislative intent is, let's get it straight—*in dealing with the subject today as a Legislature we mean by creed, religious belief and nothing else.*" [12] Senator Quinn made the same point to the Senate.[13]

Section 127 defines the terms used in the statute and excludes the following classes of employers: social and fraternal clubs, charitable, educational, and religious associations not organized for private profit, and establishments with less than six employees. Section 128 creates the State Commission Against Discrimination, composed of five members appointed by the Governor for five-year terms at a salary of ten thousand dollars annually. Section 129 directs SCAD to "formulate policies to effectuate the purposes" of the law and empowers it to make appropriate recommendations to other state agencies and officials.

Section 130 sets forth the "functions, powers and duties" of SCAD: to announce rules for the execution of its task; to "receive, investigate and pass upon" complaints of unlawful discrimination in employment; to "hold hearings, subpoena witnesses, compel their attendance, administer oaths, take the testimony of any person under oath, and in connection therewith, to require the production for examination of any books or papers relating to any matter under investigation or in question" before it; to create "advisory agencies and conciliation councils" composed of "representative citizens" to study any kind of discrimination and to help achieve the purposes of the statute and the civil rights section of the state constitution.

Section 131 declares the following types of discrimination, on the ground of race, creed, color, or national origin, to be an "unlawful employment practice": an employer's refusal to hire any individual or his discrimination against any one in pay or the terms of employment; a labor union's exclusion of any person, or its discrimination against any of its members or against an employer or any person working for an employer; an employer's or an employment agency's written or oral statement or job application form calling for information from a prospective employee that expresses or shows intent to use any criterion other than "bona fide occupational qualification;" an employer's, labor union's, or employment agency's discharge or other discrimination against a person who has opposed these unlawful practices or who has "filed a complaint, testified or assisted in any proceeding" under the statute.

Section 132 prescribes the method for handling complaints. "Any person claiming to be aggrieved" under the act may file a complaint with SCAD. The chairman of SCAD then assigns the case to one of the commissioners, who investigates the matter. If the commissioner finds that "probable cause exists for crediting the allegations of the complaint," he tries to eliminate the unlawful practice by "conference, conciliation and persuasion." "The members of the commission and its staff shall not disclose what has transpired in the course of such endeavors." If these methods fail to accomplish the elimination of the unlawful practice (or before that if the conditions warrant) the commissioner calls for a hearing of the case before three members of SCAD. At this hearing the commissioner who has investigated the case may participate only as a witness, and nothing that occurred during the efforts at conciliation may be accepted as evidence. If after the hearing the Commission finds the law has been violated, it states its findings of fact and issues an order to the respondent to cease and desist from the unlawful practice. The respondent may be required to hire, reinstate, or upgrade a worker, or to perform any "affirmative action . . . as, in the judgment of the commission, will effectuate the purposes" of the statute.

Section 133 provides for judicial review of an order by SCAD, and SCAD may obtain a court order for the enforcement of its own orders. Section 134 provides a maximum jail sentence of one year and a maximum fine of $500 for any person, employer, labor union, or employment agency willfully impeding the Commission's work or willfully violating its order.

Before the passage of the law the executive committee of the New York State Bar Association opposed its enactment on the ground that it was an unconstitutional infringement of freedom of contract; it would cause business firms to leave the state; it tried to legislate morality; it could not be enforced; and it would actually intensify group hostility and cause riots.[14]

Even Assemblyman Ives, who sponsored the bill and served as chairman of the Temporary Commission which proposed it, doubted that the problem of employment discrimination could be solved by legislation. It was only after a study of the subject that he became convinced that the law was an appropriate means in this area of group relations.[15]

The most important feature of the Ives-Quinn law is its provision for full use of the coercive power of the state in cases where conciliation has failed to eliminate a verified discriminatory practice. The State Commission Against Discrimination thus has a number of techniques by which to achieve the purposes of the statute, ranging from persuasion to court enforcement of its orders. In a sense, of course, there is really no "persuasion" under the statute, for the suspected violator knows, when he talks with SCAD, that the full power of the law can be applied. If, therefore, he appears quite willing to be "persuaded" it is because he knows that he can be forced to do what he might not be persuaded to do. In testifying in 1947 before a United States Senate subcommittee on a federal bill similar to the New York law, the first chairman of SCAD pointed out that while this reserve power did not mean that conferences were conducted under duress, it did make the respondent "more willing to sit down and realize he had to make certain concessions."[16] Unfortunately, the interplay between persuasion and coercion in the enforcement of the law cannot be studied in detail since the Commission is forbidden, under Section 132, to reveal what transpires in the course of its conferences to settle cases by conciliation.

OPERATION AND ENFORCEMENT

It is easier to review the work of the State Commission Against Discrimination than to assess its effects precisely. This is true of almost any agency but especially of this one because the possible criteria for an assessment are neither clear nor easy to apply. It is nevertheless immediately apparent from the Commission's reports that the law which it administers has certainly reduced discrimination in employment in New York State. In this section we shall examine SCAD's general approach to the enforcement of the law and its operations since its effective date, July 1, 1945.

The Commission, following the tone of the Law Against Discrimination, emphasizes that conciliation and education are the chief methods by which employment discrimination is to be eliminated. The first is the technique applied in the cases the Commission handles, and the second, directed at the community as a whole, aims "to create a climate of public opinion which would be favorable to the administration of the Law." [17] SCAD fully appreciates the danger involved in applying punitive measures to long-standing patterns of behavior based upon human attitudes. It therefore seeks a type of compliance with the law which is voluntary in some degree. "It would be of little avail if compulsory action on the basis of individual complaints resulted in temporary compliance which could only be maintained by a policing operation that in the end would assume formidable proportions." [18]

The Commission has energetically adhered to this view of its tasks and has resisted "alike the pressure of those who would attain the objectives of the Law by the quick resort to its punitive features and those who stubbornly oppose any governmental intervention in the conduct of their business affairs." [19] SCAD, seeing two methods of administering the law, has tried to do its job "in an atmosphere of cooperation. The alternative to this is to administer the Law in an atmosphere of conflict." [20] It is doubtful that these are the only alternatives. As we shall see later, minority groups which have criticized SCAD as too "lenient" have not stressed the "*punitive* features" of the law, but rather those sanctions in it which lie somewhere between the conciliation process and the punitive features. Such sanctions are the holding of a hearing and the issuance of a cease-and-desist order. Neither of these is a resort to the punitive features of the law (presumably administering the act in "an atmosphere of conflict"), and yet both are somewhat more harsh than efforts at conciliation and compromise ("an atmosphere of cooperation"). As of the end of 1950, SCAD had found it necessary upon only two occasions to invoke its powers beyond the conciliation process.[21]

To assess the effects of the law and the Commission's work is especially difficult. How, for example, is one to answer such questions as these: How many employers, employment agencies and labor unions have reduced or eliminated discriminatory practices merely because the law had been enacted? How many employers have voluntarily gone far beyond the law's requirements in eliminating employment discrimination, and how far have they gone? How many employers have eliminated discrimination as a result of their knowledge of the Commission's work, without ever becoming parties to a case? How many employers, once in contact with the Commission, manage to continue to discriminate illegally? Some of these questions can be given approximate answers, but only after a lengthy field study using data which SCAD regards as confidential, while others are hardly answerable at all in the present state of social science.

Criteria for Evaluation

The basic difficulty in assessing the separate roles of the law and of the agency in the elimination of discrimination is that decisive criteria are not available. If we measure the effect of the law by the number of Negroes or Jews employed compared to the rest of the population, we may be overlooking the fact that other influences are at work here too, such as the federal wartime FEPC and the sustained high rate of employment since 1941. If we were to judge by public attitudes and opinions, how could we separate out the influence of this particular law in New York State? If we judge by the reduction in the number of discriminatory want ads in the newspapers, we would overlook the possibility that discrimination can be practiced at the next stage, in the employer's office, by those who hire. If we judge by the number of complaints received by the Commission, we must then realize that not all persons who are discriminated against know they can appeal to a state agency, and not all who know of the law go so far as to complain to the Commission.

The best measure is the degree to which members of minority groups, through action by the Commission, are admitted to jobs and into industries from which they were previously barred. Such a measure would be compounded of two elements: (1) the number of persons who have actually obtained jobs in firms or industries and at levels from which the groups to which they belong had been excluded; (2) the number of industries, firms, and types of work, with the number of jobs they include, from which members of minority groups had been barred but which have been opened to them by SCAD action.

This is actually the criterion which the Commission itself uses (though unsystematically), as it has indicated in its 1948 annual report: "By far the greatest number of complaints are filed charging discrimination by reason of race and color and in some measure the gauge of progress may be determined by the extent of opportunity of employment, hitherto denied, which has been created for this group." [22] But the Commission has not attempted to apply this test systematically. It objects to the compiling of data on "the number of proscribed individuals who are now employed as compared to those employed prior to the passage of the Law." Though this is not really a valid criterion anyway, the Commission's objection to it is somehow based on its rejection of the "quota system of employment" of minority groups.[23]

By excluding the method of evaluation decribed above, the

Commission makes it impossible for others to use it, since it alone possesses the necessary data, which it now considers confidential. (This policy is discussed at greater length below, in the section of this chapter dealing with SCAD's relations with the community.) Having neglected the problem of scientific self-evaluation, SCAD falls back upon such spotty, generalized, and impressionistic statements as the following:

> Even to the casual observer it is evident that significant progress in employment and opportunities has been made in the State of New York since the enactment of the Law Against Discrimination. Negro girls, for instance, are now employed in the telephone exchanges as operators or clerks or both in all the cities in the metropolitan area and in eleven cities upstate, and Negro men have for the first time been enrolled in classes in telephone installation. The community is aware of the changing picture in the department store field as evidenced by the increasing number of Negro girls employed in clerical capacities in administrative and executive offices and on the selling staffs. Nor is the community unmindful of the expanding opportunities for employment of Negro men and women in banking and life insurance institutions.[24]

The Commission is aware of the difficulties involved in the evaluation of the law's accomplishments.[25] It is constantly impressing upon employers that they must not think in terms of group membership but only in terms of individual ability. SCAD hesitates to conduct a census of the hiring of members of minority groups because that would entail requesting employers to ask for the information which the Commission asked them to ignore. Some firms have replied, in answer to the Commission's request for such data, by repeating all the strictures first uttered by the Commission itself. A second difficulty is that in evaluating the effects of the law, one tends to think in terms of quotas—how many Negro clerks have been hired in proportion to the total population of the Negro community? Yet SCAD constantly reiterates that quota employment is not compliance with the law. How many members of a minority group must an employer hire, then, to comply? No specific amount, the Commission answers, merely all those who best qualify for each opening.

These are genuine problems the Commission faces in assessing its work, yet they do not appear to be insoluble. It is hardly conceivable that its own preachments should be an effective barrier to self-evaluation. In the present stage of the law's operation it seems unnecessary to judge its effectiveness by measuring its achievements according to some standard of what is the "proper" number of members of minority groups for each type of job in each firm or industry. A more simple test, the increase in the jobs held by, and the openings available to, such employees from year to year, should be adequate for the present and well into the future.

There is still another aspect to the problem of evaluating the Law Against Discrimination and SCAD's administration of it, and to evaluating any piece of legislation in the area of group relations. To what extent, it may be asked, does the law succeed in eliminating prejudice, not merely discrimination? It is an explicit or unstated assumption of most advocates of this kind of legislation that the removal of intergroup barriers by law will eventually lead to the reduction of the prejudice which is said to be the motivation for discriminatory practices. The Lavanburg Foundation has sponsored a study of a biracial housing project in Pittsburgh which shows, according to one of the directors of the study, that "under appropriate institutional and administrative conditions, the experience of interracial amity can supplant the fear of interracial conflict." [26] Are the "institutional and administrative conditions" which result from the Ives-Quinn law likewise the appropriate ones to bring about such a change? The answer to this question can be obtained only with the sponsorship of SCAD. The procedure would be to test a group of workers for racial prejudice in an establishment which the Commission finds has excluded members of minority groups. After the company has complied with the law, and previously barred persons are employed, another test can be administered to the same group of workers at certain intervals of time. Such a series of tests would permit some definite conclusions as to the role of law and coercion in the elimination of intergroup hostility; it would show where the coercion and the sanctions are effective and where this feature of a legal system must not be applied. It is doubtful, however, that such tests would reveal much except after an interval of some years.

This limitation, indeed, applies to many of the statements in this chapter, especially to the trends reported in the next section. This study deals with only five and a half years of a new type of law, and this fact must be taken into account throughout.

Statistical Summary

Most of the complaints filed with SCAD charge discrimination because of race and color, that is, they charge anti-Negro employment policies. The proportion of such charges to the total number of complaints is rising. (See Table 2.*)

* The tables which follow have been prepared from data in the text and tables of SCAD's annual reports. Beginning with the annual report for 1947, SCAD has presented the data for the year just ended and for the cumulative period since July 1, 1945. To obtain the annual data for earlier periods, given in the tables which follow, it has been necessary to subtract the annual data for the later periods from the cumulative totals since July 1, 1945. SCAD from time to time reclassifies cases closed in previous years. The result is that adding the annual totals across a table does not always yield the exact cumulative total given in the last column. Another discrepancy is that the total number of cases for a particular period of time in one table is sometimes different from the total for the same period of time in another table. This is the result of (a) the necessity to compute the data for some periods from the cumulative data for longer periods, and (b) the fact that in some of its statistical tables SCAD has given as the total number of cases for a given period the number of individuals who filed claims, while in other tables for the same period it has given the number of different individual respondents—these two totals need not be the same.

TABLE 2

Basis of Discrimination Alleged in Verified Complaints Filed: July 1, 1945–December 31, 1950

BASIS OF DISCRIMI-NATION	JULY 1, 1945, TO JUNE 27, 1946		JULY 1, 1945, TO DEC. 31, 1946		JAN. 1, 1947, TO DEC. 31, 1947		JAN. 1, 1948, TO DEC. 31, 1948		JAN. 1, 1949, TO DEC. 31, 1949		JAN. 1, 1950, TO DEC. 31, 1950		JULY 1, 1945, TO DEC. 31, 1950	
	Num-ber	Per-cent	Num-ber	Per-cent	Num-ber	Per-cent	Num-ber	Per-cent	Num-ber	Per-cent	Num-ber	Per-cent	Num-ber	Per-cent
Race or color	207	56	365	63	322	75	198	73	235	75	166	65	1,295	70
Creed	89	24	121	21	51	12	49	18	48	15	51	20	305	16
National origin	60	16	68	12	3	1	9	3	15	5	21	8	115	6
Other	14	4	24	4	51	12	17	6	17	5	19	7	145	8
Totals	370	100	578	100	427	100	273	100	315	100	257	100	1,860	100

TABLE 3

Type of Respondent in Verified Complaints Filed: July 1, 1945–December 31, 1950

TYPE OF RESPONDENT	JULY 1, 1945, TO JUNE 27, 1946		JULY 1, 1945, TO DEC. 31, 1946		JAN. 1, 1947, TO DEC. 31, 1947		JAN. 1, 1948, TO DEC. 31, 1948		JAN. 1, 1949, TO DEC. 31, 1949		JAN. 1, 1950, TO DEC. 31, 1950		JULY 1, 1945, TO DEC. 31, 1950	
	Number	Per cent	Number	Per cent	Number	Per cent	Number	Per cent	Number	Per cent	Number	Per cent	Number	Per cent
Employer	313	85	455	85	381	80	235	86	226	72	215	84	1,512	81
Employment agency	8	2	14	3	30	6	26	10	42	13	31	12	144	8
Labor union	32	9	40	7	66	14	12	4	42	13	8	3	172	9
Other	17	5	28	5	...	...	...	...	5	2	3	1	32	2
Totals	370	101	537	100	477	100	273	100	315	100	257	100	1,860	100

TABLE 4

Type of Discrimination Alleged in Verified Complaints Filed:
July 1, 1945–December 31, 1950

TYPE OF DISCRIMINATION	JULY 1, 1945, TO DEC. 31, 1947 [a]		JAN. 1, 1948, TO DEC. 31, 1948		JAN. 1, 1949, TO DEC. 31, 1949		JAN. 1, 1950, TO DEC. 31, 1950		JULY 1, 1945, TO DEC. 31, 1950	
	Number	Per cent	Number	Per cent	Number	Per cent	Number	Per cent	Number	Per cent
Application for employment denied	445	44	142	52	141	45	111	43	823	44
Dismissal from employment	210	21	64	23	50	16	65	25	390	21
Conditions of employment	148	15	18	7	23	7	28	11	220	12
Employment agency referral withheld	35	4	23	8	38	12	27	11	123	7
Union membership withheld	38	4	1	...	9	3	2	1	50	3
Conditions of union membership	67	7	10	4	33	10	6	2	122	6
Other	62	6	15	6	21	7	18	7	132 [b]	7
Totals	1,005	101	273	100	315	100	257	100	1,860	100

a Data for shorter period not available.
b Includes 20 complaints not related to employment.

TABLE 5

Verified Complaints and Commission-Initiated Investigations Opened and Closed: July 1, 1945–December 31, 1950

TYPE OF PROCEEDING	JULY 1, 1945, TO DEC. 31, 1946	JAN. 1, 1947, TO DEC. 31, 1947	JAN. 1, 1948, TO DEC. 31, 1948	JAN. 1, 1949, TO DEC. 31, 1949	JAN. 1, 1950, TO DEC. 31, 1950	JULY 1, 1945, TO DEC. 31, 1950
Verified complaints						
Opened	536	472	273	315	257	1,860
Closed	421	297	453	282	289	1,743
Commission-initiated investigations						
Opened	174	137	80	90	101	600
Closed	146	110	98	88	114	562
Totals—Complaints and investigations						
Opened	710	609	353	405	358	2,460
Closed	567	407	551	370	403	2,305

TABLE 6

Disposition of Closed Cases of Verified Complaints: July 1, 1945–December 1, 1950

DISPOSITION OF CLOSED CASES	JULY 1, 1945, TO JUNE 27, 1946		JULY 1, 1945, TO DEC. 31, 1946		JAN. 1, 1947, TO DEC. 31, 1947		JAN. 1, 1948, TO DEC. 31, 1948		JAN. 1, 1949, TO DEC. 31, 1949		JAN. 1, 1950, TO DEC. 31, 1950		JULY 1, 1945, TO DEC. 31, 1950	
	Num-ber	Per-cent	Num-ber	Per-cent	Num-ber	Per-cent	Num-ber	Per-cent	Num-ber	Per-cent	Num-ber	Per-cent	Num-ber	Per-cent
Lack of jurisdiction	69	24	71	17	20	7	13	3	15	5	20	7	136	8
Withdrawn	15	5	14	3	7	2	5	1	9	3	8	3	42	2
Dismissed, lack of evidence of discrimination	77	27	131	31	114	39	242	53	109	39	123	43	723	42
Dismissed, lack of evidence, but other discrimination found and eliminated	122 [a]	43 [a]	109	26	67	23	85	19	67	24	73	25	403	23
Sustained, discrimination eliminated			96	23	87	29	108	24	82	29	65	22	439	25
Totals	283	99	421	100	295	100	453	100	282	100	289	100	1,743	100

[a] Only one figure given for these two categories.

During the period 1945–46, covering the first eighteen months of the law, 65 percent of the complaints charged discrimination because of race and color. During 1947 this category was 75 percent of the total. In 1948 it was 73 percent, in 1949 it rose again to 75 percent, but in 1950 it fell to 65 percent. Meanwhile, complaints charging discrimination because of creed, involving mainly Jews, declined both relatively and absolutely until 1950. During the first eighteen months of the law such cases were 21 percent of the total; they were 12 percent of the total in 1947, rose to 18 percent in 1948, declined to 15 percent in 1949, and rose to 20 percent in 1950.

Employers are the main objects of charges in complaints filed with SCAD (see Table 3). From the inception of the law until the end of 1950, employers were the respondents in 81 percent of all complaint cases. The proportion of employment agencies as respondents has been rising slowly, although the absolute number from July, 1945, through July, 1950, is only 144. During the first eighteen months of the law agencies were the respondents in only 3 percent of all cases, but this proportion rose to 6 percent during 1947, to 10 percent in 1948, and to 13 percent in 1949, and it fell slightly to 12 percent in 1950.

There have been no significant changes in the kind of discrimination charged in the complaints filed with the Commission since 1945. For the entire period to the end of 1950, 44 percent of the complaints charged denial of application for employment, 21 percent charged dismissal from employment, 12 percent charged discrimination in the conditions of employment, and 23 percent made other charges (see Table 4).

The data on the number of complaints filed annually are obtainable only since 1947 (see Table 5). During 1947 SCAD received 376 complaints, in 1948 only 273, in 1949 the number rose to 315, and in 1950 it declined to 257. The Commission was able to close 297 complaint cases in 1947, 453 in 1948, 282 in 1949, and 289 in 1950. In 1947 SCAD opened

137 investigations of its own, without complaints, and closed 110; in 1948 it opened 80 and closed 98; in 1949 it opened 90 and closed 88; in 1950 it opened 101 and closed 114. From its inception to the end of 1950 the Commission received 1,860 verified complaints, of which it closed 1,743. During the same period the Commission opened 600 investigations independently, of which it closed 562.

During 1950 SCAD reviewed the practices of 231 employers, employment agencies, and labor unions who were respondents in cases previously closed but which came up for reexamination during the year. In addition, SCAD completed in 1950 examinations of the application forms used by 703 establishments.[27] It was during the years 1945–46 that the Commission appears to have accomplished the bulk of the task of eliminating preemployment discrimination inquiries, for its 1946 report asserted they were "now the rarity, rather than the rule." [28]

From July, 1945, to the end of 1950 2 percent of the complaints filed were withdrawn and 8 percent were discontinued because SCAD lacked jurisdiction over them. About two fifths of the complaints (42 percent) were dismissed for lack of evidence of the discriminatory practice charged. In another 23 percent of the complaints SCAD did not find the respondent guilty of the charge specified in the complaint but did find and eliminate through conciliation some form of employment discrimination. And in 25 percent of the complaints the Commission upheld the complainant and eliminated the illegal practice by conciliation (see Table 6). Thus in about two thirds (65 percent) of the complaints SCAD did not find sufficient evidence to uphold the specific charge of discrimination. This proportion increased until 1949. In the first eighteen months of the law's operation, SCAD found insufficient evidence to uphold 57 percent of the complaints filed; in 1947 this proportion rose to 62 percent and in 1948, to 72 percent; in 1949, however, it declined to 63 percent of the cases decided by

SCAD, although in 1950 it rose again to 68 percent. Meanwhile, the proportion of complaint cases in which the Commission found evidence of other discrimination, though not of the specific charge, declined until 1949. In its first eighteen months SCAD found and eliminated such discrimination in 26 percent of the complaint cases it received; in 1947, in 23 percent of the cases; in 1948, in 19 percent. But in 1949 the proportion rose to 24 percent and in 1950 to 25 percent. The proportion of complaints which SCAD has upheld has fluctuated from 23 percent in its first eighteen months to 29 percent in 1947, to 24 percent in 1948, to 29 percent in 1949, and down to 22 percent in 1950.

The Commission itself does not present the data in precisely this way and has not commented on the large proportion of complaints (65 percent) in which it found insufficient evidence to support the specific charge of discrimination, and the small proportion of cases (25 percent) in which it did sustain the complainant's claim. This proportion rises to 28 percent if we omit those cases withdrawn by the complainant and those over which the Commission did not have jurisdiction. Two commissioners, asked about these data, denied that the difficulty of proving discrimination is the reason for the small proportion of cases in which the specific complaint was sustained.[29] Apparently, then, the explanation is that the complaints filed with SCAD are weak ones, or that SCAD's standards of evidence of proof of discrimination by a respondent are rather high.

The Commission presents its data in another way. From July, 1945, to the end of 1950 SCAD dealt with 986 different respondents, of whom 617, or about 65 percent, were found to have practiced some form of discrimination forbidden by the law. All of these respondents eliminated the discriminatory practice through conciliation.[30]

SCAD, as has been indicated, considers not only the specific charges in a complaint it receives, but uses the occasion to inquire into the respondent's general employment policies. While it sustained only about a quarter of the complaints it received to the end of 1950, the Commission found in almost as many cases (23 percent of all complaint cases) some form of employment discrimination which it proceeded to eliminate by conference and conciliation. By this practice SCAD makes each case yield the utmost results.

Compliance by Employers

When they face a statute such as the Law Against Discrimination, employers are subject to contradictory impulses. On the one hand they tend to resent further governmental jurisdiction over their business affairs, especially so where personal attitudes toward other groups are involved. On the other hand, it would seem that the Ives-Quinn law should be welcomed by employers since it expands their sources of labor supply. Of course, before the enactment of minimum wage and hour laws and the tremendous growth of trade unionism during the late 1930s, the usual result of larger labor supply was the possibility of reducing wages and increasing the workday. Even though such results are almost entirely precluded now, an increase in labor supply should theoretically be welcomed by employers, who could select more efficient workers from a larger group.

While employers as a group have not looked upon the law as a boon, most of them reached by the Commission have apparently abandoned their early opposition. SCAD's first chairman, testifying in 1947 before a Senate subcommittee on a federal fair employment practice bill, stated: "We were confronted with the fact that when the [New York State] bill was considered before the legislature there was strong opposition, particularly on the part of . . . management." [31] At the joint legislative committee hearing on the Ives-Quinn bill in February of 1945, the following business groups spoke against its enactment: Broadway Association, Bronx Board of Trade, Brooklyn Chamber of Commerce, Buffalo Chamber of Commerce, Chamber of Commerce of the Borough of Queens, Chamber of Commerce of the State of New York, a group of employment agencies, New York Board of Trade, Real Estate Board of New York, West Side Association of Commerce, Associated Industries of New York State, New York State Laundry Owners Association.[32] In a resolution sent to the Governor of New York State, the State Chamber of Commerce opposed the bill on the grounds that it would make New York less desirable for employers and workers, might attract unwelcome persons from outside the state, and might lead to race riots and pogroms.[33] Once the initial lack of knowledge was remedied by the Commission and the provisions of the law explained, according to SCAD's first chairman, "a great deal of the opposition which had been apparent during the legislative consideration was gradually broken down, and we were—frankly, I was myself amazed, not at the opposition which developed but at the extent of the cooperation which we got from management and from the large industrial groups, such as Associated Industries of the State of New York and merchants' associations." [34]

That opposition on the part of employers should decline after the enactment of the law is not surprising. If we assume that employers want as little governmental regulation of their hiring policies as possible, it is to be expected that they would make at least the minimum compliance with the law in order to avoid dealing with the enforcing agency. Interviews with the personnel managers of thirty-two companies in New York, New Jersey, and Connecticut, and the experience of the field staff of the Committee on Discrimination in Employment of the New York State War Council with 175 companies, supports this expectation: "Once confronted with the legal necessity of hiring the Negro, many managers, supervisors and foremen have exhibited the same earnest desire to make a success of it as they have in tackling any other problem of production and management. And they have succeeded." [35]

In dealing with management, SCAD, according to one commissioner,[36] has found that top-level executives are more conciliatory than those at the middle levels. There appear to be good reasons for this difference. Top executives have the authority to make whatever concessions the firm will make, whereas those lower in the hierarchy must await the decisions made above. Top executives do not deal so directly with the workers as do middle-level executives, and hence their decision is less likely to be affected by their own personal attitudes towards minority groups. The relationship between workers and top-level management is as purely economic and devoid of sentiment as any relationship can be. To the middle-level executives the employment of minority group members is a social as well as an economic decision, involving interpersonal relations more intimate than those between workers and the highest levels of management.

The early fears of opponents of the law have not been realized: industries have not been driven from the state by the law; there have been only a few cases in which individual workers refused to work alongside members of minority groups employed as a result of the law; there has been no unfavorable response from department store customers since the employment of Negro salesgirls. "The experiences of the commission, therefore," according to a joint statement by its first two chairmen, "lead to the conclusion that the bogies and phantoms urged in opposition to the passage of the law have vanished in the light of experience." [37]

Opponents of the proposed legislation feared that a flood of cases would follow its enactment. This has not occurred. Indeed, minority groups which want to strengthen the law's operation have argued that SCAD handles a small number of cases. A 1948 report of the Committee to Support the Ives-

Quinn Law (sponsored by representatives from the Urban League of Greater New York, the National Association for the Advancement of Colored People, and the American Jewish Congress) asserted that this situation is the result of neglect on the part of SCAD and the civic and social agencies that favor the law, and is not an indication that there is little employment discrimination.[38]

With regard to the number of complaints it receives, the Commission is caught between two fires. If it receives or initiates a large number of cases, the law may be said to be creating a "nuisance" for business. If there are few cases, the law may be said to be unnecessary or the Commission lax. While there is no "correct" number of cases that should arise in a given period of time, it is probably true that changes in SCAD's methods of case settlement and publicity would bring complaints to it at a greater rate and would give it a case load more nearly equal to that of similar agencies. The Committee to Support the Ives-Quinn Law prepared data which show that SCAD during 1947 had a case load of 485, a staff of twenty-two and a budget of $420,000; the New York State office of the federal FEPC during the year ending June 30, 1944, had a case load of 820, a staff of four and a budget of about $50,000; the New York State Labor Relations Board during 1946 had a case load of 2,024, a staff of twelve to fourteen, and a budget of about $450,000. From these data the Committee concluded that SCAD, for its budget and staff, carries a small case load and takes too long to settle complaints.[39]

There are several possible explanations for the small number of complaints filed with SCAD. First, as SCAD itself has pointed out,[40] the high level of employment has meant that workers have not felt the same need for protection from discrimination that they might feel if jobs were scarcer. Second, workers who identify themselves with minority groups learn which types of jobs, firms, and industries are closed to them, hence avoid applying and have no occasion to file a complaint.

In 1948 the Research Committee on Intergroup Relations and the Commission on Community Interrelations of the American Jewish Congress sponsored a study of the attitudes, with respect to employment discrimination, of 504 New York City residents.* The study showed that Jews believe their freest occupational opportunities are in small business and the professions, and that Negroes see their freest opportunities in manual labor and domestic service.[41] These judgments seem to correspond to the facts of economic life.

Third, it takes time for workers to learn about the law. SCAD has an educational and a publicity program, but only a small part of it appears to have as its purpose the dissemination of information in such a way as would substantially increase the number of cases.[42] The New York City study just referred to revealed that only 8 percent of those asked knew that New York State has a law against discrimination in employment which is enforced by an official agency to which complaints may be brought. Thirty-nine percent did not know the law exists; 30 percent knew it exists but could give no details about it, and 23 percent knew that it exists and that it deals with employment discrimination.[43] Thus only one person in twelve knew more about the law than was actually revealed in the circumstances of the interview (about employment discrimination) and in the question itself: "Do you know about the New York State Law against Discrimination?"

Fourth, the small amount of evidence available indicates that minority groups as well as the public in general are skeptical about the efficiency of the Ives-Quinn law. Of the 504 New York City residents interviewed in the aforementioned study, 56 percent said they did not believe the law is "efficient," 19 percent said they did not know or were undecided, and only 25 percent said they believed the law efficient. Of the Jewish

* This sample of 504 New York City residents does not appear to be a representative one. This fact, however, is irrelevant here since the study's results are not interpreted as reporting the views of the entire population of the city, but only as a rough indication of opinion.

respondents 69 percent said they did not believe the law efficient, and 52 percent of the Negroes asked took the same position.[44] The accuracy of and the foundation for these opinions are irrelevant to the fact that a law in which so large a proportion of the population lacks faith is not likely to be invoked as frequently as one which people believe efficient. This situation may have changed since the study was made in 1948, but there are no further data on the subject.

Fifth, if we judge by SCAD's disposition of complaint cases (already discussed earlier in this section), then we must conclude that complainants are not likely to encourage others to file complaints. As we have already seen, to the end of 1950 SCAD found that 65 percent of the complaints it received could not be sustained after investigation, and only about 25 percent were sustained (see Table 5). Regardless of whether or not SCAD could do anything else but decide each complaint case as it did, when two out of three complainants find their charges not sustained (though SCAD finds evidence of *other* discrimination in about a third of these cases), it is probable that few workers come away from an experience with SCAD in a mood to recommend the same procedure to their friends among the minority groups.

Sixth, the length of time SCAD takes to settle complaint cases, too, probably discourages potential complainants who know of this situation. To the end of 1947, covering two and a half years, SCAD has stated, the "average time required to dispose of a complaint case . . . was three months." [45] This is obviously too long a period to be effective for a worker who has experienced discrimination, since it is not likely that he can afford to remain unemployed for more than a few weeks while his complaint is being handled. If many weeks go by and the Commission has not yet come to a decision, the worker probably has to get another job. When he does, the chances are he is no longer interested in the one where he experienced the discrimination. There is another clue to the length of time SCAD devotes to each complaint case. In 1948 the Commission closed 453 complaint cases, of which 180 (or 40 percent) had been opened during 1948, whereas 273 cases (or 60 percent) had been opened before 1948. In 1949 the Commission closed 282 complaint cases of which 183 (or 65 percent) had been opened during that year and 99 (or 35 percent) in earlier years. In 1950 the Commission closed 289 such cases, of which 172 (or 59 percent) had been opened in that year and the remaining 117 in earlier years.[46] The Commission, as we shall see in a later section, is aware of this problem. Much of the delay in the settlement of complaint cases is unavoidable. A field investigator must make one or more trips to the respondent's place of business. The commissioner assigned to a case has to hold one or more conferences with the respondent or his representative and with the complainant. Many persons are often involved, and visits, schedules, and so on, must be synchronized. Three months is probably too long for the complainant, but some delay seems inevitable.

Since SCAD does not make public the provisions of its settlement of complaint cases, it is impossible to assess this aspect of the Commission's work. But its first chairman told a United States Senate subcommittee that fewer than 243 persons had actually obtained jobs as a result of filing complaints with the Commission from its inception in July of 1945 to June 1, 1947.[47] Such a record, it must be noted, is not one to encourage the filing of complaints. The Commission, however, has noted that "in a substantial proportion of the complaints . . . the complainant has taken the position that it is not his desire to obtain action which will affect him directly, but only that the Commission proceed to eliminate the unlawful employment practice or policy which resulted in the incident of which he complains." [48]

It is apparent that the mere opportunity to report discrimination to a state agency empowered to eliminate it is a genuine source of satisfaction to persons who believe they are victims of discrimination.

It would be interesting to learn systematically what is the reaction of complainants to their experiences with SCAD; it would be equally interesting to learn the attitudes of employer-respondents. Such studies, of course, could be undertaken only with the Commission's sponsorship. Here again one of the Commission's preachments seems to block reliable self-evaluation, for it assures all parties to its cases that their names will not be made public or used in any way not relevant to a proceeding without their permission. Again it appears odd that SCAD should be effectively barred in this way. Probably it could undertake or sponsor this kind of study, and still not violate its assurances, by explaining the purposes the study would serve and by guaranteeing anonymity as when the interviewees were parties to a case.

Since the Commission had not found it necessary to bring a single complaint case to a hearing before 1949, the three minority agencies which sponsored the Committee to Support the Ives-Quinn Law, asserting that this situation "hardly seems to be the result of chance," claimed that SCAD might be "willing to settle for less than full compliance with the letter and spirit of the law, in order to avoid the public hearing stage." [49] In response to the Committee's request that SCAD set forth its standards for adjustment of complaint cases,[50] the second chairman of SCAD described certain "minimum" and "variant" bases of conciliation.[51]

The minimum bases call for a commitment by the respondent that: (1) his employment policies will conform to the law and that he will make this known to all persons in his organization who deal with employment matters; (2) the SCAD poster stating the rights and obligations of persons affected by the law will be displayed in such a way that employees and applicants can see it; (3) no oral or written inquiries will be made that may reveal an applicant's race, creed, color, or national origin; (4) his employment pattern will in the future, dependent upon job openings and the qualifications of those who apply for them, show the inclusion of members of all minority groups. Some of the "variant" bases of conciliation are a commitment by the respondent to: (1) hire the complainant; (2) offer the complainant the next opening; (3) give the complainant back pay; (4) upgrade the complainant; (5) use employment agencies which will refer workers on a non-discriminatory basis; (6) investigate the attitudes of his personnel workers and take steps to eliminate any prejudices they have which may hinder them from meeting the requirements of the law; (7) make periodic reports to SCAD showing those applicants selected and rejected, and the basis for each type of action. In summary, the chairman stated, the Commission may during a conciliation "require a respondent to do anything which the Law says the Commission may require him to do after the conduct of a formal public hearing." This general statement and most of the foregoing "minimum" and "variant" bases for adjustment of complaints were set forth by SCAD in its 1948 report.[52]

Two features about employers' compliance with the law are of special importance. First, as the Commission points out, "the successful treatment of each case, although reflecting statistically only one complainant and one respondent, may and does in many cases affect thousands of persons in this State." [53] The New York Telephone Company and Montgomery Ward are each one case, but the significance of their genuine compliance with the law is considerable, since they themselves not only employ thousands of workers but their employment practices are likely to influence those of other large firms in similar fields of business. Second, SCAD constantly watches out for mere token compliance, the hiring of one or a few Negroes or Jews, for example, primarily for the purpose of claiming compliance with the law. SCAD does not tell an employer how many members of a minority group he must have; it only asserts that he must employ such persons on the same basis he uses in hiring other workers. The Commission can determine whether or not compliance is genuine and continuing by examining the application blanks filled out by the prospective employees. If they reveal discrimination even after the employer has once complied with the law, the Commission may reopen proceedings against the firm.

Just as it is difficult to measure precisely the effect of the Ives-Quinn law and the success of the Commission in administering it, so it is difficult to determine exactly to what extent employers comply with the law. We have reviewed SCAD's data on compliance, but there remains one other important source, the reports of discriminatory job orders received by the New York State Employment Service (N.Y.S.E.S.). When the N.Y.S.E.S. receives a discriminatory request from an employer, the rules of the agency provide that a record must be made of it and that the employer must be asked to amend his request in accordance with the Ives-Quinn law.[54] Despite the law, the official state employment agency continues to receive hundreds of illegal requests each year. Though the number declined considerably after the passage of the act, there are still a surprising number of requests of this kind, and an equally surprising number which cannot be relaxed by the state employment agency officials. The N.Y.S.E.S. sends this information to SCAD, but the latter has not, to the knowledge of this writer, commented on this matter in its annual reports or in its literature. About 80 to 90 percent of these requests discriminate against Negroes and less than 10 percent against Jews. The probability is, further, that the number of such discriminatory job orders is under-reported. During 1948 one of the community councils created by SCAD claimed that the N.Y.S.E.S. offices in one county were not reporting to that agency's headquarters the discriminatory job orders they received. After a conference with N.Y.S.E.S. officials the local offices were directed to make the reports in conformity with N.Y.S.E.S. policy.[55]

During 1944 the N.Y.S.E.S. received 999 discriminatory job orders, of which it was able to change 591, leaving 408 requests which employers refused to amend. In 1945, during half of which year the Ives-Quinn law was in effect, the number of requests fell to 697, of which 554 were amended, leaving 143 unchanged with regard to their discriminatory features. Since 1945 the total number of requests received has declined, but the proportion of employers who are willing to amend their discriminatory requests has also declined except for 1949. Thus 79 percent of the discriminatory requests made in 1945 were amended, 72 percent in 1946, 58 percent in 1947, 54 percent in 1948 and 57 percent in 1949. In 1949, three and a half to four and a half years after the passage of the Ives-Quinn law, 410 discriminatory requests from employers were reported by the state's employment agency, of which 233 were amended. This seems like a large number of illegal requests, but it is small compared to the 565,569 nonagricultural placements the N.Y.S.E.S. made in 1949.[56]

Of the employers who make these discriminatory requests about 15 percent, according to an official estimate, are fully subject to the Ives-Quinn law and are probably aware of that fact.

Compliance by Employment Agencies

Private employment agencies have not very often appeared before SCAD as respondents in complaint cases or investigations initiated by the Commission. From July, 1945, to the end of 1950 agencies were named as respondents in 144 complaint cases and in 45 investigations begun on the Commission's own initiative.[57] SCAD has found discriminatory practices among agencies in higher proportion than among employers and labor unions. Of 134 complaint cases against employment agencies closed to the end of 1950, the specific charge of the complainant was upheld in 45 percent, but only in 28 percent of the cases in which a complaint was lodged against an employer, and in 9 percent of the 129 complaints against a labor union. In the Commission-initiated cases, discrimination was found in 77 percent of the 422 cases closed to the end of 1950 involving employers and in 58 percent of the 38 cases involving unions, but in 91 percent of the 53 cases involving private employment agencies.[58]

It would seem reasonable to expect that employers who want to circumvent the Ives-Quinn law would resort to private employment agencies willing to help them. Such a claim was made, in extreme form, by Representative John E. Rankin of Mississippi, testifying before a Senate subcommittee in 1947 on a federal fair employment practice bill. Mr. Rankin stated: "The businessmen in New York tell me that they have had to resort to employment agencies to get around this thing [the Ives-Quinn law], and in those employment agencies they have a string of questions . . . that get around these regulations, and they tell me that there is hardly a Negro in New York can get by them." [59]

The Commission has been aware of the challenge employment agencies represent to the full enforcement of the law. Commenting in its 1946 annual report that the private agencies present a "real difficulty," the Commission stated: "There can be little doubt that some employers have sought to evade the provisions of the Law Against Discrimination by job orders placed with these agencies in which limitations as to race, color, creed, and national origin are openly or tacitly conveyed to the agency." In attempting to eliminate such practices, SCAD has studied the work of the agencies, conferred with them and their legal advisers, and observed that improper questions have been excluded from their application blanks. The Commission also noted progress in its efforts to get the agencies to reject discriminatory job orders. In addition it has developed, with the New York City Commissioner of Licenses, a procedure for invoking the latter's regulatory powers where conciliation fails to eliminate unlawful practices.[60]

That the Commission has as yet not achieved much success in this area is shown by the fact that private employment agencies are willing to accept discriminatory job orders even on the telephone from persons who have not identified themselves or their firms, according to three studies conducted by the Commission on Law and Social Action of the American Jewish Congress. In 1945, soon after the enactment of the Law Against Discrimination, 102 employment agencies, of which 92 specialized in white-collar jobs, were personally called upon. Of these 102, 30 were "not openly hostile to the law but were set upon circumventing it"; "35 were not even willing to give it lip service"; and "only 37 or one-third had a friendly, cooperative attitude toward the policy expressed in the law." Unfortunately, the survey does not indicate the criteria used to classify the attitudes of the employment agencies. The following year the same organization made a telephone survey of 121 agencies in Manhattan, Brooklyn, and Queens which supply white-collar workers, including 65 agencies covered in the 1945 study. Of the 121 agencies telephoned anonymously, 107 (88 percent) said they would fill the request for a "white Protestant stenographer," and only 14 refused.[61] Early in 1949 the American Jewish Congress made a third survey, this time covering 255 Manhattan agencies supplying stenographers and other office personnel. Nine gave replies too uncertain to be classified. Of the 246 agencies giving definite replies, 158 (or 64.2 percent) said they would fill the discriminatory request, whereas 88 (or 35.8 percent) refused it. These figures show a substantial change in the policy of private employment agencies but indicate, nevertheless, that they still engage in a good deal of illegal discrimination. If such a large proportion are willing to accept a discriminatory order from an anonymous telephone caller, it is safe to assume that even more would do so when contact is more personal.[62]

Employment agencies have shown some measure of opposition to the work of SCAD. In November of 1946 the Commission adopted a General Regulation requiring that all employers, employment agencies, and labor unions covered by the law post in their establishments a notice prepared by the Commission setting forth the main provisions of the Ives-Quinn law. Some employment agencies in New York City, the Commission reports, "have refused to comply with the regulation on the ground that the Commission is without power to adopt a regulation requiring the posting of a notice." Though the Commission believes it does have this power, it sought in 1949 an amendment to the Law Against Discrimination requiring the posting of such a notice. Two bills [63] were introduced, one in each state legislative body, but both died in committee. As a result, the Commission decided to "proceed against the recalcitrant employment agencies by way of criminal proceedings." By agreement with New York City's Chief Magistrate, all cases involving charges of willful interference with SCAD in the performance of its duty or violation of its orders, it announced, would be handled by a court especially created to deal with violations of orders of New York City and State departments and commissions.[64]

The employment agencies' opposition reached the point in 1950 where an official of the Association of Private Office Personnel Agencies brought suit against SCAD, challenging some of its rulings on preemployment inquiries and the validity of its regulations requiring the posting of a notice, provided by the Commission, giving information about the Ives-Quinn law and where complaints may be filed.[65]

The Commission has successfully sponsored an amendment to the General Business Law of New York State which helps to solve another problem regarding employment agencies. The names of some agencies, such as American-Jewish Employment Exchange and Japanese Employment Agency, immediately suggest that they accept job orders from employers and make referrals on the basis of race, color, creed, or national origin. Recognizing that an agency's name may be a business asset, SCAD did not ask the Legislature to outlaw such names which were already in use but requested it to refuse a license to prospective agencies which planned to adopt such names. As to those agencies already in operation under such names, the law requires that they expressly indicate that they do not discriminate in violation of the law.[66]

During 1949 the Commission began a general investigation into the practices of fee-charging employment agencies to "ascertain the facts and, if necessary, to provide a basis for remedial action." [67] No special program, however, was announced as a result of it.[68]

Compliance by Labor Unions

In SCAD's dealing with illegal discrimination by labor unions its chief success has come not as a result of complaint cases but through investigations begun on its own initiative. To the end of 1950 the Commission had received a total of 172 complaints against unions, of which it had closed 129. In only 11 of these 129 cases had SCAD sustained the complainant's charge of illegal discrimination. To the end of 1950 the Commission had initiated 50 investigations of union practices, of which it had completed 44. Of these 44, SCAD had found discrimination in 26 cases and had eliminated the illegal practices through conciliation.[69]

Probably the Commission's most substantial achievement with respect to discrimination by unions has been the elimination of provisions in union constitutions and by-laws excluding Negroes entirely or denying them the full privileges of membership. In 1948 SCAD concluded a survey of thirty-eight unions to determine the extent of such discriminatory rules, and succeeded in getting the following eight unions to remove discriminatory provisions from their constitutions or by-laws: [70] Air Line Dispatchers; Blacksmiths, Drop Forgers

and Helpers; International Association of Machinists; Maintenance of Way Employes; Railroad Yardmasters; Railway and
Steamship Clerks, Freight Handlers, Express and Station Employes; Sheet Metal Workers; Switchmen's Union.

The following nine unions have made such discriminatory
provisions inoperative in New York State: National Associa-
tion of Letter Carriers; Locomotive Engineers; Locomotive
Firemen and Enginemen; Railroad Telegraphers; Railroad
Trainmen; Railway Carmen; Railway Conductors; Railway
Mail Association; Rural Letter Carriers' Association.

Some of these unions, the Commission has reported, complied with the law on their own initiative, some "complied
readily" upon the Commission's request, and some "complied
only after the exertion of strenuous effort." SCAD pointed
out that it is not convinced, merely because the survey has
been concluded, that the discriminatory admissions practices
of unions have been entirely eliminated, nor even that all discriminatory provisions have been removed from union constitutions and by-laws. "Pending and future cases involving such
clauses or practices," it stated early in 1949, "will, however,
be handled on an individual case basis." [71]

Seniority Rules and Vocational Training

In its efforts to break up long-standing discriminatory patterns in employment, the Commission meets problems that it
can do little to solve directly or immediately. Two such problems are seniority and the need for expanded job-training
programs. While the Law Against Discrimination aims to open
all job levels to all groups in the state, it also has the effect
of breaking up the traditional pattern of "Negro jobs." Just as
Negroes may not be excluded from jobs merely on account of
race or color, so no class of jobs may be reserved exclusively
for Negroes. Thus it is illegal to exclude white waiters in
restaurants where all the waiters have been traditionally Negroes, or to exclude whites from holding bus boy jobs where

these have been held traditionally by Filipinos. While this type of breakup of customary employment patterns is not nearly so important as opening up new opportunities to members of minority groups, both processes, if carried out over a period of years, will accomplish the law's aim to make employment a matter of ability and not of race, color, creed, or national origin.

Seniority achieved through company policy or contracts with trade unions often perpetuates past employment discrimination. How to deal with this problem, which runs into an issue on which unions are very touchy, has been under informal and formal discussion in the Commission.[72] In its annual report for 1948, SCAD noted that the railroad brotherhoods, for example, have extensive seniority arrangements which continue past discriminatory practices: "In every category of employment there exist formidable lists of furloughed employees with prior claims on job vacancies which militate against an immediate visible change in the pattern of employment save by assault on the principle of seniority." [73]

The second chairman of the Commission, testifying in 1947 before a Senate subcommittee on a federal fair employment practice bill, described, in the course of proving a different point, how a minority group is discriminated against because of previous unfair employment patterns perpetuated through seniority arrangements. In a large industrial city in upstate New York, members of the Italian community felt they were being discriminated against in postwar discharges, and "a good deal of racial bitterness" resulted. But investigation "disclosed that the Italians had been discharged solely on the basis of seniority, that there was no racial discrimination whatsoever." [74]

Industrial training, especially for Negroes and Puerto Ricans, is essential if the purposes of the Ives-Quinn law are to be realized to the full. Much potential discrimination in skilled trades and white-collar jobs is probably concealed, since so few Negroes and Puerto Ricans are qualified for them by training and experience. As these and other groups develop the skills which will enable them to hold better jobs, they can further test the law and enter new occupations. The Commission has considered this problem from the start of its work, and it reported in 1948: "Plans for close cooperation between the New York State Apprenticeship Council and the Commission are presently being formulated in order to insure that opportunity for training shall not be restricted by reason of race, creed, color or national origin." [75] The second chairman of the Commission pointed out to minority group leaders at a meeting sponsored in 1948 by the Committee to Support the Ives-Quinn Law that they could aid in strengthening the enforcement of the law if they helped "to prepare the members of minority groups to become skilled and qualified to take their places on a competitive basis in this industrial society." [76]

When training schools are open to all minorities and when they qualify for the higher-paying jobs the Ives-Quinn law can then operate at greater strength to raise their occupational and income level.

SCAD'S RULINGS AND POLICIES

In administering the Law Against Discrimination, SCAD, of course, works in a legal area that has not been fully charted, and it is anxious to proceed cautiously and upon the basis of principles that have been verified to the greatest possible extent. The administration of such laws so clearly affects their efficacy that a detailed examination of SCAD's rulings, policies, and procedures becomes necessary if we are to understand the role of the Ives-Quinn law in the elimination of discrimination.

Rulings

On four occasions SCAD has made public a comprehensive set of rulings dealing with one or more phases of the Law Against Discrimination. The first set was presented June 1, 1946, and dealt only with preemployment inquiries.[77] More comprehensive collections of rulings on this subject and other matters were included in the annual reports for 1948, 1949, and 1950.[78] In its rulings, as a whole, the Commission has strengthened the law considerably, and, as it points out, "has followed the statutory mandate of liberal construction." [79] With respect to preemployment inquiries, especially, SCAD has done a thorough job. It has proscribed inquiries as to race, religion, color, and national origin as well as other inquiries from which it is possible to determine these characteristics. Thus an applicant may be asked whether he is a citizen of the United States, but not whether he is a native-born or a naturalized citizen. Questions about the applicant's place of birth, or that of his parents or close relatives, are likewise forbidden. The statute, SCAD points out, "does not restrict an employer's right to fix the qualifications necessary for satisfactory job performance. It merely requires that the same standards of qualification be applied equally to all persons." [80]

In its 1948 annual report the Commission published a large number of rulings referring to the meaning, under the law, of employers, employees, labor organizations, employment agencies, verified complaints, services of governmental agencies, exclusiveness of remedy under the act, preemployment inquiries, bona-fide occupational qualifications, and help-wanted and situations-wanted advertisements. The following paragraphs summarize a number of the more important rulings SCAD has made.

Employers. (1) SCAD has jurisdiction over state and municipal agencies and other subdivisions of the state but not over the United States Government, its subdivisions, agencies, and instrumentalities.[81] (2) SCAD has jurisdiction over a maritime company when an unlawful practice is alleged to have been committed in the state, even if the company is engaged in interstate or foreign commerce.[82] (3) SCAD has jurisdiction over railroad employment within the state.[83] (4) SCAD has jurisdiction over an employer who has a total of six or more employees even if they are so distributed among several establishments that each has fewer than six.[84]

Employees. A "maid" employed regularly in a business establishment is *not* in "domestic service," which is excluded from the law's coverage.[85]

Labor Organizations may not exclude persons on the basis of race, creed, color, or national origin, maintain auxiliary unions for persons of a particular race, creed, or national origin, or deny any privilege to members on such a basis.[86]

Employment agencies come within SCAD's jurisdiction even if they are nonprofit agencies or are operated in conjunction with an educational institution otherwise exempt from the law.[87]

Verified complaints. (1) Verified complaints may be filed by employers whose employees "refuse or threaten to refuse to cooperate with the provisions of the Law." [88] (2) A membership corporation whose purposes are embraced by the law may file a verified complaint under Sections 131.3, which forbids discriminatory preemployment inquiries, and Section 131.5, which provides against inducing others to violate the law.[89] (3) An employer who places a discriminatory job order with an employment agency is violating the law no matter what action the agency takes.[90] (4) An employment agency that accepts a discriminatory job order is violating the law.[91] (5) A person who is required to fill out an application form, in order to obtain employment, which contains unlawful questions, may file a complaint even if he does not complete the form or does not submit it to the employer.[92]

Preemployment inquiries. Discrimination because of political creed is not covered by the law, which forbids discrimination on the basis of religious creed.[93]

Policies

Expediting Settlement of Complaints. SCAD has been criticized by minority groups for taking too much time in settling complaint cases. During 1948, SCAD attempted to reduce the time per case by determining as quickly as possible the merits of the complaint, notifying the complainant and respondent of the decision, and then conducting the ancillary investigation into the latter's whole employment record (although it denied that this survey results in any appreciable delay).[94] In its annual report for 1948, nevertheless, the Commission reaffirmed its policy of studying a respondent's overall employment pattern, even though the result may delay the disposition of the specific complaint. The reasons given by the Commission for this policy are that the specific complaint frequently cannot be decided without such a larger study; that the larger study proceeds simultaneously with the investigation of the specific complaint; and that the individual complaint cannot be fully remedied unless the respondent's overall employment policy is corrected if it is discriminatory. This statement suggests that the Commission does not intend to apply this technique more widely in the immediate future unless "the exceptional case proves to be the normal case." [95] The annual reports for 1949 and 1950 make no reference to this matter.

Hearings. Until late in 1949 SCAD frequently pointed out that it had not yet found it necessary to bring any case to a hearing and that it had adjusted all its cases by conciliation while adhering to the letter and spirit of the law. In 1949 it ordered one case for a hearing, but that case was settled before the hearing actually was held. In 1950 SCAD ordered and held a hearing in one case. No employer, one commissioner wrote,[96] "has elected to hazard the stigma of discrimination by going to a hearing." The implication is that the dislike of exposure has made respondents so conciliatory that no hearings had to be called. The wartime federal FEPC, too, found this dislike of exposure,[97] yet that agency nevertheless found it necessary to hold hearings from time to time. SCAD does not disclose enough of its records to enable others to determine whether or not hearings have been avoided at the expense of the spirit of the law.

Disclosure of Data. Following its interpretation of that part of Section 132 of the Law Against Discrimination which prohibits the Commission and its staff from disclosing what transpires during the conciliation of complaint cases, SCAD has withheld certain information from the public. It has not been entirely clear, however, just what SCAD withholds on this statutory ground and what it withholds merely as a matter of policy. It would be helpful in evaluating the Commission's work if there were available a description of the results of the conciliations it achieves with each respondent, but it does not prepare such information for the public. What the law forbids, it would seem, is the disclosure of what occurs *during* negotiations in the conciliation process, and not the *results* of that process. In its annual reports since 1946, SCAD has presented summaries of selected cases; there would seem to be no legal restriction against its publication of a summary of the adjustment provisions in all its cases.

SCAD has shifted the ground upon which it has based at least one of its nondisclosure policies—that regarding the names of complainants and respondents. The Commission has steadily adhered to the rule of not revealing such names except upon the consent of both parties to a case. In its first annual report SCAD held that it was forbidden by law to reveal names.[98] In its 1947 report the Commission implied, without expressly stating, the same notion.[99] But in its reply of November 5, 1948, to the Committee to Support the Ives-Quinn Law, the Commission referred to nondisclosure of names as a "policy" it has "adopted" and which is subject to change.[100] And in its 1948 report SCAD likewise called its nondisclosure of names a policy.[101]

Finally, SCAD appears to withhold data merely on the ground that they might be misinterpreted. Thus it rejected a recommendation that it make public the length of time elapsing between the opening and closing dates of complaint cases apparently because such data "would be conducive to misunderstanding." [102] It would seem to be a fairer procedure for SCAD to reveal all significant facts, release of which the Law Against Discrimination does not prohibit, present its own interpretation and warnings if necessary, and permit others to analyze the data as they see fit.

SCAD'S RELATIONS WITH THE COMMUNITY

The educational features of the Law Against Discrimination put the Commission into contact with the community through its relations with civic groups working in the same field and through the community councils which the law empowers it to create. Since the success of the law is admittedly [103] dependent upon its reception by the people of New York State, it is appropriate to examine the relations between SCAD and those community agencies.

Administrative law in the federal and New York State governments has recognized the value of civic agencies in the enforcement of law. Trade unions have played a highly important role in the enforcement of the National Labor Relations Act, and the New York Society for the Maintenance of Public Decency (formerly the New York Society for the Suppression of Vice) was chartered by New York State in 1873 to aid in enforcing state and federal laws against obscenity.

The Critics

Very early in its career SCAD was vigorously criticized by the very minority and civic groups that had most earnestly supported the bill which became the New York State Law Against Discrimination. The American Civil Liberties Union, in February of 1946, held a meeting to decide how to "make the work of the State Commission Against Discrimination effective." [104] The following month the chairman of the City-wide Citizens Committee on Harlem asserted that the Commission "must be persuaded or forced to change its attitude toward its job. It must see itself as a dynamic agency . . . abandon secrecy and an excess of caution . . . work in both the higher and lower levels of employment . . . speed up its timid approaches to publicity and education." [105] Early in 1947 the Citizens Union urged an amendment to the law to enable organizations to file charges of discrimination.[106] In April the Welfare Council of New York City pointed out that the Commission had made a good beginning but must publicize its work more widely if it was to achieve maximum effectiveness.[107]

Such civic groups face a dilemma when they want to act on their beliefs that the Commission can vastly improve its administration of the law. They want to put pressure on SCAD to alter certain practices, yet they do not want to give the general impression that the principle behind the law is being questioned.

The Commission is aware of this dilemma. Two members, in April of 1946, publicly chided critics of SCAD who "borrow the arguments of those who oppose this type of legislation not only in fact but in principle." Asserting that SCAD welcomed constructive criticism, they expressed the hope that in the future its critics would not "provide ammunition and comfort to those who oppose antidiscrimination laws everywhere." [108]

An interesting conjuncture of criticisms from those who

oppose antidiscrimination laws and those who favor them occurs in regard to the unexpectedly small number of complaints SCAD has received. Those opposed to the Ives-Quinn law have argued that the small number of complaints proves there is really no need for the law. One such critic asserted in January of 1947 that advocates of the law had claimed, before its enactment, that 15,000 complaints were ready for filing before it went into effect on July 1, 1945, and that the small number of complaints actually received to the end of 1946 refuted the charges of widespread employment discrimination.[109] During a Senate subcommittee hearing in 1947 on a federal fair employment practice bill Senator Ellender (Dem., La.) asked the first chairman of SCAD whether he had expected more complaints than were received. "Frankly," he answered, "we expected more cases." And Senator Ellender observed, "Which, of course, leads me to believe that there is more talk about the matter [widespread employment discrimination] than truth." [110] Later on the same day the second chairman of the Commission remarked that "we have always lived well within our budget and we will not spend more than 75 percent of our budget this year." To which Senator Ellender replied, "There are so few cases I wonder why you do not cut it in half?" [111]

Criticism of SCAD for the small number of complaints it has received has been leveled also by groups who want to strengthen the Ives-Quinn law. Thus the Committee to Support the Ives-Quinn Law has protested that "very little use is made of the law" and that SCAD is in part responsible for the small number of complaints filed with it.[112]

The Committee to Support the Ives-Quinn Law during 1948 persistently prodded SCAD to take a more "militant" view of its tasks. The Committee was formed early in 1948 to help "dispel . . . civic inertia and individual apathy" in group relations and to influence SCAD's policies and procedures.[113] In a memorandum to SCAD, dated April 20, 1948, the Committee made recommendations on the disposition of individual complaints, publicity for SCAD's work, and investigations on an industry-wide scale.[114] To these recommendations SCAD replied in a lengthy memorandum dated November 5, 1948, in which it found the Committee's suggestions already in effect or unacceptable in the best interests of the enforcement of the law.[115] Dissatisfied with this response and with the work of SCAD, Committee representatives early in 1949 presented their criticisms of SCAD before the Governor in Albany,[116] but the Committee to Support the Ives-Quinn Law does not appear to have moved SCAD in any direction.

Yet minority group agencies can exert a salutary influence upon the Commission. For example, it was after the American Jewish Congress had asked for a ruling that the Commission outlawed discriminatory situations-wanted advertisements.[117] In addition, it was in cases initiated by the Congress that SCAD brought the employment bureaus of educational institutions within the law's coverage,[118] announced that a civic agency could file complaints under Sections 131.3 and 131.5 of the law,[119] and held, on the basis of a statistical study of a firm's employment practices and of the neighborhood population, that minorities as a group and not merely certain individuals were at a disadvantage in applying for employment.[120]

SCAD, however (for a time, at least), made it clear that it did not wholeheartedly welcome the activity of agencies such as the Committee to Support the Ives-Quinn Law. The second chairman of the Commission in 1949 charged the latter group with "drumming up" many complaints that could not be sustained.[121] In May of 1948 he told representatives of the Committee and of other groups that SCAD wanted "the benefit of advice from any group of citizens of this State." [122] Yet in describing six means by which these groups could help in "strengthening the administration of the law," he did not mention the value of suggestions to the Commission itself on its own policies and procedures.

During 1950 the Commission's relations with civic agencies apparently became more intimate and less strained. In addition to other contacts with SCAD, the representatives of twenty-six voluntary agencies met with the commissioners and offered various suggestions, some of which SCAD accepted.[123] Such give and take between the Commission and interested agencies can lead to that close and sustained cooperation between the Commission and the law's supporters which will insure greater knowledge of and compliance with it. Although the voluntary agencies had worked hard to secure passage of the Ives-Quinn law, they have neglected thus far to establish an appropriate role for themselves in helping to give the law greater meaning for those groups it was intended to protect.

Publicity

Since the law which SCAD administers is a pioneering effort one would expect that the agency would seek the widest publicity for its accomplishments, both to encourage persons who might benefit from the law and to discourage those who might violate it. A pioneering law, in a new field of such profound concern to a very large proportion of New York State's multigroup population, should be making stirring news more often than it does, according to critics of the Commission. From its inception in July, 1945, until the end of 1948, SCAD issued only about twenty publicity releases, excluding those announcing addresses by its members and staff, which reported facts about the law's accomplishments.[124]

Local Community Councils

Under the terms of Section 130.8 of the Ives-Quinn law the State Commission Against Discrimination is brought into contact with the community in a rather direct way. This provision empowers SCAD to "create such advisory agencies and conciliation councils . . . as in its judgment will aid in effectuating the purposes of this article [the "Law Against Discrimination"] and of section eleven of article one of the constitution of this state [the civil rights section]." These agencies and councils, the statute continues, may, under the direction of SCAD, study discrimination in any field; promote cooperation among the state's various national, religious, and racial groups; and make recommendations to SCAD on policy, procedure, and educational programs. Members of these agencies and councils serve without pay, but certain expenses they may have are met by the state. In 1945 SCAD established a council in Buffalo; in 1946, in Syracuse, Onondaga County, Albany, and Westchester County; in 1947, in New York City, Broome County, and Troy. The annual report for 1948 mentioned no new councils added to these seven. The 1949 report likewise mentions no new councils but indicates the replacement of the New York City Council by four separate county councils for Kings, Manhattan, Queens and Richmond. In 1950 councils were organized in Bronx County and in Rochester.[125]

The wording of the statute makes it clear that two different types of boards were intended by Section 130.8, "advisory agencies" and "conciliatory councils." But their functions are then described jointly, so that there is no indication that each type is to carry on separate activities. It appears that the "advisory agencies" were intended to study discrimination and make recommendations as to SCAD's policies and procedures, while the "conciliation councils" were meant "to foster . . . cooperation and conciliation among the groups and elements of the population of the state." The Commission, in establishing these boards, has at least formally, though not in practice, combined in them all the functions outlined in the statute, even to the extent of assisting, upon request, "in the process of conciliation on pending cases of alleged discrimination." [126] Thus far, however, the Commission has not made such a request of any of its advisory councils in a case in which SCAD has had enforcement jurisdiction. In 1949 SCAD sponsored informal discussions with representatives of the hotel industry

as the first step in the establishment of industry advisory councils. The Commission has authorized councils in the fields of
banking, insurance, and public utilities. This program, instituted in 1948, may, if expedited and carried through consistently, lead to much more effective application of SCAD's
powers to the tasks assigned it by the Ives-Quinn law.[127]

To illustrate the relations between the Commission and the
community through these advisory councils we shall consider
the record of the New York City Council of SCAD until its
dissolution at the end of 1948. New York City is, of course,
the Commission's most important area of operation. Of 1,005
complaints filed with the Commission from its inception until
the end of 1947, 862, or 86 percent, originated in New York
City. Since the commissioners find most of their case work in
New York City, they have had more direct contact with the
council there than with any other council in the state. Finally,
the New York City Council had many national figures of
great influence in industry, politics, and education. The work
and record of this council, however, is not discussed here as
necessarily representative of the other councils.

The level on which the New York City Council of SCAD
could operate is indicated in its attempt to persuade the Metropolitan Life Insurance Company to reconsider its policy of
excluding Negroes from its "Stuyvesant Town" housing project for 8,000 families. Mr. James G. Blaine, president of the
Marine Midland Trust Company, was authorized by the Council to confer with executives of the company. At a Council
meeting in September of 1947 Mr. Blaine reported that he was
studying the evidence on interracial housing communities pre-
paratory to asking for such a conference. At the same meeting, Mr. Winthrop Rockefeller, stating that he had already
talked with Mr. Frederick H. Ecker, chairman of the board
of the Metropolitan Life Insurance Company, advised against
pressing the issue at that time. At the November meeting of the
Council, Mr. Blaine reported that he had conferred with Mr.

Ecker. The Council agreed that another such meeting would be advisable in the spring of 1948, but the minutes of the Council's sessions do not indicate that it was held.[128]

Much of the Council's work, however, was undertaken in a more formal manner, on less difficult problems, and with more success or promise of success. One of the more active groups in the Council was the committee on discrimination in medical institutions, which carried out two significant projects. In the fall of 1947 its chairman met with the Mayor of New York City, the Commissioner of Hospitals, and two members of the Mayor's Committee on Unity to press for the admission of Negroes to the professional staffs of city hospitals. The Commissioner of Hospitals accepted the responsibility for providing such opportunities for Negroes and it was agreed to hold another conference in six months or a year to determine what progress had been made.[129] The Council's committee on discrimination in medical institutions in June of 1948 brought SCAD's attention to the fact that the New York State Joint Hospital Survey and Planning Commission was contemplating a substantial increase in hospital facilities in New York City. The Council resolved that the planning commission be urged to establish nondiscriminatory standards of appointment and employment in the new facilities, and that other SCAD councils take up the matter in their own localities.[130] A few months later a letter from the chairman of SCAD was read at the regular meeting of the Council, stating that he had conferred with the chairman of the planning commission, who asserted that "insofar as the Joint Commission has to do with the erection and operation of any of the hospitals proposed by the Joint Commission, the hospitals will be operated under a nondiscriminatory policy." [131]

The New York City Council of SCAD functioned under several limitations. Perhaps because of the prominence of its members and their involvement in many activities attendance at Council meetings was poor. In its report for 1947 [132] SCAD listed thirty-one members of the Council (reduced by a few resignations), yet only an average of fourteen attended the ten meetings in 1947 and an average of nine members attended the ten meetings in 1948.[133] The Council, too, had to function within the narrow lane marked out by the Commission. At a public meeting sponsored in May of 1948 by the Committee to Support the Ives-Quinn Law, one of the most active Council members complained of the restraints imposed by the second chairman of SCAD: "He has constantly urged concentration upon the problems of discrimination in employment, to the exclusion, so far as he has been able to influence our Council, of other phases of discrimination. This attitude, I believe, is not in accord with the stated purposes of the Ives-Quinn Act." [134] At the Council meeting in January of 1948, one of the members suggested that a monthly newsletter be circulated to keep the members better informed of the Commission's work. The second chairman of SCAD, according to the minutes,[135] "expressed approval of the suggestion and agreed to prepare and distribute among all Council members throughout the state a brief monthly digest of interesting and significant accomplishments of the Commission and of the various Councils of the Commission." This material was not circulated up to the end of 1948, when the New York City Council was dissolved by the Commission. It does not appear, from the minutes of the Council meetings, interviews with Council members, and the literature distributed by SCAD that the councils were given any more details of the work of the Commission than were made public to any interested person or group.

The statute, in Section 130.8, gives SCAD a considerable degree of control over the councils it establishes. The Commission is empowered to "create" the councils. The Commission may authorize a council to carry on certain studies, to foster good will among the various groups in the state, and to make recommendations to the Commission itself. SCAD has interpreted these powers to mean that, in general, the councils must obtain the Commission's approval before they make public their views and findings; that the Commission alone appoints council members, and chairmen and vice chairmen of council committees; [136] and that the Commission may dissolve councils.[137] The manner of its dissolution of the New York City Council reveals the Commission's interpretation of its total power with respect to the councils. At the Council's meeting in December, 1948, attended by ten members, the chairman, according to the minutes, "outlined a suggested plan for the dissolution of the present New York City Council and the establishment of councils in each of the five counties of New York City with an overall greater New York Council. After some discussion the members present expressed approval of the plan." The second chairman of SCAD, the minutes conclude, "then stated that the Commission would act on the matter at its next regular meeting." [138] The plan for the creation of five county councils was not a new one, for SCAD's first annual report [139] mentioned that the New York City Council would be "followed by the establishment of Borough Councils throughout the city." The minutes of the Council's last meeting, however, give no intimation as to how its dissolution was to be effected, nor any hint as to the action which soon followed. On December 16, a week after this Council meeting, the Commission unanimously passed a series of resolutions dissolving the Council as of December 31, 1948, and establishing a council for each county of New York City and a Greater New York City Council, of which the Commission would name all the members, chairmen, and vice chairmen. Membership in the Council was terminated by letter from the chairman of SCAD.[140]

Although there does not seem to have been similar friction between the Commission and its other community councils, there is no evidence that these councils play a more independent role elsewhere in the state.

SCAD's Reply to its Critics

The Commission has, of course, been aware of the criticism of its work which has come from persons and groups opposing the goals of the Ives-Quinn law as well as from those supporting these goals. In an address [141] in 1951 Commissioner Caroline K. Simon dealt directly with the criticisms made by the latter group; her comments, since they refer to several issues mentioned in this chapter, warrant extended quotation here:

Our "friendly critics" say that the publicity policy of the Commission is not a strong one; that the length of time it takes to settle cases is too long; that the Commission relies on complaints filed with it rather than on systematic studies of areas of discrimination; that the Commission does not disclose the basis on which cases are settled "informally" (our conciliation agreements), and finds "probable cause" in a small number of cases.

Take our publicity policy first: I am sure no one can really believe that it is apparent only to him but not to the Commission that the field of discrimination provides opportunity for sensational headlines. We are quite aware that we could whoop it up by adopting a type of press release such as, "SCAD forces department store to hire Negro" or "SCAD gives stinging rebuke to utility." We probably wouldn't even need a complaint case to get our name in the newspapers under such devices as, "SCAD plans full scale investigation into charges of anti-Semitism against the B chain" or "SCAD subpoenas president of local factory."

We believe, however, that our publicity program should serve a more important function than sensationalism and artificial stimulation. It is aimed at establishing a solid base of understanding and acceptance of the purposes and terms of the Law. It is directed to worker and employer, to labor union and employment agency, to the student preparing himself to take his place in the community, to the vocational counsellor who advises the student, to parent-teacher groups, to service clubs, to all those facets in our society in which there should be an awareness that in this state you have the right to be judged on the basis of your skills. . . .

The complaint that the Commission takes too long to close its cases actually stems from the Commission's practice of making inquiry into a respondent's overall policies and practices and its resultant employment pattern in the course of investigating a specific complaint case. The Commission reported on this subject in its 1948 Report of Progress.

The Commission has recognized the possibility that this practice may result in delay in disposing of the complainant's individual grievance. After careful consideration the Commission determined to continue its policy in all but exceptional cases. . . .

The charge that the Commission relies on complaints filed with it rather than on the systematic studies of areas of discrimination is hardly warranted. The Commission has always taken the position that it must do more than simply deal with complaints; and in its 1948 Report of Progress it formally announced its conviction that major emphasis must increasingly be given to an effort to prevent and eliminate discrimination on an industry basis.

One aspect of this effort has been the action of the individual investigating commissioner in conferring with official representatives of an industry of which a particular respondent is a part. The most recent effort of the Commission has been a program for the formation of industry-wide committees to work in cooperation with the Commission. Some of these committees have already been formed and others are in the process of being established. . . .

The suggestion that the Commission does not disclose the basis on which cases are settled informally is also not borne out by the facts. . . .

The Commission follows no mysterious system in bringing about these agreements nor has it withheld a description of the terms used by it in its various conciliation agreements.

In its last three annual reports the Commission has included detailed descriptions of illustrative cases together with the terms of the conciliation agreements, and in its last two annual reports it has also added a separate section called "Patterns of Conciliation" to show additional examples of terms of conciliation in particular cases. . . .

With respect to the final criticism, that the Commission finds probable cause in only a small number of cases, it seems reasonable to believe that no one would wish the Commission to find probable cause to credit the allegations of a complaint where there was no basis, in fact, for such a determination. It also seems to be overlooked in such criticism that in any case, whether or not probable cause is found, the Commission does not close the case until it has assured itself that the respondent is fully aware of the requirements of the Law. Each and every complaint before the Commission is treated as an opportunity for implementing the Commission's educational program and there is no case which can correctly be said to have had no action taken on it and no result achieved other than "investigation made—case dismissed."

THE IVES-QUINN LAW AND ITS SIGNIFICANCE

An evaluation of the way in which the New York State Law Against Discrimination has functioned to control discriminatory employment patterns should include two elements: first, an assessment of the actual operation of the law and the way it is enforced by the State Commission Against Discrimination; and second, a conclusion as to whether or not law is an appropriate means by which to control discrimination in employment, and if so, precisely in what way it is appropriate.

Undoubtedly, as the foregoing sections have shown, the Ives-Quinn law has reduced the amount of discrimination in employment and has opened new job opportunities to members of minority groups. A study which the U. S. Bureau of the Census made for the Urban League of Greater New York shows that, whereas in 1940 64 percent of the employed Negro women in New York City were in domestic service and 40 percent of the employed Negro men were in service occupations, by 1947 these proportions had declined to 36 percent and 23 percent respectively. In 1940 only 3 percent of Negro women workers held clerical sales jobs, but in 1947, 13 percent held such jobs. In 1940 20 percent of employed

Negro men held semiskilled jobs, but by 1947 this proportion had increased to 30 percent. The Urban League asserted that these gains were the result of its own efforts, the New York State Commission Against Discrimination, and the federal wartime FEPC.[142] Here again we face the problem of how to evaluate the results of the New York State law where other influences, such as the wartime labor shortage and the activities of private and federal agencies, are working in the same direction.

Although it is easy to show that the Ives-Quinn law has broadened employment opportunities for minorities, it is more difficult to appraise SCAD's role precisely. The Commission, enforcing an act with "educational" features as well as sanctions, has stressed the former. In its report for 1946 SCAD stated that its experience confirmed "the contention of the framers of the law that legislation devised to change discriminatory attitudes and behavior must be rooted in educational processes, supplemented and complemented by legal sanctions." [143] In its 1947 report SCAD observed that the sanctions in the Ives-Quinn law enable it "to do a thorough educational job." [144] The Commission's educational functions, apparently, are carried out not only in its public speeches by commissioners and the staff, distribution of literature, cooperation with community groups, and programs in the schools but also in the very process of conciliation in settling cases. The law presupposes that its sanctions and punitive features are also "educational" influences, but the Commission has only twice brought into action this potential educational force. This stress on the cautious use of compulsory powers goes far back into the early history of the Ives-Quinn law even before its enactment. The Temporary Commission Against Discrimination, whose work led to the framing of the law, in its report to the Governor and the Legislature in 1945, called upon the people of the state to fulfill the objective of the proposed legislation voluntarily, so that there would be no "need for frequent

invocation of the compulsory powers contained therein." [145]
The chief legislative sponsor of the bill, Assemblyman Ives,
likewise emphasized the importance of "education." [146] SCAD's
emphasis in part flows directly from the law itself, which requires that conferences be held to conciliate cases before sanctions are applied. In these conferences the Commission, of
course, is bound by law to try to educate and persuade the
respondent.

The legal sanctions in the Ives-Quinn law, the hearing and
the cease-and-desist order, which are still short of the law's
punitive provisions, are nevertheless themselves excellent means
for "educating" violators, potential violators, and the community in general. The Commission's emphasis on "education"
in the sense of sheer persuasion short of the use of the law's
sanctions deters it from using its full powers, all of which likewise serve an educational function. It was precisely the realization that persuasion was hardly effective that impelled the
New York State Legislature to enact the Ives-Quinn law.[147]

It was largely because of widespread skepticism of the
efficacy of legislation in the elimination of employment discrimination that the state officials emphasized the "educational"
features of the law rather than its sanctions and punitive measures, and warned against enforcement by presumably "vision-
ary" social reformers who would resort to compulsion too
easily. Governor Dewey wrote to a Congressman from New
Jersey in December of 1945: "If it [the Law Against Dis-
crimination] were left to a collection of reformers and social
dreamers it would crash with a mighty bang and perhaps take
down a good segment of our economy with it. In New York
I appointed a group of very sound high-minded people who
made it a living reality." [148] And the second chairman of the
Commission told a United States Senate subcommittee in 1947,
"If a law of this sort were turned over, let us say, to pressure
groups, it would not last very long." [149]

If we judge the Commission by its disposition of cases and

general approach, it appears that it defines its own role as a broadly educational one. SCAD's main function seems to be to reach as many employers as possible and to get across to them its "educational" message rather than to obtain a satisfactory settlement for the individual complainant. This judgment is consistent with the fact that (as we saw earlier) SCAD has sustained only about one quarter of all the complaints brought to it to the end of 1950, and has denied the validity of the specific claims of discrimination made in about two thirds of all the complaints it has received in the same period. It is consistent, also, with the fact that SCAD does not make a greater effort to increase its complaint caseload, and (to the end of 1948, a least) took an average of three months to settle complaints. This definition of its own role, it must be stressed, is not explicitly stated by the Commission, but it follows from its work. It was, however, almost stated plainly in 1947 by the first chairman, when he said, "The mere passing on an individual complaint and the restoration to service, to employment, of the individual complainant means nothing unless we can get a conversion on the part of the employer, and a change in the pattern; *therefore we have deemed it more important to effect a conciliation whereby an employment pattern will be changed and a number of John Does employed, rather than merely to make a finding in a specific instance.*" [150]

Nothing the Commission has done since the resignation of its first chairman in April of 1947 has indicated that it has substantially altered this viewpoint.

In its first five and a half years the Commission seems to have relied too much upon individual complaints and upon the unsystematic initiation of cases of which it was informed in various other ways. It has been clear that ultimately the Commission would have to go out and systematically select areas for study and correction instead of relying so heavily upon individual complaints, which is at best a slow and haphazard way of reaching the discriminators. It might be wiser for

SCAD (and for other state and municipal agencies which administer antidiscrimination laws) to recognize explicitly what it seems to feel implicitly—that the most important matter is not the settlement of individual cases but the opening of new job opportunities for minority groups. If it drew this conclusion directly, the Commission would initiate its own cases in a planned, systematic way, and use the individual complaints as a supplement and as a means of satisfying the worker who feels he has been discriminated against. Such a program would represent full appreciation of the implications of the Ives-Quinn law and the new type of statute it fathered—that is, that employment discrimination is a danger to the entire community best neutralized by an agency of the community especially designated for this purpose. The Commission has stressed the importance of action with respect to whole industries, but, as we saw above, it has thus far moved slowly in implementing this stated policy.

Recently, however, SCAD has given more attention to its liaison with committees representing various industries and has asserted that it has "recognized from the very beginning of its work that the prevention and elimination of discrimination will not be accomplished solely on the basis of complaint cases or upon the use of its enforcement powers alone." [151]

Although the State Commission Against Discrimination has administered the law cautiously, there is no doubt by now that a measure such as the Ives-Quinn act is appropriate to achieve its end, the reduction of employment discrimination. It has become evident that the relationship of employer to worker is so devoid of personal sentiment under present conditions of large commercial and manufacturing enterprises, has become so purely an economic tie, that it becomes a fit subject for legal control. The employer-worker relationship in the United States has for more than a generation been regulated as to sanitation, accidents on the job, child and female labor, wages, hours, unionism, and so on. It is not surprising, therefore, to see that the community insists, through its government, that employment be based solely upon ability, that considerations of race, color, creed, and national origin are irrelevant to employment in an age when it has become almost purely an economic bond.

The relationship among workers is less purely an economic one than that between worker and employer, yet even this relationship, under present work arrangements, is losing its noneconomic aspects. That is why, for example, the New York State War Council found that a forthright statement by management generally prevented workers who said they would not work alongside Negroes from actually refusing to do so once the change was made.[152] The federal wartime FEPC made the same finding.[153] SCAD's experience with the reaction of workers to the opening of job opportunities to previously barred members of minority groups confirms the conclusions of these earlier agencies.[154] Still another kind of evidence of the willingness of workers to accept minority group members as fellow employees, even if less willing to accept them as neighbors or guests, appears in a 1948 public opinion poll. Of 2,508 respondents, 67 percent said they preferred not to have minority group members move into their neighborhoods, 60 percent preferred not to have them in their homes as guests, but only 46 percent preferred not to work with them side by side at equal jobs. To 48 percent of the respondents it made "no difference" if they worked under such conditions.[155]

If law cannot reach private tastes and inclinations, that is no longer proof that law cannot reduce employment discrimination, for under present conditions employment is not a matter of private taste. As an economic, relatively impersonal relationship, it is a fit subject for legal control, as the experience reviewed in this chapter clearly shows.

CHAPTER FIVE

Law and the Control of Prejudice and Discrimination

POLITICAL OBEDIENCE

IT IS probably a fruitless question, for our purposes in this investigation, to ask why men obey laws. Both conformity and nonconformity to law seem to be deeply rooted in human beings. As R. M. MacIver says, "Law-abidingness is the pragmatic condition of and response to the whole firmament of social order." [1] Though men do not obey all laws in the same degree and in the same spirit, they are in general law-abiding.

In less secularized times and countries than the contemporary United States, the law has usually had a certain magic or divine aspect of which some traces still exist. Some of the greatest religious teachers, such as Moses and Mohammed, are also called lawgivers, and other lawgivers have claimed to speak for the deity or have been considered the deity.[2] The sacred books of the world's leading religions are also books of law. Even in our own day law is still looked upon as the codification of the morality to which a community adheres, and it therefore still has an inviolate quality. George H. Mead, asserting that we respect law as law because it is our common instrument of defense and attack and because it binds those who obey against those who disobey, has suggested this imperious aspect of law: "The majesty of the law is that of the sword drawn against a common enemy." [3]

With the entire physical, moral, and symbolic force of the state behind it, law is truly an efficacious means to control behavior. Yet it has limitations, and there are tasks for which it is not appropriate. Roscoe Pound listed its limitations as follows: (1) The law deals with facts but we may be wrong as to what we take as facts. (2) Many duties, such as gratitude, "morally are of great moment but defy legal enforcement." (3) There are certain ways of injuring others—for example, through domestic intrigue—which are difficult for law to restrain effectively. (4) Many injuries—for example, to one's feelings and mental health—cannot be prevented or adequately remedied by law. (5) In important phases of law enforcement it is still necessary for individuals to set the legal machinery in motion, and individuals are often loath to do so.[4]

More broadly, it has been argued by many writers that law can control only the external actions of persons—it can make us act in certain ways, but it cannot make us act from certain motives. Where law requires for compliance a particular attitude and inclination or taste, it is not the appropriate means for control. This view has been put forward by political thinkers at least as far back as Aristotle.[5] In a democracy, where public opinion must be considered, such limitations upon law operate with added strength.

Applied to the problem of eliminating prejudice and discrimination, these limitations are said to preclude the possibility of influencing such attitudes and patterns of behavior by legislation. "You can't legislate goodness," it is often pointed out. A good moral principle, then, is not one that must necessarily find expression in specific statutes. Morality, Bentham claimed, can command that every person do what will benefit the entire community, but there are many acts, beneficial or harmful to the group, which law ought not to command or to forbid. "In a word," he concluded, "legislation has the same centre with morals, but it has not the same circumference." [6] Yet we are not satisfied merely to accept a moral rule. When a moral rule, such as the one asserting that each man should be judged only as an individual, becomes widely accepted as a verbalism, men seek to embody the principle in a legal measure. That is the problem the United States faces in its intergroup relations: how to guarantee the effective functioning of the equalitarian doctrine most Americans seem to accept on the verbal level.

While it is true that the province of law is "external" behavior, it is also true that in an urban, secular society an increasing number of relations fall within this province. Thus the range of behavior that can be called "external" is enlarged. At the same time, law can influence "external" acts which affect or constitute the conditions for the exercise of the private inclinations and tastes that are said to be beyond the realm of law. "Are not our most private feelings and beliefs," asks Felix S. Cohen, "molded, in part at least, by our personal contacts, our economic circumstances, our education, our opportunities for recreation and work? And in all these fields of activity does not the law again and again intervene, for better or for worse?" [7] Another writer makes the point more forcefully: "I believe that the reduction or elimination of discrimination will inevitably lead to the reduction of and make for the elimination of bias and prejudice. I submit that external attitudes and behavior influence internal convictions and emotions of normal men and women. This conclusion rests basically upon my conviction that a life of mental reservations, of hypocritical compliances and hidden hostility is a burden unbearable for the majority of decent human beings." [8]

Thus the frequently expressed notion that law can influence only external actions must, when we apply it to intergroup relations, be balanced by two further considerations: first, that what appears not to be an "external" action may actually be an "external" action under certain conditions; second, that the "external" actions and situations which can be influenced by law in turn influence the inclinations, tastes, and attitudes which law cannot reach directly. Law itself is not meant to make people good or happy; rather, it promotes the situations under which people will be encouraged to do the "good" that the prevailing morality favors, or to become "happy" according to a particular notion of happiness.

Law embodies, to some degree, the leading notions of morality in a community. Those who break the law reveal themselves as nonconformists; in our day of mass communications, Lazarsfeld and Merton point out, the publicity given to those who repudiate the group norms "exerts pressure for a single rather than a dual morality by preventing continued evasion of the issue. It calls forth public reaffirmation and (however sporadic) application of the social norm." If the authority of law is ranged against discriminatory behavior, those who break the law by discriminating in the proscribed way are branded as nonconformists. Such legislation brings into unity the legal system and the system of morality in the United States. What Lazarsfeld and Merton say of publicity may also be said of law, the violation of which brings publicity: it "closes the gap between 'private attitudes' and 'public morality.' " [9]

LAW AND THE MORES

Sociologists, concerned with persisting and influential forms of group life, have been inclined to stress the enduring qualities of customs and deeply rooted beliefs and their virtual imperviousness to the planned social changes embodied in legislation and other legal forms. Herbert Spencer and William Graham Sumner, two thinkers who exerted considerable influence on the generation of sociologists just now expiring, emphasized the subordination of law to custom and the mores.[10] As recently as 1937 one writer published an entire treatise built around the Spencerian notion that "etiquette" as a form of control is not only prior to law but survives conflicts with the law.[11] In the last decade this heavy emphasis upon the mores has come under attack. Gunnar Myrdal has argued that to conceive of the mores as a static, homogeneous set of group values is to overlook, especially in Western society, the differences within the groups that are said to accept the mores. According to MacIver "the mores are not the static and irresistible force suggested by Sumner. They are full of inconsistencies and strains, unliberated tendencies in many directions, responsive adjustments to new situations well conceived or ill conceived." [12]

More than a quarter-century ago Walter Lippmann pointed out the important part stereotypes play in the formation of "public opinion." Our opinions and attitudes, he claimed, are the results of the stereotypes we acquire with the moral codes we accept.[13] Now law can choose among these moral codes. Many Americans believe, for example, both that an individual's opportunity for "success" should not be limited except by his own ability, and that Negroes are inferior. The law can find some support in public opinion for reinforcing either of these values. And law itself can shape the stereotypes and the codes that accompany them. The writer of the Spencerian study of racial "etiquette" just referred to recognizes the influence of law upon custom (while insisting that the more fundamental relationship is the opposite one) when he points to the disappearance of the Negro-white "etiquette" characteristic of slavery.[14]

In certain decisions reviewed in Chapter Two, the United States Supreme Court during the late nineteenth century discussed the relationship between law and public opinion or the mores in much the same terms as these questions are discussed today. "Legislation," according to a seven-to-one majority in 1896,[15] "is powerless to eradicate racial instincts or to abolish distinctions based upon physical differences. . . . If one race be inferior to the other socially, the Constitution of the United States cannot put them upon the same plane." The lone dissenter in the case took a contrary position. "What can more certainly arouse hate," he asked, "what more certainly create and perpetuate a feeling of distrust between these races, than state enactments, which, in fact, proceed on the ground that colored citizens are so inferior and degraded that they cannot be allowed to sit in public coaches occupied by white citizens?" [16] Nearly twenty years before this case, in 1879, a seven to-two majority of the Court subscribed to a view similar to this one, but even more specific as to the influence of law upon public opinion. Invalidating a state law excluding Negroes from juries, the Court declared that such legislation "is practically a brand upon them, affixed by law, an assertion of their inferiority, and a *stimulant to that race prejudice* which is an impediment to securing to individuals of the race that equal justice which the law aims to secure to all others." [17]

Law, then, capable of choosing among moral codes, as Pound puts it, "maintains one set of values against another." [18] The relation of law to public opinion is a complex one, for we must first know what we mean by "public opinion," then determine its "state," and, finally, consider that on leading political and social issues there is usually a range of public opinion rather than just *a* public opinion. The theory that people will obey laws they like and disobey those they dislike, Pound claims, is too simple "under the conditions of the urban industrial society of today." In some matters, he adds, the welfare of society requires that law make habits instead of waiting for them to grow. This necessitates a study of "the limits of effective legal action." [19] Just how far can law go in sustaining one code against another, one value against another? Where the law has some genuine support in the community it can at least begin a rapid process of chipping away at discriminatory behavior and prejudicial attitudes. One student of the subject goes so far as to claim, upon good evidence, that "the attitude of prejudice, or at least the practice of discrimination, can be substantially reduced by authoritative order." And he points to what he considers the effectiveness of the Soviet Union's laws against anti-Semitism,* the successful elimination of segregation in certain units of the United States Army during World War II and in Catholic schools in St. Louis, Missouri in 1946, and to a study (to be considered in some detail later in this chapter) of customers' reactions to Negro salespersons in New York City department stores.[20]

Recently there has accumulated considerable evidence suggesting that once a genuine breach is made in a discriminatory system, further gains tend to follow rapidly. Thus, in January, 1948, the United States Supreme Court held that Oklahoma must provide an equal law-school education for Negro applicants at the same time as for others.[21] A few weeks later the president of the University of Arkansas announced that Negroes would be admitted, on a segregated basis, in its graduate schools.[22] Around the same time the trustees of the University of Delaware voted to admit Negroes to courses of study not available at the institution for Negroes, the Delaware State College.[23] The following semester, in October, regents of the University of Oklahoma ordered the admission, in segregated classes, of a Negro graduate student, in compliance with a federal court ruling that Negroes must be provided equal educational opportunities.[24] In August the University of Arkansas admitted a Negro to its medical school on an unsegregated basis, and the following month it admitted a Negro to the law school on the same basis. At first the Negro law student sat in a corner, surrounded by a rail, but later the rail was removed as a "physical inconvenience." [25] In November the president of the University of Maryland announced that beginning in the fall Negroes would be admitted to the graduate school on the same basis as white students.[26] In December the curators

---

* The relevance of this example, which refers to the effectiveness of law in combating manifestations of *folk anti-Semitism* in Russia, is not vitiated by the recent revival of *official* anti-Semitic discrimination in the Soviet Union as reported, for example, in Solomon M. Schwarz, *The Jews in the Soviet Union* (sponsored by the American Jewish Committee: Syracuse University Press, 1951), Part II, Chapter VII.

of the University of Missouri recommended changes in state laws to permit admission of Negroes to courses of instruction not available to them at Lincoln University, the state college for Negroes.[27]

All of these changes, some not at all explicitly required by the court decisions preceding them, were taken within twelve months of the Supreme Court decision of January, 1948. Such events confirm Dicey's observation that "no facts play a more important part in the creation of opinion than laws themselves." [28]

THE PREJUDICED PERSONALITY AND SOCIAL CONTROL

It would seem elementary that in order to select effective means of controlling discrimination we should first have some verified knowledge of the nature and extent of the prejudice that admittedly lies back of discriminatory behavior. Yet it is only in the last decade or so that scholars have been studying prejudiced persons in such a way as to provide reliable hypotheses as to the means that are likely to be effective in controlling their attitudes and actions. And the organizations attempting to eliminate prejudice and discrimination have hardly begun to apply the few dependable discoveries that psychologists and sociologists have already produced.[29]

Several typologies of prejudice and discrimination have been advanced in recent years; some are more useful than others for our purpose in this inquiry, and some are overlapping. Horkheimer's typology [30] is one, for example, that offers us little guidance for selection of methods of control. He lists such anti-Semitic types as the "born anti-Semite," "religious and philosophical anti-Semitism," "backwoods" or "sectarian anti-Semite," "vanquished competitor," "Jew-baiter," and "fascist anti-Semite." Merton has put forth [31] an inclusive typology of both prejudice and discrimination. He lists four combinations of these two elements, as follows: the unprejudiced non-

discriminator (or all-weather liberal), the unprejudiced discriminator (or fair-weather liberal), the prejudiced nondiscriminator (or fair-weather illiberal), and the prejudiced
discriminator (or all-weather illiberal). Each one, Merton
points out, requires certain "treatment." "Policies designed to
curb discrimination must be oriented toward differences in
the composition of a population with respect to the four types
here under discussion." [32]

MacIver and Stone (the former with some reservations) [33]
advance two types of prejudiced persons, based upon the origin
and function of the bias. The first, more inclusive kind of prejudice is acquired imperceptibly as a result of indoctrination;
it presumes the existence of prejudice in the social group, and
the individual takes on this value as he takes on others the
group imparts. Most prejudiced persons, MacIver says, probably are of this type. The second type of prejudice, far from
being an expression of individual conformity to the group's
values, is an expression of the individual's inability to achieve
a satisfying sort of conformity. Some persons, needing an outlet for tensions and traumas, find it in hostility, often in extreme prejudice against certain groups exposed because of
their inferior position in the community.

The third of the useful typologies, offered by N. W. Ackerman and M. Jahoda on the basis of studies of twenty-seven
persons who expressed anti-Semitism while undergoing psychoanalytic treatment, is very similar to the MacIver-Stone
typology. Ackerman and Jahoda state: "First, there is the anti-
Semite whose hostility to the Jews seems mainly the expression
of social conformity to the attitude of the dominant group; this
conformity, however, represents in part the patient's defense
against anxiety. Second, there is the anti-Semite whose motivation for hostility to the Jews is patterned by some basic distor-
tion in his own personality structure to which his anti-Semitism
has a specific relation. Actually, all our cases represent a fusion,
in varying proportion, of both levels of correlation. The first

level illuminates the nature of the anti-Semitic reaction at the group psychological level of adaptation; the second, at the individual level of adaptation." [34]

There is considerable agreement among these three typologies. It is clear that Merton, MacIver-Stone, and Ackerman-Jahoda are referring to the same type when they delineate the prejudiced nondiscriminator (or fair-weather illiberal), and the person who acquires prejudice chiefly through the process of taking on the values of the group to which he belongs. Again they mean roughly the same person when they speak of the prejudiced discriminator (or all-weather illiberal) and the person whose prejudice is an outlet for personality disorder. Corresponding in some degree to one element in this typology of personality, MacIver has set forth a typology of situations with respect to the practice of discrimination and segregation. [35] One of these situations, which he calls the "indifferent equilibrium," is relevant, in one of its two sides, to the first of the personality types just mentioned. In the "indifferent equilibrium" the "conditions and sentiments" that maintain discrimination and segregation are balanced by other conditions and sentiments which, given the opportunity to express themselves, would reject the discriminatory practices. Forthright action and confident leadership can in the "indifferent equilibrium" precipitate change away from (or toward) discriminatory behavior.

The prejudiced nondiscriminator, the unprejudiced discriminator, and those who acquire prejudice as they acquire other group values, as well as the "indifferent equilibrium," are all clearly susceptible to legal measures discouraging discrimination. The fact that this type is the more prevalent under normal conditions, MacIver asserts, is a strong argument for the kind of institutional changes that are embodied in laws. [36] Merton describes the prejudiced nondiscriminator as "the man of prejudice who does not believe in the creed but conforms to it in practice through fear of sanctions which might otherwise be visited upon him." [37] He concludes that "the seemingly most appropriate tactic" for this type is "a change in the institutional and legal environment." [38]

Agencies aiming at the improvement of intergroup relations, as we have already remarked, have been slow to apply these hypotheses based upon the most reliable knowledge we have of prejudice. Merton properly argues that merely knowing "that ethnic discrimination is rife in a community does not, therefore, point to appropriate lines of social policy. It is necessary to know also the distribution of ethnic prejudices and basic motivations for these prejudices as well." [39] Accordingly, he calls for periodic tests to determine the "relative proportions in various areas of these four prejudice-discrimination types" as a guide to effective policy.[40]

The execution of this reasonable proposal can provide an opportunity for an interesting test of the influence of legal measures. What would be the relative proportions of the four types in a given community, on various socioeconomic levels, before and after the administration of an effective law against discrimination in employment or in places of public accommodation? It is very likely that the effect of such a law would be to increase substantially the proportion of prejudiced non-discriminators (or fair-weather illiberals). In other words, anti-discrimination laws probably reveal that a community has a larger porportion of this group amenable to just such laws than prior study would indicate. Law influences conduct and verbal responses in such a way that the discovery, by psychological tests, of only a low proportion of persons we suspect can be persuaded by law to change their behavior and attitudes would not be a convincing argument against this method of social control. The law not only makes prejudiced nondiscriminators alter their behavior; it probably also affects the prejudiced discriminator, bringing his response to the law closer to that of the type previously suspected of being rather amenable to the influence of legal measures.

Thus far we have been discussing mainly the prejudice that is acquired when the individual takes on the values of the group to which he belongs. But what of the appropriateness of legal measures for the other kind of prejudice, which is acquired as part of a serious personality disorder and which has a definite function in the character structure of the prejudiced? For this type, too, we shall see, law is an effective means of control at least of discriminatory acts if not also of prejudicial attitudes. In recent years there has accumulated an abundance of evidence to support this conclusion.

Studies of prejudiced persons show them to be conventional in morality, that is, they are conformists. This is a major conclusion in *The Authoritarian Personality*,[41] the most thorough study of prejudice that has yet appeared, as well as in several of the other volumes in the "Studies in Prejudice," sponsored by the American Jewish Committee. The same conclusion appears in still other studies. The Hartleys, from a personality study of the five most tolerant and the five least tolerant among thirty-four college students, assert that the latter show greater "acceptance of conventional mores." [42] Frenkel-Brunswik, Levinson, and Sanford's clinical analysis of women exhibiting a relatively high degree of ethnocentrism shows that such persons accept "conventional moralism." [43] In other places Frenkel-Brunswik and Sanford report that "the most outstanding feature of the anti-Semitic college women, derived from our small sample, seems to be a restricted, narrow personality with a strict conventional super ego, to which there is complete surrender." [44] Among ethnocentric children, too, Frenkel-Brunswik found similar qualities. Such children show greater conformity toward their parents and toward approved social values.[45] Anxiety feelings, these researches have found, accompany this urge to conformity. Prejudiced persons fear they do not achieve the conventionality toward which they strive, and hence strive all the more toward this goal. In response to a question asking for one's most em-

barrassing experience, persons high on the anti-Semitic scale
tended to mention public breaches of manners and conventions,
while those lowest on the scale tended to mention failures in
personal relations and feelings of inadequacy.[46] Ackerman
and Jahoda likewise found anxiety feelings to be characteristic
of the anti-Semites.[47]

There is agreement among the students of prejudiced personalities not only on conformity, but also on the notion that
this conformity is superficial, part of an ambivalent system
of conformity—hostility to the same symbols. Beneath the
overt personality and attitudes of anti-Semites Frenkel-Brunswik and Sanford find, through projective tests, a covert personality tending toward destructiveness and hatred of authority.[48] Ackerman and Jahoda report that their anti-Semitic
cases "had the urge to conform, but unconsciously they re-
sented the compulsory submission and reacted with destruc-
tive rebellion." [49] Frenkel-Brunswik concludes that the conformity of ethnocentric children conceals "violent underlying
destructiveness, dangerous to the very society to which there
seems to be conformity." [50] This ambivalence, according to
Ackerman and Jahoda,[51] is merely one manifestation of the
prejudiced person's confused and unstable image of himself.
Such persons have no clear notion of group membership. They
want to conform, but fear submission; they want to appear
to be the same as other people but are incapable of genuine
identification with others. As a result their group loyalties are
shifting ones, temporary havens where they draw courage by
association with the powerful, the privileged, and the prestige-
ful. Resentful of the Jews, whom they see as nonconformists,
they attack those who are weak but are willing to seek the
approval of Jews who have power or high status. Their aggres-
siveness is stimulated by the weak, their conformity by the
strong. At this point Frenkel-Brunswik's studies of ethnocentric
children support the findings of Ackerman and Jahoda; such
children show aggressive tendencies toward minorities and

"generalized rejection of all that is weak or indifferent." [52]

Incidental confirmation of the uncertainty of the prejudiced personality in the face of authority and the accomplished fact emerges from a 1947 study [53] of customer reactions toward the integration of Negro salespersons in New York City department stores. A brief summary of the New York State Law Against Discrimination was given to 256 respondents who had been placed in five categories, from least prejudiced (Group One) to most prejudiced (Group Five). They were then asked their opinion of such a law. Approval of the law, as might be expected, decreased from Group One to Group Five. More significant for us at this point, however, are the proportions of the "no opinions." In Group One (least prejudiced) only 2 percent had no opinion; in Group Two, 10 percent; in Group Three, 14 percent; in Group Four, 19 percent; in Group Five (most prejudiced), 25 percent. Thus, as prejudice rises, uncertainty as to opinion of the law (a power symbol) also rises along with certain disapproval of it.

This study [54] incidentally confirms still another of the findings of the students of the prejudiced personality, that is, the need such personalities have for identifying themselves with the dominant group or the majority. Each of the 256 respondents, placed in the five categories according to degree of prejudice, was asked to estimate the proportion of the rest of the population that objects to the employment of Negro salespersons. Of those in Group One (least prejudiced) 13 percent replied that they thought "most" people would object, and 19 percent that about half the general population would object. In Group Two, the respective proportions were 20 percent and 34 percent; in Group Three, 29 percent and 27 percent; in Group Four, 62 percent and 14 percent; in Group Five (most prejudiced), 92 percent and 8 percent. Thus, as prejudice rises the tendency to think the rest of the people share one's own values also rises, until in the most prejudiced group not a single respondent said that only a few others or none shared his opinion as to the employment of Negro sales-persons. On this point the most prejudiced showed no uncertainty—no one said he had no opinion on this subject. How correct each of the five groups was in estimating is shown by their own responses to the same question; 70 percent of all the respondents said they would approve the hiring of Negro salespersons, 17 percent said they would disapprove, and 13 percent had no opinion.[55]

What do these conclusions about the prejudiced personality suggest with respect to law as a means of control of bias and discriminatory behavior? For this type of prejudice institutional changes would seem to be most effective. Tolerance propaganda through the mass media of communication, it appears, affects this group not at all, for the persons in it draw too much sustenance from their bias to give it up merely in response to words which they can refuse to listen to, misinterpret, or use to reinforce their established values.[56] Ackerman and Jahoda point out [57] that persons with character weaknesses are susceptible to social pressures and propaganda, but only to the kind which sustain their values, not to the kind (in favor of tolerance, for example) which gives little gratification. The extremely prejudiced person has a high stake in his bias, which may function to keep his personality integrated; he does not easily succumb to verbalisms which attack his way of maintaining his own equilibrium.

The specific types of institutional change that probably can modify extreme prejudice are the slow but fundamental adjustments in the economic and political system. Changes leading to the generation of less hostility or to its direction into less harmful channels are the ones likely to affect deeply rooted prejudice, but these take many years to work themselves out and to become apparent. The bearing of law upon such alterations in our way of life is somewhat remote and is beyond our present concern. But law can still function to aid in controlling the discriminatory behavior of the extremely prejudiced, as well as in establishing and supporting the institutions which favor the modification of their values and attitudes.

Law is an effective means for reducing the discrimination or overt antiminority conduct of the extremely prejudiced. We have seen that the personality studies have found such persons to be conformists of a certain kind, respecters of power, scorning the weak but toadying to the strong. One of the few constants in their behavior is submission to the symbols of power. Law, when it is backed by the full panoply of the state and has strong support in at least some sections of the community, is just such a symbol. Even if law did nothing but reduce discrimination by such persons it would be accomplishing something of value in a multigroup democracy. But there is evidence that antibias laws can also influence the conditions under which our attitudes are developed and maintained.

Most investigators seem to agree that prejudice is acquired through contact with the attitude of prejudice itself, and not through contact with the groups that are the objects of prejudice. This conclusion and the evidence for it are advanced by Murphy and Likert, by Frenkel-Brunswik and Sanford, by Ackerman and Jahoda, and by Horowitz.[58] There is further agreement that intergroup contact under certain conditions tends to reduce discriminatory acts, lessen hostility, alter stereotypes, and modify prejudices. Newcomb points out that group hostility is constantly reinforced for the individual who has little or no contact with persons outside the group which shares his values.[59] Investigators are careful to point out that intergroup contact in which the traditional superior-subordinate relations prevail is not likely to result in a reduction of prejudice, but that such a reduction is achieved when the contact is on equal terms, is sustained, and is reinforced by other institutional patterns.[60] Lewin and MacIver [61] suggest that prejudice can be reduced by inducing in the biased person a feeling of belonging to a larger authoritative, powerful group which includes the object of his prejudice.

Now law is a particularly appropriate means by which to increase intergroup contact on an equal level. We saw in previous chapters how the United States Supreme Court tended to sustain laws facilitating interracial contact of the superior-subordinate type and tended to invalidate those facilitating such contact on a level of equality. Law, having thus supported intergroup barriers, can serve to remove other legal barriers and to favor such institutional arrangements as are conducive to peaceful, equal intergroup contacts. In the field of employment, housing, and education, law can eliminate the conditions that set groups apart and can encourage those that bring them together. As Mead observed, "We cannot make persons social by legislative enactment, but we can allow the essentially social nature of their actions to come to expression under conditions which favor this." [62]

Thus we have seen the efficacy of law in controlling the behavior of persons who acquire prejudice as they acquire other social values from the group to which they belong, and the behavior of those whose prejudice is more deeply rooted in personality disorders. If law could do no more than this, it would be improving the welfare and status of minorities, giving them a feeling of genuine participation in the life of the community, and fulfilling the obligations and the promise of democracy. But, as we have seen, law can do even more. It is one of the great movers and changers of basic institutions of all kinds and can help in establishing the conditions which favor group equality in a free society.

INSTITUTIONS, ATTITUDES, AND ACTIONS

The embodiment of creeds in legal institutions not only registers the community-wide acceptance of values but can reinforce those values. Prejudice, as distinguished from discrimination, is volatile, changing and difficult to measure, Mac-Iver points out. For this reason, he adds, changes registered in institutions tend to endure, are not easily undone, and have a way of encouraging usages that are congenial to their preservation.[63]

While there are many laws that have little or no observable effect, a law that is incorporated into a vast regulative network tends to be obeyed. Law, as an accomplished fact, is likely to be taken as something already established and it influences even those opposed to it. Thus, Dicey observed in 1914 in another context, "the legislation of collectivism has continued now for some twenty-five or thirty years, and has itself contributed to produce the moral and intellectual atmosphere in which socialistic ideas flourish and abound. So true is this that modern individualists are themselves generally on some points socialists." [64] A social security law, for example, which sets up a vast administrative apparatus, collects large amounts of money which it distributes systematically, and induces certain expectations in the community, is not likely to be rescinded by a new administration; rather it is accepted in its fundamentals, and differences in policy revolve around the machinery of administration or the extension of the law, but not around the law itself.

We have already seen that law does not change attitudes directly, but that by altering the situations in which attitudes and opinions are formed, law can indirectly reach the more private areas of life it cannot touch directly in a democratic society. This conclusion rests upon a presumed difference, for which there is considerable evidence, between attitudes and behavior. These two categories are not unrelated, and both are in turn related to those situations over which law has some control. Dewey, for example, goes even further, emphasizing that attitudes cannot be altered except through alterations in actions and in the environment. "The idea that dispositions and attitudes can be altered by merely 'moral' means conceived of as something that goes on wholly inside of persons," he has argued, "is itself one of the old patterns that has to be changed. Thought, desire and purpose exist in a constant give and take of interaction with environing conditions." [65]

It is precisely the difference between stated attitudes and actions that enables law to reduce overt discriminatory acts while not attempting directly to affect prejudicial attitudes. The accomplished fact is more likely to influence the attitudes and behavior of the person who is not strongly attached to a value than one for whom the value plays a highly important role in the functioning of his total personality. Studies of public opinion show, says Hadley Cantril, that after the repeal of the arms embargo, the enactment of a conscription law, and the repeal of neutrality legislation, there was a rise of about 10 percent in the opinion favorable to these actions. Cantril offers as a "law" of public opinion: "When an opinion is held by a slight majority or when opinion is not solidly structured, an accomplished fact tends to shift opinion in the direction of acceptance." [66]

Similar evidence is given in the aforementioned study, by Saenger and Gilbert, of customer reactions to the employment of Negro sales personnel in New York City department stores. At the time of the study, in the spring of 1947, most of the nine stores in which customers were approached had hired Negroes as wrappers and cashiers before hiring them as salespersons, and most of the stores had several times as many Negroes in these two jobs as in sales jobs. Only 2 percent of the respondents said they disapproved of Negroes as wrappers, 5 percent disapproved of them as cashiers, but 17 percent disapproved of Negroes as sales clerks. "It seems probable," the authors conclude, "that these differences in attitude reflect the difference between reacting to an event *before* it takes place and *after* it has taken place. In the latter situation the attitude of disapproval toward Negro employees seems almost to have disappeared." [67]

In answering a question as to prejudice or as to intention with respect to members of minority groups, an individual does not encounter the same conditions he encounters in a situation which challenges his values, and in which he deals not only with generalized stereotypes but with specific persons in a specific context of social relations. That the stated attitude often differs from the action is shown in a report,[68] by La Piere, of his travels with a Chinese couple who were "charming" and spoke excellent English. During 1930–32 La Piere and the couple traveled twice across the United States and up and down the Pacific Coast. They asked for service at sixty-seven hotels, auto camps, and tourist homes, and were refused in only one place; they asked for service at 184 restaurants and cafes, and were served in all of them. Six months after being served at each of the sixty-six sleeping places and the 184 eating places, La Piere sent a mail questionnaire asking if "members of the Chinese race" could be accommodated. Replies came from forty-seven sleeping places and eighty-one eating places. Of the former, 91 percent said such persons would *not* be accommodated, and of the latter 92 percent made the same discriminatory response.

In their department store study Saenger and Gilbert present further evidence of the discrepancy between stated attitudes and actions performed in a specific context in which other attitudes and drives are called into play. They report interviews with two sets of white persons. The first group consisted of 114 persons observed making a purchase from a department store clerk (sixty-one from Negro clerks and fifty-three from white clerks); the second group, of 142 persons in the streets and parks near the nine stores in which the first group made purchases. The first group, the "observed sample," were actual customers; the second group, the "street sample," were potential customers. All the individuals in both samples were placed in the five categories, according to degree of prejudice, mentioned earlier in this chapter. The main question the investigator sought to answer was: Does prejudice against Negro sales clerks lead to discrimination by white customers? The answer, in this study, is no, and there is a variety of evidence for it.[69]

As the authors point out, if there were a tendency for prejudiced persons to avoid the stores employing Negro clerks, then there should be a higher proportion of prejudiced persons among the potential than among the actual customers. But this is not the case, for only 14 percent of the "street sample" of potential customers and 20 percent of the "observed sample" of actual purchasers said they disapproved when asked what they would think if all New York City department stores employed Negro sales personnel. Thus those who disapproved of Negro clerks did not tend to avoid the stores employing them. Following the same supposition, the authors ask whether prejudiced persons tend to avoid the Negro clerks in the department stores. If they did, then we should expect a higher proportion of prejudiced persons among those observed purchasing from white clerks than among those purchasing from Negro clerks. But there is in fact no significant difference here, for 20 percent of the buyers from Negro clerks said they would disapprove of the policy of employing Negro clerks in all department stores, whereas 21 percent of those buying from white clerks expressed this attitude. Thus prejudice toward the employment of Negro clerks did not cause customers to avoid them in the stores. Some of the other attitudes and desires entering into the specific situation which the prejudiced customer faces in a store are, according to Saenger and Gilbert, the "desire to buy conveniently and cheaply," feelings which tend to contradict prejudice, the tendency to conform to "group values, as expressed particularly in the state law against discrimination," and the "reluctance to challenge a *fait accompli*." [70]

One further significant result emerges from this study by Saenger and Gilbert. Of the 256 respondents in both samples, twelve said they would not buy in a store with Negro clerks. But five of these twelve had been actually observed not only in such a store but at a counter where there was a Negro clerk, and two of the five had been observed talking to a Negro clerk.[71] In another report on the same study Saenger asserted that nine respondents said they would never buy from a Negro clerk, but three of them had been observed buying from a Negro clerk "less than an hour before they were interviewed." [72]

These empirical studies show again that law can reduce discrimination and influence attitudes. The department store data are particularly pertinent because it is only since the enactment of the New York State Law Against Discrimination in 1945 that department stores have taken on Negro salespersons in the numbers now easily visible.[73]

LAW IN URBAN SOCIETY: ITS POTENTIAL AND SOME PROBLEMS

Law as a formal, codified regulatory system administered by a special agency of the community is, of course, a characteristic of politically organized societies. Within such societies, however, the role of law differs. As interpersonal contacts increase and become more casual and fleeting, as population density grows, and as individual or group interests proliferate, law functions in more and more areas where less formal controls previously sufficed to maintain the conditions of social order and the protection of society's manifold interests. These are the traits of urban society.

Rural or folk societies have some rules and controls that may be as rigid as law and as effectively enforced, but their regulatory systems are more customary than our own, more integrated in their means of control, and their institutions show less differentiation.[74] More and more of the functions carried out by the family and the home in a relatively informal system of face-to-face relations are being assumed, in urban areas, by the state and by voluntary associations more intimately subject to government than is the family.[75] As our society becomes more urbanized, the situations actually brought under legal controls increase vastly. Public opinion and custom, as Durkheim has pointed out,[76] are less binding in urban than in rural areas. In our world, compartmentalized but interdependent, the main agency of social control is the state, which becomes increasingly appropriate in an increasing number of contemporary relations.[77]

We have reviewed the advances in minority status and welfare, the changing role of the Supreme Court, the operation of the New York State Law Against Discrimination, and the evidence from sociology, social psychology, and psychoanalysis. All this evidence indicates that law in our society is a formidable means for the elimination of group discrimination and for the establishment of conditions which discourage prejudicial attitudes. Law, we find, has certain potentialities in this area of human behavior. It can codify our society's loftiest ideals rather than its basest practices—that is, the legal machinery can be withdrawn from the support of discriminatory patterns. This is, of course, a rather negative function, but there are others more positive. Law can withhold certain privileges from the discriminators. It can put the state's influence and power on the side of those who are discriminated against and give them effective means for defending themselves. Law can also help establish those fundamental conditions of social life which encourage free association of all groups on a level of equality and which discourage prejudicial attitudes. Frequently, as we have seen in earlier chapters, favorable laws can be the wedge for advances in the status and welfare of groups which are made the objects of unfair discrimination. In summary, law can affect our *acts* and, through them, our *beliefs.*

Proper legal controls fortify the unprejudiced and the believers in fair play. They also weaken the position of those who discriminate whether out of some deep personality disorder or merely to conform to the values of their own groups. The demonstration by government that it supports the interests of all groups seeking only free and active participation in democracy is likely to reinforce the very freedom under which such an official policy can evolve. "Only where the various loyalties of men," says MacIver, "can live together, interadjusted within the same framework of . . . law, can the firmament of order be sustained." [78]

NOTES

BOOKS cited in these notes, but not in full, are listed with full data in the Bibliography.

CHAPTER ONE

1. See G. T. Stephenson, *Race Distinctions in American Law*, pp. 112, 115; Franklin Johnson, *The Development of State Legislation Concerning the Free Negro*, Part II.

2. W. W. Davis, "The Federal Enforcement Acts," in *Studies in Southern History and Politics*, pp. 223–26.

3. Johnson, *op. cit.* (in note 1 *supra*), p. 30 and Part II; Stephenson, *op. cit.* (in note 1 *supra*), pp. 120–21.

4. See W. L. Fleming, *Documentary History of Reconstruction*, II, 381–83.

5. Francis Biddle, "Civil Rights and the Federal Law," in Carl Becker *et al.*, *Safeguarding Civil Liberty Today*, p. 131.

6. See President Franklin D. Roosevelt's campaign address at the Commonwealth Club, San Francisco, September 23, 1932, in *The Public Papers and Addresses of Franklin D. Roosevelt*, I, 742–56; R. Pound, *Social Control through Law*, p. 25; John Dewey, *Liberalism and Social Action*, pp. 54–55; L. M. Hacker, *The Shaping of the American Tradition*, pp. 1125–26. On the changes in the role of the state in England, which later American developments resemble closely, see A. V. Dicey, *Lectures on the Relation between Law and Public Opinion in England during the Nineteenth Century*, 2d ed., Lectures IV, VII, VIII.

7. Walter White, *A Man Called White*, pp. 169–70.

8. U.S. Bureau of Census, *Statistical Abstract of the United States 1947* (Washington, D.C., 1947), Table 19, p. 20.

9. J. A. Burdine, "Trends in Public Administration in the South," *The Journal of Politics*, X (1948), 426–30.

10. H. W. Odum, "Social Change in the South," *The Journal of Politics*, X (1948), 251–53.

11. R. B. Vance, *All These People*, pp. 267–69.

12. U.S. Bureau of Labor Statistics, Bulletin 898, *Labor in the South* (Washington, D.C., 1947), Table 2, p. 7, and Table 13, p. 28.

13. U.S. Bureau of Census, *op. cit.* (in note 8 *supra*), Table 14, p. 16.

14. W. S. Thompson and P. K. Whelpton, "Changes in Regional and Urban Patterns of Population Growth," *American Sociological Review*, V (1940), 927, Table 4.

15. U.S. Federal Works Agency, *Summary of Relief and Federal Work Program Statistics, 1933–1940* (Washington, D.C., 1941), Table 1, p. 21.

16. U.S. Works Progress Administration, Division of Social Research, Research Monograph IV, *Urban Workers on Relief* (Washington, D.C., 1936), Part I, Tables 1, 2, 3, pp. 6–8.

17. U.S. Works Progress Administration, *Final Report on the W.P.A. Program, 1935–1943* (Washington, D.C., 1947), Table 25, p. 45.

18. Gunnar Myrdal, *An American Dilemma*, I, 488–89.

19. R. J. Bunche, "The Political Status of the Negro," V, 1054–55.

20. Richard Sterner, *The Negro's Share*, pp. 298–304.

21. R. C. Weaver, *The Negro Ghetto*, pp. 74–75.

22. Sterner, *op. cit.* (in note 20 *supra*), pp. 317–18.

23. Weaver, *op. cit.* (in note 21 *supra*), pp. 157, 162 f.

24. See C. S. Johnson and associates, *To Stem This Tide: a Survey of Racial Tension Areas in the United States.*

25. R. C. Weaver, *Negro Labor*, pp. 6–7, 107.

26. U.S. Committee on Fair Employment Practice, *Final Report, June 28, 1946* (Washington, D.C., 1947), pp. viii–ix.

27. U.S. Bureau of Labor Statistics, "War and Post-War Trends in Employment of Negroes," *Monthly Labor Review*, LX (1945), 2–4.

28. S. L. Wolfbein, "Post-War Trends in Negro Employment," *Monthly Labor Review*, LXV (1947), 664–65.

29. U.S. Bureau of Labor Statistics, Bulletin 618, *Handbook of American Trade-Unions* (Washington, D.C., 1936), pp. 40–48.

30. H. R. Northrup, *Organized Labor and the Negro*, pp. 3–5.

31. Railway Mail Association v. Corsi, 326 U.S. 88 (1945); Steele v. Louisville and Nashville R.R., 323 U.S. 192 (1944); Brotherhood of Locomotive Firemen v. Tunstall, 332 U.S. 841 (1947). See also *New York Times*, January 27, 1948, p. 19.

32. N.Y. State Commission Against Discrimination, *1948 Report of Progress*, pp. 35–36.

33. *New York Times*, August 11, 1948, p. 46.

34. *Ibid.*, April 21, 1948, p. 3.

35. L. P. Jackson, "Race and Suffrage in the South Since 1940," *New South*, Vol. III, Nos. 5–6 (1948), pp. 1, 3 f., 25, Charts I and II.

36. National Association for the Advancement of Colored People and American Jewish Congress, *Civil Rights in the United States in 1948: a Balance Sheet of Group Relations*, p. 10.

37. Data on the Negro in the armed forces may be found in Myrdal, *op. cit.* (in note 18 *supra*), I, 419–23; Johnson, *op. cit.* (in note 24 *supra*), Chapter VII; White, *op. cit.* (in note 7 *supra*), Chapters XXXI, XXXII; Roi Ottley, *Black Odyssey*, pp. 288–303; U.S. Department of the Army, "The Negro in the Army: Policy and Practice," by James C. Evans (Washington, D.C., 1948).

38. Executive Order 9981, reprinted in *Freedom to Serve: Equality of Treatment and Opportunity in the Armed Services. A Report by the President's Committee on Equality of Treatment and Opportunity in the Armed Services* (Washington, D.C., 1950), p. xi.

39. *Ibid.*, pp. 5, 21.

40. *Ibid.*, pp. 6 f.

41. U.S. Department of the Interior, *People in Motion: the Postwar Adjustment of Evacuated Japanese Americans* (Washington, D.C., n.d.), p. 48.

42. See *ibid.*, p. 22. See also National Association for the Advancement of Colored People and American Jewish Congress, *Civil Rights in the United States in 1949*, p. 16.

43. Public Law 863, 80th Congress.

44. Tadayasu Abo et al. v. Clark et al., Furuya et al. v. Same, 77 F. Supp. 806 (1948).

45. Acheson v. Murakami et al., 176 F. 2d 953 (1949). *New York Times*, October 27, 1949, p. 17.

46. Public Law, 567, 80th Congress.

47. For example, *Civil Rights in the United States*, annual survey published by American Jewish Congress and National Association for the Advancement of Colored People; and American Jewish Committee, *The People Take the Lead: a Record of Progress in Civil Rights, 1947 to 1952* (New York, 1952).

48. These figures were compiled from the appropriate numbers of the *Congressional Index Service*, Commerce Clearing House, Inc., N.Y. Twenty-nine relevant headings in the index were examined. Those bills whose titles indicated intent to advance minority interests, in any way or area, were included in the compilation. The compilation does not include antilynching bills, which go back as far as 1890, and of which nearly 200 were introduced to the end of 1948, because the introduction of such bills has been a response to different pressures than the introduction of the bills included in the compilation. See D. O. Walter, "Proposals for a Federal Anti-Lynching Law," *American Political Science Review*, XVIII (1934), 436–42, and *Anti-lynching*, Hearings before Subcommittee No. 4 of the Committee on the Judiciary, House of Representatives, 80th Congress, 2d Session (Washington, D.C., 1948), pp. 185–88.

49. See R. K. Carr, *Federal Protection of Civil Rights*, pp. 24 ff.; Biddle, *op. cit.* (in note 5 *supra*), pp. 134–35.

50. See Carr, *ibid.*, Chapters II, III, VI.

51. Biddle, *op. cit.* (in note 5 *supra*), pp. 134–35.

52. Carr, *op. cit.* (in note 49 *supra*), p. 210.

53. See L. C. Kesselman, *The Social Politics of FEPC*.

54. See W. Maslow, "FEPC—a Case History in Parliamentary Maneuver," *The University of Chicago Law Review*, XIII (1946), 407–44.

55. U.S. Committee on Fair Employment Practice, *First Report, July 1943–December 1944* (Washington, D.C., 1945), and *Final Report, June 28, 1946* (Washington, D.C., 1947). M. Ross, *All Manner of Men, passim*. R. M. MacIver, *The More Perfect Union*, pp. 153–63.

56. Executive Order 9808, December 5, 1946.

57. *To Secure These Rights: the Report of the President's Committee on Civil Rights* (Washington, D.C., 1947), p. 166.

58. *Higher Education for American Democracy: a Report of the President's Commission on Higher Education* (Washington, D.C., 1947), II, 35.

59. *Ibid.*, p. 29, note 1.

60. *Ibid.*, pp. 44, 68.

61. "Message from the President of the United States Transmitting His Recommendations for Civil Rights Program," House of Representatives, 80th Congress, 2d Session, Document No. 516, February 2, 1948.

62. "Address of the President of the United States Delivered Before a Joint Session of the Senate and the House of Representatives," House of Representatives, 80th Congress, 2d Session, Document No. 734, July 27, 1948.

63. Executive Order 9980, July 26, 1948.

64. Executive Order 9981, July 26, 1948.

65. American Jewish Congress, Commission on Law and Social Action, *State Anti-Discrimination and Anti-Bias Laws* (New York, 1948).

66. American Council on Race Relations, Chicago, *Report*, IV (Aug. 1949), Supplement.

CHAPTER TWO

1. The texts of these five laws may be found in R. K. Carr, *Federal Protection of Civil Rights*, Appendix 1.

2. Slaughter House Cases, 83 U.S. 36 (1873).

3. *Id.* at 71.

4. *Id.* at 73–75.

5. *Id.* at 95–96.

6. See Colgate v. Harvey, 296 U.S. 404, 445–46 n. 2 (1935).

7. Minor v. Happersett, 88 U.S. 162 (1874).

8. *Id.* at 170–71.

9. *Id.* at 175.

10. U.S. v. Cruikshank, 92 U.S. 542 (1876).

11. Carr, *op. cit.* (in note 1 *supra*), p. 219.

12. U.S. v. Cruikshank, 92 U.S. 542, 551–59 (1876).

13. U.S. v. Reese, 92 U.S. 214 (1876).

14. Colgate v. Harvey, 296 U.S. 404 (1935).

15. Colgate v. Harvey, 296 U.S. 424 (1935).

16. *Id.* at 443.

17. *Id.* at 445–46 n. 2.

18. Hague v. C.I.O., 307 U.S. 496 (1939).

19. *Id.* at 521 n.

20. Madden v. Kentucky, 309 U.S. 83 (1940).

21. *Id.* at 90, 92–3.

22. Munn v. Illinois, 94 U.S. 113 (1877).

23. Chicago, Milwaukee and St. Paul Ry. v. Minnesota, 134 U.S. 418 (1890).

24. E. S. Corwin, *The Twilight of the Supreme Court*, pp. 77–78.

25. Hurtado v. California, 110 U.S. 516 (1884).

26. *Id.* at 541.

27. Maxwell v. Dow, 176 U.S. 581 (1900).

28. Twining v. New Jersey, 211 U.S. 78 (1908).

29. *Id.* at 110.

30. Chicago, B. and Q. R.R. v. Chicago, 166 U.S. 226 (1897).

31. Gitlow v. New York, 268 U.S. 652 (1925).

32 *Id.* at 666.

33. Fiske v. Kansas, 274 U.S. 380, 387 (1927).

34. Near v. Minnesota, 283 U.S. 697 (1931).

35. Civil Rights Cases, 109 U.S. 3 (1883).

36. *Id.* at 26.

37. Prigg v. Pennsylvania, 41 U.S. 539 (1842).

38. *Id.* at 615.

39. Civil Rights Cases, 109 U.S. 3, 53 (1883).

40. *Id.* at 7.

41. U.S. v. Cruikshank, 92 U.S. 542 (1876).

42. Civil Rights Cases, 109 U.S. 3, 50 (1883).

43. Hall v. de Cuir, 95 U.S. 485 (1877).

44. *Id.* at 485–90.

45. Louisville, N.O. and Texas Ry. v. Mississippi, 133 U.S. 587 (1890).

46. *Id.* at 591.

47. *Id.* at 594.

48. Plessy v. Ferguson, 163 U.S. 537 (1896).

49. *Id.* at 543.

50. *Id.* at 544.
51. *Id.* at 551.
52. *Id.* at 552.
53. *Id.* at 559.
54. McCabe v. Atchison, Topeka and Santa Fe Ry., 235 U.S. 151 (1914).
55. *Id.* at 161.
56. Buchanan v. Warley, 245 U.S. 60 (1917).
57. Corrigan v. Buckley, 271 U.S. 323 (1926).
58. *Id.* at 330–32.
59. Berea College v. Kentucky, 211 U.S. 45 (1908).
60. G. T. Peterson, "The Present Status of the Negro Separate School as Defined by Court Decisions," *Journal of Negro Education*, IV (1935), 364–65.
61. See Pauli Murray, ed., *States' Laws on Race and Color*, p. 14. See also M. R. Konvitz, *The Constitution and Civil Rights*, p. 230.
62. U.S. Office of Education, Statistical Circular No. 239, *Statistics of Education of Negroes, 1945–46* (Washington, D.C., 1948), Table 5; also Statistical Circular No. 286, *Negro Public Schools in States Maintaining Segregated School Systems, 1948–49* (Washington, D.C., 1951), Table 3.
63. Yick Wo v. Hopkins, 118 U.S. 356 (1886).
64. Truax v. Raich, 239 U.S. 33 (1915).
65. *Id.* at 41.
66. Strauder v. West Virginia, 100 U.S. 303 (1879).
67. *Id.* at 308–09.
68. Virginia v. Rives, 100 U.S. 313 (1879).
69. *Id.* at 323.
70. *Ex parte* Virginia, 100 U.S. 339 (1879).
71. Guinn v. U.S., 238 U.S. 347 (1915).
72. *Id.* at 367.
73. Nixon v. Herndon, 273 U.S. 536 (1927).
74. Nixon v. Condon, 286 U.S. 73 (1932).
75. Grovey v. Townsend, 295 U.S. 45 (1935).
76. See Carr, *op. cit.* (in note 1 *supra*), p. 57.
77. *Ex parte* Yarbrough, 110 U.S. 651 (1884).
78. U.S. v. Mosley, 238 U.S. 383 (1915).
79. U.S. v. Gradwell, 243 U.S. 476 (1917).

80. U.S. v. Bathgate, 246 U.S. 220 (1918).

81. Clyatt v. U.S., 197 U.S. 207 (1905).

82. *Id.* at 215.

83. C. W. Collins, *The Fourteenth Amendment and the States*, pp. 46–47.

84. *Ibid.*, p. 68.

85. *Ibid.*, p. 47.

86. Figures tabulated from list of cases in Felix Frankfurter, *Mr. Justice Holmes and the Supreme Court*, Appendix I, pp. 97–137.

87. Slaughter House Cases, 83 U.S. 36, 81 (1873).

88. Berea College v. Kentucky, 211 U.S. 45 (1908).

89. *Id.* at 54.

90. H. E. Flack, *The Adoption of the Fourteenth Amendment*, p. 94.

91. *Ibid.*, pp. 96–97.

92. *Ibid.*, p. 277.

93. Max Weber, "Class, Status, Party," in H. H. Gerth, and C. W. Mills, eds., *From Max Weber*, pp. 188–89.

94. R. M. MacIver, *Society, its Structure and Changes*, pp. 84–85.

95. Gunnar Myrdal, *An American Dilemma*, I, 667–68.

96. R. M. MacIver, *The More Perfect Union*, p. 25.

97. See *ibid.*, pp. 25–26.

98. Weber, *op. cit.* (in note 93 *supra*), p. 189.

99. *Ibid.*, pp. 405–9.

100. Myrdal, *op. cit.* (in note 95 *supra*), I, 106–7.

101. *Ibid.*, I, 60–61.

102. E. F. Waite, "The Negro in the Supreme Court," *Minnesota Law Review*, XXX (1946), 219–304.

103. Franklin Johnson, *The Development of State Legislation Concerning the Free Negro*, p. 45.

104. H. W. Odum, *Race and Rumors of Race*, Chapters VII, VIII.

105. J. W. De Forest, *A Union Officer in the Reconstruction*, p. 28.

106. See, e.g., B. H. Nelson, *The Fourteenth Amendment and the Negro Since 1920*, p. 167.

107. R. W. Logan, ed., *The Attitude of the Southern White Press toward Negro Suffrage, 1932–1940.*

108. C. S. Johnson, *Patterns of Segregation,* p. 159.

109. Weber, *op. cit.* (in note 93 *supra*), p. 190.

110. Plessy v. Ferguson, 163 U.S. 537, 543 (1896).

CHAPTER THREE

1. R. M. MacIver, *The More Perfect Union,* p. 169.

2. Smith v. Allwright, 321 U.S. 649, 665 (1944).

3. United States v. Butler, 297 U.S. 1, 62 (1936).

4. C. E. Hughes, *Addresses and Papers of Charles Evans Hughes,* p. 139.

5. Chambers v. Florida, 309 U.S. 227, 241 (1940).

6. United States v. Carolene Products, 304 U.S. 144, 152, 152 n. 4 (1938).

7. Hague v. C.I.O., 307 U.S. 496, 521 n. 1 (1939).

8. Colgate v. Harvey, 296 U.S. 404 (1935).

9. Madden v. Kentucky, 309 U.S. 83 (1940).

10. Edwards v. California, 314 U.S. 160 (1941).

11. *Id.* at 177.

12. *Ibid.*

13. *Id.* at 182.

14. Snowden v. Hughes, 321 U.S. 1, 7 (1944).

15. Hague v. C.I.O., 307 U.S. 496, 521 n. 1 (1939).

16. Adamson v. California, 332 U.S. 46, 61–62 (1947).

17. Edwin Borchard, "The Supreme Court and Private Rights," *Yale Law Journal,* XLVII (1938), 1063.

18. Munn v. Illinois, 94 U.S. 113 (1877) (due process does not prevent state from fixing minimum rates charged by company).

19. E.g., Chicago, Milwaukee and St. Paul R.R. v. Minnesota, 134 U.S. 418 (1890). See E. S. Corwin, *The Twilight of the Supreme Court,* pp. 77–78.

20. Railroad Commission v. Rowan and Nichols Oil Co., 310 U.S. 573, 581 (1940).

21. This process is described and analyzed in J. R. Green, "The Bill of Rights, the Fourteenth Amendment and the Supreme Court," *Michigan Law Review,* XLVI (1948), 869–910.

22. Betts v. Brady, 316 U.S. 455, 461–62 (1942).
23. *Id.* at 474, 476–77.
24. 332 U.S. 46 (1947).
25. 325 U.S. 91 (1945).
26. This section has recently been amended slightly and re-numbered. Compare 18 U.S.C. § 242 (1948) with 35 STAT. 1092 (1909), 18 U.S.C. § 52 (1946).
27. Virginia v. Rives, 100 U.S. 313 (1879), and *Ex parte* Virginia, 100 U.S. 339 (1897).
28. *Ex parte* Virginia, 100 U.S. 347 (1879).
29. Screws v. United States, 325 U.S. 91, 111 (1945).
30. See C. H. Pritchett, *The Roosevelt Court.*
31. Strauder v. West Virginia, 100 U.S. 303 (1879).
32. 294 U.S. 587 (1935).
33. *Id.* at 596.
34. Pierre v. Louisiana, 306 U.S. 354 (1939).
35. Smith v. Texas, 311 U.S. 128 (1940).
36. Hill v. Texas, 316 U.S. 400 (1942).
37. Akins v. Texas, 325 U.S. 398 (1945).
38. *Id.* at 410.
39. Patton v. Mississippi, 332 U.S. 463 (1947).
40. 295 U.S. 45 (1935).
41. United States v. Classic, 313 U.S. 299 (1941).
42. *Id.* at 307. Sections 51 and 52 have been renumbered. See 18 U.S.C. §§ 241, 242 (1948).
43. United States v. Classic, 313 U.S. 299, 314 (1941).
44. *Id.* at 330.
45. United States v. Gradwell, 243 U.S. 476, 488 (1917).
46. 321 U.S. 649 (1944).
47. *Id.* at 661.
48. *Id.* at 660.
49. *Id.* at 663.
50. *Id.* at 664.
51. *Id.* at 666.
52. *Ibid.*
53. Quoted in Note, "Negro Disenfranchisement—a Challenge to the Constitution," *Columbia Law Review,* XLVII (1947), 78.
54. 72 F. Supp. 516 (E.D.S.C. 1947).

55. *Id.* at 527.

56. *Id.* at 521.

57. Rice v. Elmore, 165 F. 2d 387 (4th Cir. 1947).

58. Rice v. Elmore, 333 U.S. 875 (1948).

59. Brown v. Baskin, 78 F. Supp. 933 (E.D.S.C. 1948).

60. *Id.* at 937.

61. *Id.* at 941–42.

62. 322 U.S. 385 (1944).

63. Francis Biddle, "Civil Rights and the Federal Law," in Carl Becker *et al.*, *Safeguarding Civil Liberties Today*, p. 137.

64. Davis v. Schnell, 81 F. Supp. 872 (S.D. Ala. 1949).

65. Schnell v. Davis, 336 U.S. 933 (1949).

66. L. P. Jackson, "Race and Suffrage in the South Since 1940," *New South*, III (1948, No. 5–6), 11.

67. *New York Times*, June 28, 1948, p. 12.

68. R. C. Weaver, *The Negro Ghetto*, p. 211.

69. Buchanan v. Warley, 245 U.S. 60 (1917).

70. Corrigan v. Buckley, 271 U.S. 323 (1926).

71. Weaver, *op. cit.* (in note 68 *supra*), p. 255.

72. *Brief for United States as Amicus Curiae*, p. 38, Shelley v. Kraemer and McGhee v. Sipes, 334 U.S. 1 (1948); Hurd v. Hodge and Urciolo v. Hodge, 334 U.S. 24 (1948).

73. Hurd v. Hodge and Urciolo v. Hodge, 334 U.S. 24 (1948).

74. Shelley v. Kraemer and McGhee v. Sipes, 334 U.S. 1 (1948).

75. *Id.* at 13–14.

76. Dorsey et al. v. Stuyvesant Town Corporation et al., 299 N.Y. 512, 87 N.E. (2d) 541 (1949).

77. Dorsey et al. v. Stuyvesant Town Corporation, 339 U.S. 981 (1950).

78. Mitchell v. United States, 313 U.S. 80 (1941).

79. Morgan v. Virginia, 328 U.S. 373 (1946).

80. *Id.* at 380–81.

81. Whiteside v. Southern Bus Lines, 177 F. 2d 949 (6th Cir. 1949).

82. Bob-Lo Excursion Co. v. Michigan, 333 U.S. 28 (1948).

83. *Id.* at 32, 35.

84. Henderson v. U.S., 339 U.S. 816 (1950).

85. *Id.* at 825.

86. Missouri, *ex rel.* Gaines v. Canada, 305 U.S. 337 (1938).

87. Sipuel v. Board of Education, 332 U.S. 631 (1948).

88. *New York Times,* January 13, 1948, p. 1.

89. Fisher v. Hurst, 333 U.S. 147, 150 (1948).

90. *New York Times,* February 1, 1948, p. 14.

91. Sweatt v. Painter, 339 U.S. 629, 631 (1950).

92. *Id.* at 633, 634, 636.

93. McLaurin v. Oklahoma, 339 U.S. 637, 641–42 (1950).

94. McCready v. Byrd, 73 Atl. (2d) 8 (Md.) (1950).

95. Byrd v. McCready, 340 U.S. 827 (1950).

96. Steele v. Louisville & Nashville R.R., 323 U.S. 192 (1944).

97. Betts v. Easley, 161 Kan. 459, 169 P. (2d) 831 (1946).

98. Railway Mail Association v. Corsi, 326 U.S. 88 (1945).

99. U.S. Department of the Interior, War Relocation Authority, *The Relocation Program* (Washington, D.C., 1946), pp. 1–8.

100. U.S. District Court, Western District of Washington, No. 498, oral opinion by Judge Black, April 15, 1942, quoted in full in H. R. Rep. No. 2124, 77th Cong., 2d Sess., Select Committee Investigating National Defense Migration, Fourth Interim Report, 1942, pp. 44, 47.

101. 320 U.S. 81 (1943).

102. *Id.* at 83.

103. *Id.* at 101.

104. *Id.* at 100.

105. *Id* at 111.

106. *Id* at 113.

107. 323 U.S. 214 (1944).

108. *Id.* at 218.

109. *Id.* at 216.

110. *Id.* at 225–26.

111. *Id.* at 233.

112. *Id.* at 243.

113. *Ex parte* Mitsuye Endo, 323 U.S. 283 (1944).

114. Oyama v. California, 332 U.S. 633 (1948).

115. *Id.* at 641–43.

116. Takahashi v. Fish and Game Commission, 334 U.S. 410 (1948).

117. *Id.* at 412.

118. *Id.* at 419, 421.

119. E. F. Waite, "The Debt of Constitutional Law to Jehovah's Witnesses," *Minnesota Law Review*, XXVIII (1944), 209.

120. Lovell v. Griffin, 303 U.S. 444 (1938).

121. Schneider v. Irvington, 308 U.S. 147 (1939).

122. Cox v. New Hampshire, 312 U.S. 569 (1941).

123. Jones v. Opelika, 316 U.S. 584 (1942).

124. Jones v. Opelika, 319 U.S. 103 (1943); Murdock v. Pennsylvania, 319 U.S. 105 (1943).

125. Jamison v. Texas, 318 U.S. 413 (1943).

126. Largent v. Texas, 318 U.S. 418 (1943).

127. Follett v. McCormick, 321 U.S. 573 (1944).

128. Marsh v. Alabama, 326 U.S. 501 (1946).

129. *Id.* at 506.

130. *Id.* at 507–8.

131. Minersville School District v. Gobitis, 310 U.S. 586 (1940).

132. West Virginia State Board of Education v. Barnette, 319 U.S. 624 (1943).

133. Taylor v. Mississippi, 319 U.S. 583 (1943).

CHAPTER FOUR

1. See the compilations in State of New York, Executive Department, State Commission Against Discrimination (SCAD), *Compilation of Laws Against Discrimination Because of Race, Creed, Color or National Origin* (New York, 1948); American Jewish Congress, Commission on Law and Social Action, *State Anti-Discrimination and Anti-Bias Laws* (New York, 1948); M. R. Konvitz, *The Constitution and Civil Rights*.

2. R. G. Weintraub, *How Secure These Rights? An Anti-Defamation League Survey*, p. 33.

3. See Morroe Berger, "Fair Employment Practice Legislation," *The Annals of the American Academy of Political and Social Science*, CCLXXV (1951), 34–40.

4. New York Laws 1945, c. 118; New York Executive Law, art. 12, §§ 125–36.

5. See Berger, *op. cit.* (in note 3 *supra*).

6. New York State, *Report of the New York State Temporary Commission Against Discrimination*, Legislative Document (1945) No. 6, pp. 15–20; also SCAD, *op. cit.* (in note 1 *supra*).

7. New York State, *op. cit.* (in note 6 *supra*), p. 21.

8. New York State War Council, Committee on Discrimination in Employment, *Report, March, 1941 to July, 1944* (1944), pp. 5, 118.

9. Phillips Bradley *et al.*, eds., *Fair Employment Legislation in New York State* (Albany, 1946), pp. 8–9.

10. New York State, *op. cit.* (in note 6 *supra*), p. 48.

11. Bradley, *op. cit.* (in note 9 *supra*), pp. 14–15.

12. New York State Legislature, "Debates on the Proposed Law Against Discrimination (Ives-Quinn Bill)," Assembly Chamber and Senate Chamber, February 28, 1945, p. 123.

13. *Ibid.*, p. 26.

14. H. Spitz, "The New York State Law Against Discrimination," *New York State Bar Association Bulletin*, XX (1948), 8.

15. U.S. Senate, 80th Congress, 1st Session, Hearings before a Subcommittee of the Committee on Labor and Public Welfare, on S. 984, *Anti-Discrimination in Employment* (1947), testimony of U.S. Senator Irving M. Ives, p. 6.

16. *Ibid.*, p. 338.

17. State of New York, Executive Department, State Commission Against Discrimination [SCAD], *Annual Report, January 1, 1948–December 31, 1948* (New York, 1949), p. 7. See also *Annual Report, January 1, 1946–December 31, 1946*, Legislative Document (1947) No. 53 (Albany, 1947), p. 7, and *Annual Report, January 1, 1947–December 31, 1947* (New York, 1948), p. 22. Hereafter SCAD's annual reports will be referred to by the period they cover; the report covering July 1, 1945, to June 27, 1946, is referred to as SCAD, *Annual Report*, 1945–46, and the others as SCAD, *Annual Report*, 1946, 1947, 1948, 1949, or 1950.

18. *Annual Report*, 1948, p. 9.

19. *Ibid.*, p. 8.

20. *Ibid.*, p. 12.

21. *Annual Report*, 1950, p. 71 (all references to the 1950 *Annual Report* of SCAD are to the mimeographed edition); *Annual Report*, 1949, p. 8.

22. *Annual Report*, 1948, p. 11; *Annual Report*, 1946, p. 7; *Annual Report*, 1947, p. 8. SCAD, "Memorandum Report of State Commission Against Discrimination Re Recommendations of Committee to Support the Ives-Quinn Law" (mimeographed, New York, November 5, 1948), p. 7.

23. *Annual Report*, 1948, pp. 10–11.

24. *Ibid.*, p. 11.

25. Interview with a commissioner, June 8, 1949.

26. R. K. Merton, "The Self-Fulfilling Prophecy," *The Antioch Review*, VII (1948), 210.

27. *Annual Report*, 1950, App. A, Table 1.

28. *Annual Report*, 1946, p. 7.

29. Interviews with commissioners, January 11 and 17, 1949.

30. SCAD, *Annual Report*, 1950, App. A, Table 7.

31. Testimony of Henry C. Turner (see note 15 *supra*), p. 324.

32. New York State Assembly, "Hearings on A.I. 883, Assembly Print 1138, by Mr. Ives Before the Assembly Ways and Means Committee and Senate Finance Committee," February 20, 1945, pp. 2, 14, 58 (copy in New York City office of SCAD).

33. *New York Times*, February 12, 1945, p. 32.

34. Testimony of Henry C. Turner (see note 15 *supra*), p. 324.

35. J. A. Davis, "How Management Can Integrate Negroes in War Industries," Committee on Discrimination in Employment, New York State War Council, 1942, p. 3.

36. Interview with a commissioner, January 14, 1949.

37. Statement of Henry C. Turner and Charles Garside (see note 15 *supra*), p. 327.

38. Anne Mather, "Report on the Experience of the Urban League, NAACP, and American Jewish Congress with the State Commission Against Discrimination" (mimeographed), Urban League of Greater New York, March 11, 1948, p. 6.

39. The Committee's report does not indicate how the figure of 485 was obtained for 1947. Our data in Table 4 show that SCAD during 1947 received 472 complaints and opened 137 investigations on its own initiative, and that it closed 297 complaint cases and 110 investigations.

40. SCAD, *Annual Report*, 1947, p. 10, and *Annual Report*, 1948, p. 83.

41. Gerhart Saenger and N. S. Gordon, "The Influence of Discrimination on Minority Group Members in its Relation to Attempts to Combat Discrimination," *The Journal of Social Psychology*, XXXI (1950), 97, 99 (Table 5).

42. SCAD's educational and publicity program are discussed in each *Annual Report:* for 1945–46, p. 13; for 1946, p. 14; for 1947, pp. 18–21; for 1948, pp. 68–74; for 1949, pp. 47–67; for 1950, pp. 80–99.

43. Saenger and Gordon, *op. cit.* (in note 41 *supra*), Table 11, p. 103.

44. *Ibid.*, Table 13, p. 105.

45. SCAD, "Memorandum Report" (cited in note 22 *supra*), p. 3.

46. *Annual Report*, 1948, App. A, Table 5; *Annual Report*, 1949, p. 16; *Annual Report*, 1950, p. 9.

47. Testimony of Henry C. Turner (see note 15 *supra*), pp. 329–31.

48. *Annual Report*, 1948, p. 21.

49. Mather, *op. cit.* (in note 38 *supra*), p. 8.

50. Committee to Support the Ives-Quinn Law, "Recommendations for the Consideration of the New York State Commission Against Discrimination" (mimeographed), April 1, 1948, p. 2, and a memorandum to SCAD, "Reasons in Support of the Proposals Submitted by our Committee to the State Commission Against Discrimination, April 1, 1948" (mimeographed), April 20, 1948, p. 2.

51. SCAD Release, May 11, 1948, "Address by Charles Garside . . . before . . . Committee to Support the Ives-Quinn Law . . . May 11, 1948," pp. 4–5. See also SCAD, "Memorandum Report" (cited in note 22 *supra*), pp. 3–5.

52. *Annual Report*, 1948, pp. 19–25.

53. *Annual Report*, 1947, p. 9.

54. All data on these discriminatory job orders were obtained either in personal interview on January 17, 1949, and March 30, 1950, with the liaison officer, State Director's Office of the New York State Employment Service, or from "Summary of Discriminatory Reports," issued quarterly by the New York State Employment Service, for the years 1945–49.

55. *Annual Report,* 1948, p. 78.

56. New York State Department of Labor, Bureau of Research and Statistics of the Division of Placement and Unemployment Insurance, "Operations, Employment Service and Unemployment Insurance" (monthly), 1949.

57. *Annual Report,* 1950, App. A, Tables 4 and 8.

58. *Ibid.,* App. A, Table 7, and computations based on Table 8.

59. Testimony of John E. Rankin (see note 15 *supra*), p. 697.

60. *Annual Report,* 1946, pp. 24–25; *Annual Report,* 1949, pp. 26–27.

61. American Jewish Congress, Commission on Law and Social Action, "Survey of Private Employment Agencies," April, 1947, pp. 2–3 (on file at the New York office of the American Jewish Congress). See also *Law and Social Action,* II (1947), 48.

62. *Law and Social Action,* IV (1949), 104.

63. S.I. 1817, Print 1968, and A.I. 1869, Print 1958.

64. *Annual Report,* 1949, pp. 83–84.

65. *Annual Report,* 1950, pp. 59–60.

66. *Ibid.,* pp. 130–31.

67. *Annual Report,* 1949, pp. 68–69.

68. *Annual Report,* 1950, pp. 120–21.

69. *Ibid.,* App. A, Tables 4, 7, 8.

70. *Annual Report,* 1948, pp. 33, 35–36.

71. *Ibid.*

72. Interview with a commissioner, January 17, 1949. *Annual Report,* 1950, pp. 103–4.

73. *Annual Report,* 1948, p. 82.

74. Testimony of Charles Garside (see note 15 *supra*), p. 344.

75. *Annual Report,* 1948, p. 83.

76. SCAD Release, May 11, 1948 (cited in note 51 *supra*), p. 9.

77. SCAD, "Rulings," June 1, 1946.

78. *Annual Report,* 1948, Chapter III; 1949, pp. 21–46; 1950, pp. 27–76.

79. *Annual Report,* 1948, p. 42.

80. SCAD, "Rulings," June 1, 1946, p. 1.

81. *Annual Report,* 1948, p. 42.

82. *Ibid.,* p. 43.

83. *Ibid.,* p. 44.

84. *Annual Report*, 1948, p. 45.

85. *Ibid.*, p. 46.

86. *Ibid.*

87. *Ibid.*, p. 47.

88. *Ibid.*

89. *Ibid.*, p. 48, and *Annual Report*, 1950, p. 68.

90. *Annual Report*, 1948, p. 48.

91. *Ibid.*

92. *Ibid.*

93. *Ibid.*, p. 54, but see also *Annual Report*, 1950, pp. 64–66.

94. SCAD, "Memorandum Report" (cited in note 22 *supra*), pp. 2–3; *Annual Report*, 1948, p. 18.

95. *Annual Report*, 1948, p. 18.

96. E. A. Carter, "The New York Commission Succeeds," *Interracial Review*, XX (1947), 167.

97. U.S. Committee on Fair Employment Practice, *Final Report, June 28, 1946* (Washington, D.C., 1947), p. ix.

98. *Annual Report*, 1945–46, p. 13.

99. *Annual Report*, 1947, pp. 18–19.

100. SCAD, "Memorandum Report" (cited in note 22 *supra*), pp. 8–9.

101. *Annual Report*, 1948, p. 10.

102. SCAD, "Memorandum Report" (cited in note 22 *supra*), p. 7.

103. *Annual Report*, 1948, p. 84.

104. *New York Times*, February 27, 1946, p. 6.

105. *New York Post*, March 26, 1946, p. 20.

106. *New York Times*, February 2, 1947, p. 44.

107. *Ibid.*, April 11, 1947, p. 19.

108. *Ibid.*, April 5, 1946, p. 19.

109. *Ibid.*, January 15, 1947, p. 34.

110. Testimony of Henry C. Turner (see note 15 *supra*), p. 333.

111. Testimony of Charles Garside (see note 15 *supra*), p. 339.

112. Committee to Support the Ives-Quinn Law, "New York State Law Against Discrimination—an Appraisal and a Program" (mimeographed, undated [ca. May, 1948]), p. 2; also Mather, *op. cit.* (in note 38 *supra*).

113. Committee to Support the Ives-Quinn Law, "Recommendations for the Consideration" (cited in note 50 *supra*), p. 1.

114. See note 50 *supra*.

115. "Memorandum Report" (cited in note 22 *supra*).

116. *New York Times*, February 20, 1949, p. 48.

117. *Annual Report*, 1948, p. 63; also, *Law and Social Action*, I (1946), 20, 24.

118. *Annual Report*, 1948, p. 47; *Law and Social Action*, I (1946), 23, II (1947), 49. See also Note, "Application of the Anti-Discrimination Law to University Employment Agencies," *Columbia Law Review*, XLVII (1947), 674–75.

119. *Annual Report*, 1948, p. 48; *Law and Social Action*, I (1946), 8, 20, 33.

120. *Law and Social Action*, I (1946), 35, II (1947), 68; SCAD, Press Release, September 23, 1946.

121. *New York Times*, February 20, 1949, p. 48.

122. SCAD Release, May 11, 1948 (cited in note 51 *supra*), pp. 8–10; SCAD, "Memorandum Report" (cited in note 22 *supra*), pp. 10–11.

123. *Annual Report*, 1950, pp. 3, 96, 111–15.

124. Determined by examination of file of publicity releases, New York City Office of SCAD, January 25, 1949.

125. *Annual Report*, 1945–46, pp. 10–12; 1946, p. 27; 1947, p. 20; 1949, p. 49; 1950, p. 81.

126. *Annual Report*, 1945–46, p. 9.

127. *Annual Report*, 1948, p. 40; 1949, pp. 73–74; 1950, pp. 116–20.

128. New York City Council of SCAD, *Minutes*, June 12, September 11, October 9, November 13, 1947.

129. *Ibid.*, December 11, 1947.

130. *Ibid.*, June 10, 1948.

131. *Ibid.*, October 14, 1948.

132. *Annual Report*, 1947, p. 32.

133. New York City Council of SCAD, *Minutes*, 1947, 1948.

134. Roderick Stephens, "The Functions of Councils Under the Provisions of the Ives-Quinn Act" (typewritten ms. in file at office of Roderick Stephens, New York City).

135. New York City Council of SCAD, *Minutes*, January 8, 1948.

136. *Annual Report*, 1945–46, p. 9. See also note 133 *supra*.

137. Letter from chairman of SCAD, December 28, 1948, to Mr. Roderick Stephens, member of New York City Council of SCAD.

138. New York City Council of SCAD, *Minutes*, December 9, 1948.

139. *Annual Report*, 1945–46, p. 12.

140. See note 137 *supra*.

141. Address at annual meeting of National Probation and Parole Association, Atlantic City, N.J., May 11, 1951.

142. Urban League of Greater New York, Release, October 4, 1948, pp. 2–4.

143. *Annual Report*, 1946, p. 7.

144. *Annual Report*, 1947, p. 10.

145. New York State, *op. cit.* (in note 6 *supra*), pp. 30–31.

146. New York State Legislature, "Debates" (cited in note 12 *supra*), p. 124.

147. For a brief explanation and bibliography of the failure of antidiscrimination "educational" propaganda, see R. K. Merton, "Discrimination and the American Creed," in R. M. MacIver, ed., *Discrimination and National Welfare*, p. 118; and R. M. Williams, Jr., *The Reduction of Intergroup Tensions*, pp. 64–65.

148. Letter from Governor Thomas E. Dewey to U.S. Representative H. Alexander Smith (Rep., N.J.), dated December 21, 1945, quoted in *Law and Social Action*, I (1946), 8.

149. Testimony of Charles Garside (see note 15 *supra*), p. 344.

150. Testimony of Henry C. Turner (see note 15 *supra*), pp. 332–33.

151. *Annual Report*, 1950, p. 116.

152. Davis, *op. cit.* (in note 35 *supra*), *passim*.

153. U.S. Committee on Fair Employment Practice, *First Report, July 1943–December 1944* (Washington, D.C., 1945), p. 77, and *Final Report, June 28, 1946* (Washington, D.C., 1947), pp. xv, 4.

154. Statement of Henry C. Turner and Charles Garside (see note 15 *supra*), p. 327.

155. E. Roper, *A Study of Anti-Minority Sentiment in the United States*, p. 17, quoted in Weintraub, *op. cit.* (in note 2 *supra*), p. 42.

CHAPTER FIVE

1. R. M. MacIver, *The Web of Government*, p. 77.
2. See A. A. Schiller, "Lawgivers," in *Encyclopaedia of the Social Sciences*, IX, 275; E. Durkheim, *The Division of Labor in Society*, p. 92.
3. G. H. Mead, "The Psychology of Punitive Justice," *The American Journal of Sociology*, XXIII (1918), 587, 590.
4. Roscoe Pound, *Social Control through Law*, pp. 54–61.
5. Aristotle *A Treatise on Government* III. xvi (Everyman's ed., p. 102). Spinoza, *Tractatus Theologico-Politicus*, Chapter XVII. Montesquieu, *The Spirit of Laws*, Book XII, Chapter 4, and Book XXVI, Chapters 1, 2. Kant, *The Philosophy of Law*, pp. 20–21, 25. Bentham, *Principles of Morals and Legislation*, Chapter XVII, Nos. 15, 19 (in E. A. Burtt, ed., *The English Philosophers from Bacon to Mill*, pp. 850–51). John Stuart Mill, *On Liberty*, Chapter IV (Everyman's ed., p. 140). T. H. Green, *Lectures on the Principles of Political Obligation*, pp. 34, 36. A. V. Dicey, *Lectures on the Relation between Law and Public Opinion in England during the Nineteenth Century*, p. 138. R. M. MacIver, *The Modern State*, pp. 19–21, 153, 157, and *Community*, p. 33. M. R. Cohen, *The Faith of a Liberal*, pp. 15–16. Roscoe Pound, "Law and Morals," *North Carolina Law Review*, XXIII (1945), 191, and *Social Control through Law*, pp. 55–59.
6. Jeremy Bentham, *The Theory of Legislation*, p. 60.
7. F. S. Cohen, *Ethical Systems and Legal Ideals*, p. 272.
8. S. Polier, "Law, Conscience and Society," *Lawyers Guild Review*, VI (1946), 491.
9. P. F. Lazarsfeld and R. K. Merton, "Mass Communication, Popular Taste and Organized Social Action," in L. Bryson, ed., *The Communication of Ideas*, p. 103.
10. Herbert Spencer, *The Principles of Sociology*, II, 3–12; W. G. Sumner, *Folkways*, §§ 61–63.

11. B. W. Doyle, *The Etiquette of Race Relations in the South,* *passim.*

12. Gunnar Myrdal, *An American Dilemma,* II, 1032, 1048–55. R. M. MacIver, *The More Perfect Union,* p. 279 and Chapter VII. C. McWilliams, "Race Discrimination and the Law," *Science and Society,* IX (1945), 3–24. W. Maslow, "The Law and Race Relations," *The Annals of the American Academy of Political and Social Science,* CCXLIV (1946), 75–81.

13. Walter Lippmann, *Public Opinion,* p. 93.

14. Doyle, *op. cit.* (in note 11 *supra*), p. 135.

15. Plessy v. Ferguson, 163 U.S. 537, 551–52 (1896).

16. *Id.* at 560.

17. Strauder v. West Virginia, 100 U.S. 303, 308 (1879). (Emphasis not in original.)

18. Roscoe Pound, *The Task of Law,* p. 25.

19. *Ibid.,* p. 65.

20. Arnold Rose, " 'You Can't Legislate Against Prejudice'— Or Can You?" *Common Ground,* IX (1949, No. 3), 61–67.

21. Sipuel v. Board of Education, 332 U.S. 631 (1948).

22. *New York Herald Tribune,* January 31, 1948, p. 13, and *New York Times,* February 3, 1948, p. 27.

23. *New York Times,* February 1, 1948, p. 14.

24. *Ibid.,* October 12, 1948, p. 52.

25. National Association for the Advancement of Colored People and American Jewish Congress, *Civil Rights in the United States in 1948: a Balance Sheet of Group Relations* (New York, 1949), p. 24.

26. *New York Herald Tribune,* November 19, 1948, p. 14.

27. *New York Times,* December 3, 1948, p. 19.

28. Dicey, *op. cit.* (in note 5 *supra*), p. 465.

29. R. M. Williams, Jr., *The Reduction of Intergroup Tensions,* pp. 10–16, 71 (item 80); also MacIver, *op. cit.* (in note 12 *supra*), pp. 84–86, 240–42.

30. M. Horkheimer, "Sociological Background of the Psychoanalytic Approach," in Ernst Simmel, ed., *Anti-Semitism, a Social Disease,* pp. 4–5. See also "Research Project on Anti-Semitism," in *Studies in Philosophy and Social Science,* IX (1941), 134–37.

31. R. K. Merton, "Discrimination and the American Creed," in

R. M. MacIver, ed., *Discrimination and National Welfare*, pp. 103–10.

32. *Ibid.*, p. 121.

33. MacIver, *op. cit.* (in note 12 *supra*), pp. 195–200, and L. J. Stone's "Memorandum on Types of Prejudice," *ibid.*, Appendix Four, pp. 285–87.

34. N. W. Ackerman and M. Jahoda, "The Dynamic Basis of Anti-Semitic Attitudes," *The Psychoanalytic Quarterly*, XVII (1948), 242. See also Ackerman and Jahoda, "Toward a Dynamic Interpretation of Anti-Semitic Attitudes," *The American Journal of Orthopsychiatry*, XVIII (1948), 164, and *Anti-Semitism and Emotional Disorder*, Chapter III.

35. MacIver, *op. cit.* (in note 12 *supra*), pp. 53–61.

36. *Ibid.*, pp. 199–200.

37. Merton, *op. cit.* (in note 31 *supra*), p. 107.

38. *Ibid.*, p. 117.

39. *Ibid.*, p. 108.

40. *Ibid.*, p. 124.

41. T. W. Adorno, E. Frenkel-Brunswik, *et al.*, *The Authoritarian Personality*, especially Part II.

42. E. L. Hartley, *Problems in Prejudice*, p. 62. See also E. Hartley and R. E. Hartley, "Tolerance and Personality Traits," in T. M. Newcomb and E. Hartley, eds., *Readings in Social Psychology*, p. 530.

43. E. Frenkel-Brunswik, D. J. Levinson, and R. N. Sanford, "The Anti-Democratic Personality," in Newcomb and Hartley, eds., *op. cit.* (in note 42 *supra*), p. 540. See also, Adorno, Frenkel-Brunswik, *et al.*, *op. cit.* (in note 41 *supra*), p. 402.

44. E. Frenkel-Brunswik and R. N. Sanford, "Some Personality Factors in Anti-Semitism," *The Journal of Psychology*, XX (1945), 285. See also, Simmel, ed., *op. cit.* (in note 30 *supra*), p. 117; Adorno, Frenkel-Brunswik, *et al.*, *op. cit.* (in note 41 *supra*), p. 429.

45. E. Frenkel-Brunswik, "A Study of Prejudice in Children," *Human Relations*, I (1948), 302.

46. Frenkel-Brunswik and Sanford, in Simmel, ed., *op. cit.* (in note 30 *supra*), pp. 107–8.

47. Ackerman and Jahoda, "The Dynamic Basis of Anti-Semitic

Attitudes," *The Psychoanalytic Quarterly*, XVII (1948), 244.

48. Frenkel-Brunswik and Sanford, in Simmel, ed., *op. cit.* (in note 30 *supra*), pp. 112–15.

49. Ackerman and Jahoda, "Toward a Dynamic Interpretation of Anti-Semitic Attitudes," *The American Journal of Orthopsychiatry*, XVIII (1948), 168.

50. Frenkel-Brunswik, *op. cit.* (in note 45 *supra*), p. 306.

51. *Ibid.*, pp. 251–52, and *Anti-Semitism and Emotional Disorder*, pp. 29–32.

52. Frenkel-Brunswik, *op. cit.* (in note 45 *supra*), p. 298.

53. G. Saenger and E. Gilbert, "Customer Reactions to the Integration of Negro Sales Personnel," *International Journal of Opinion and Attitude Research*, IV (1950), 74, Table 6.

54. *Ibid.*, Table 5, p. 74.

55. *Ibid.*, Table 1, p. 61.

56. See P. F. Lazarsfeld, "Some Remarks on the Role of Mass Media in So-Called Tolerance Propaganda," *The Journal of Social Issues*, III (1947, No. 3), pp. 18–19.

57. Ackerman and Jahoda, *op. cit.* (in note 47 *supra*), p. 260.

58. G. Murphy and R. Likert, *Public Opinion and the Individual*, p. 136. Frenkel-Brunswik and Sanford, in Simmel, ed., *op. cit.* (in note 30 *supra*), p. 104. Ackerman and Jahoda, *op. cit.* (in note 47 *supra*), p. 259. E. L. Horowitz, "Development of Attitudes Toward Negroes," in Newcomb and Hartley, eds., *op. cit.* (in note 42 *supra*), p. 517. A. Rose, *Studies in Reduction of Prejudice*, pp. 11–14.

59. T. M. Newcomb, "Autistic Hostility and Social Reality," *Human Relations*, I (1947), 69, 80. See also G. H. Mead, "The Genesis of the Self and Social Control," *International Journal of Ethics*, XXXV (1925), 274–77.

60. Rose, *op. cit.* (in note 58 *supra*), pp. 8–11. MacIver, *op. cit.* (in note 12 *supra*), pp. 233–38. Williams, *op. cit.* (in note 29 *supra*), pp. 70–71. Pertinent reports on a study of two interracial housing communities, directed by R. K. Merton, are given in Lazarsfeld, *op. cit.* (in note 56 *supra*), pp. 20–21.

61. Kurt Lewin, *Resolving Social Conflicts*, pp. 66–68. MacIver, *op. cit.* (in note 12 *supra*), pp. 224–25.

62. G. H. Mead, "The Working Hypothesis in Social Reform," *The American Journal of Sociology*, V (1899), 370.

63. MacIver, *op. cit.* (in note 12 *supra*), pp. 72–73, 89.

64. Dicey, *op. cit.* (in note 5 *supra*), pp. 301–2.

65. John Dewey, *Liberalism and Social Action*, pp. 61–62. See also Williams, *op. cit.* (in note 29 *supra*), p. 46.

66. Hadley Cantril, *Gauging Public Opinion*, p. 228.

67. Saenger and Gilbert, *op. cit.* (in note 53 *supra*), p. 69.

68. R. T. La Piere, "Attitudes vs. Actions," *Social Forces*, XIII (1934), 230–37.

69. Saenger and Gilbert, *op. cit.* (in note 53 *supra*), Table 2 and pp. 58–62.

70. *Ibid.*, p. 69.

71. *Ibid.*, p. 63.

72. Gerhart Saenger, "Customer Reactions to the Integration of Negro Sales Personnel" (paper read at the 56th Annual Meeting of the American Psychological Association in Boston, September 8, 1948), p. 2.

73. See New York State Commission Against Discrimination, *Annual Report*, 1948 (New York, 1949), p. 11; C. K. Simon, "Causes and Cure of Discrimination," *The New York Times Magazine*, May 29, 1949, p. 36.

74. Paul Vinogradoff, *Custom and Right*, p. 21. Pound, *op. cit.* (in note 4 *supra*), p. 18. Walter Bagehot, *Physics and Politics*, new ed., pp. 203, 213. Robert Redfield, *The Folk Culture of Yucatan*, pp. 346-47. Georg Simmel, "The Number of Members as Determining the Sociological Form of the Group," *The American Journal of Sociology*, VIII (1902), 19. Karl Mannheim, *Man and Society in an Age of Reconstruction*, p. 276. L. Wirth, "Urbanism as a Way of Life," *The American Journal of Sociology*, XLIV (1938), p. 11.

75. See J. S. Plant, *Personality and the Cultural Pattern*, pp. 132–33, 153–54.

76. Durkheim, *op. cit.* (in note 2 *supra*), pp. 298–99.

77. Pound, *op. cit.* (in note 4 *supra*), pp. 20–25. MacIver, *op. cit.* (in note 1 *supra*), pp. 65–66.

78. MacIver, *ibid.*, p. 79.

BIBLIOGRAPHY

The following bibliography lists only materials that are not given full citation in the reference notes.

Ackerman, N. W., and M. Jahoda. Anti-Semitism and Emotional Disorder. ("Studies in Prejudice," sponsored by the American Jewish Committee, No. 5.) New York, 1950.

Adorno, T. W., F. Frenkel-Brunswik, et al. The Authoritarian Personality. ("Studies in Prejudice," sponsored by the American Jewish Committee, No. 3.) New York, 1950.

Bagehot, Walter. Physics and Politics. New ed. London, n.d.

Bentham, Jeremy. The Theory of Legislation. London, 1931.

Biddle, Francis. "Civil Rights and the Federal Law," in Carl Becker et al., Safeguarding Civil Liberty Today. Ithaca, 1945.

Bunche, R. J. "The Political Status of the Negro." Special research memorandum prepared for the Carnegie Corporation study of the Negro in the United States, in the Schomburg Collection of the New York Public Library.

Burtt, E. A., ed. The English Philosophers from Bacon to Mill. New York, 1939.

Cantril, Hadley. Gauging Public Opinion. Princeton, 1944.

Carr, R. K. Federal Protection of Civil Rights. Ithaca, 1947.

Cohen, F. S. Ethical Systems and Legal Ideals. New York, 1933.

Cohen, M. R. The Faith of a Liberal. New York, 1946.

Collins, C. W. The Fourteenth Amendment and the States. Boston, 1912.

Corwin, E. S. The Twilight of the Supreme Court. New Haven, 1934.

Davis, W. W. "The Federal Enforcement Acts," in Studies in Southern History and Politics. New York, 1914.

De Forest, J. W. A Union Officer in the Reconstruction. New Haven, 1948.

Dewey, John. Liberalism and Social Action. New York, 1935.

Dicey, A. V. Lectures on the Relation between Law and Public

Opinion in England during the Nineteenth Century. 2d ed. London, 1914.

Doyle, B. W. The Etiquette of Race Relations in the South. Chicago, 1937.

Durkheim, E. The Division of Labor in Society. Glencoe, 1947.

Encyclopaedia of the Social Sciences. 15 vols. New York, 1933.

Flack, H. E. The Adoption of the Fourteenth Amendment. Baltimore, 1908.

Fleming, W. L. Documentary History of Reconstruction. 2 vols. Cleveland, 1906–7.

Frankfurter, Felix. Mr. Justice Holmes and the Supreme Court. Cambridge, Mass., 1938.

Green, T. H. Lectures on the Principles of Political Obligation. London, 1937.

Hacker, L. M. The Shaping of the American Tradition. New York, 1947.

Hartley, E. L. Problems in Prejudice. New York, 1946.

Hughes, C. E. Addresses and Papers of Charles Evans Hughes. New York, 1908.

Johnson, C. S. Patterns of Segregation. New York, 1943.

Johnson, C. S., and associates. To Stem This Tide: a Survey of Racial Tension Areas in the United States. Boston and Chicago, 1943.

Johnson, Franklin. The Development of State Legislation Concerning the Free Negro. New York, 1918.

Kant, Immanuel. The Philosophy of Law. Edinburgh, 1887.

Kesselman, L. C. The Social Politics of FEPC. Chapel Hill, 1948.

Konvitz, M. R. The Constitution and Civil Rights. New York, 1947.

Lazarsfeld, P. F., and R. K. Merton. "Mass Communication, Popular Taste and Organized Social Action," in L. Bryson, ed., The Communication of Ideas. New York, 1948.

Lewin, Kurt. Resolving Social Conflicts. New York, 1948.

Lippmann, Walter. Public Opinion. New York, 1946.

Logan, R. W., ed. The Attitude of the Southern White Press toward Negro Suffrage, 1932–1940. Washington, D.C., 1940.

MacIver, R. M. Community. 3rd ed. London, 1924.

——— The Modern State. London, 1926.

—— The More Perfect Union. New York, 1948.

—— Society, its Structure and Changes. New York, 1931.

—— The Web of Government. New York, 1947.

Mannheim, Karl. Man and Society in an Age of Reconstruction. New York, 1940.

Merton, R. K. "Discrimination and the American Creed," in R. M. MacIver, ed. Discrimination and National Welfare. New York, 1949.

Murphy, G., and R. Likert. Public Opinion and the Individual. New York, 1938.

Murray, Pauli, ed., States' Laws on Race and Color. Cincinnati, 1951.

Myrdal, Gunnar. An American Dilemma: The Negro Problem and Modern Democracy. 2 vols. New York, 1944.

National Association for the Advancement of Colored People and American Jewish Congress. Civil Rights in the United States: a Balance Sheet of Group Relations. New York, 1948–1951 (an annual publication).

Nelson, B. H. The Fourteenth Amendment and the Negro Since 1920. Washington, D.C., 1946.

Newcomb, T. M., and E. L. Hartley, eds. Readings in Social Psychology. New York, 1947.

Northrup, H. R. Organized Labor and the Negro. New York, 1944.

Odum, H. W. Race and Rumors of Race. Chapel Hill, 1943.

Ottley, Roi. Black Odyssey. New York, 1948.

Plant, J. S. Personality and the Cultural Pattern. New York, 1947.

Pound, Roscoe. Social Control through Law. New Haven, 1942.

—— The Task of Law. Lancaster, Pa., 1944.

Pritchett, C. H. The Roosevelt Court. New York, 1948.

Redfield, Robert. The Folk Culture of Yucatan. Chicago, 1941.

Roosevelt, F. D. The Public Papers and Addresses of Franklin D. Roosevelt. 5 vols. New York, 1938.

Rose, Arnold. Studies in Reduction of Prejudice. Chicago, 1947.

Ross, Malcolm. All Manner of Men. New York, 1948.

Simmel, Ernst. Anti-Semitism, a Social Disease. New York, 1946.

Spencer, Herbert. The Principles of Sociology. 3 vols. New York, 1888.

Stephenson, G. T. Race Distinctions in American Law. New York, 1910.

Sterner, Richard. The Negro's Share. New York, 1943.

Vance, R. B. All These People. Chapel Hill, 1945.

Vinogradoff, Paul. Custom and Right. Oslo, 1925.

Weaver, R. C. The Negro Ghetto. New York, 1948.

Weaver, R. C. Negro Labor. New York, 1946.

Weber, Max. From Max Weber. Ed. by H. H. Gerth and C. W. Mills. New York, 1946.

Weintraub, R. G. How Secure These Rights? An Anti-Defamation League Survey. New York, 1949.

White, Walter. A Man Called White. New York, 1948.

Williams, R. M., Jr. The Reduction of Intergroup Tensions. New York, 1947.

LIST OF CASES

THE page references to this book listed below are to the text only, not to the Notes. Many cases are discussed in the text without being mentioned by name; the names of such cases may be ascertained by looking up in the Notes the citations indicated in the text.

INDEX

fronted with legal necessity of hiring, 131; integration into N.Y. department stores, 132, 183, 188 ff.; freest occupational opportunities, 134; handicaps to job progress, 139, 145 f.; admission to N.Y. medical institutions' staffs, 159; employment gains in N.Y.: agencies responsible, 164 f.; *see also entries under* Constitution: Amendments; Law Against Discrimination, N.Y.; Supreme Court

Newcomb, T. M., and E. L. Hartley, 185

New Deal, 31, 32; government given more power under, 8, 14, 15; alliance of Southern Democrats, 15, 19; effect of federal programs upon Negroes, 19-23

New Hampshire, 106

New Jersey, 106, 109

New Mexico, 35, 55

New Orleans, *Slaughter House Cases*, 40

New York City, Commissioners, 141, 159; Mayor, 159

New York City, riots, 18

New York City Council of SCAD, 158

New York Society for the Maintenance of Public Decency, 152

New York Society for the Suppression of Vice, 152

New York State, a pioneer in antidiscrimination laws, 109; fields covered, 110; *for agencies and laws of, see their titles, e.g.,* Apprenticeship Council; Employment Service; Law Against Discrimination; etc.

New York State Bar Association, 114

New York State Chamber of Commerce, 131

New York Telephone Company, 138

North Carolina, 9, 16, 55

Northrup, Herbert, 25

Odum, H. W., 16, 66

Office of Education, U.S., 55

Oklahoma, 16, 21, 54, 55; constitutional amendment requiring literacy test, 58-60

Oklahoma, University of, Court's ruling re admission of Negroes, 95 ff., 176

Oregon, 29

Oyama, Kajiro, and son, 103

Pennsylvania, 107

Peonage, outlawed, 13, 39, 60

Permits and licenses, 106

Persuasion, *see* Conciliation

Population, urban, of the U.S., 17

Pound, Roscoe, 171, 175

Precedent, extent to which followed by Court, 72

Preemployment discrimination inquiries, 128, 148, 150

Prejudice and discrimination, advocated approach to, 111, 116; extent to which law can control, 120, 170-93 *passim* (*see also* Law); typologies, 177 ff.

Prejudiced personality and social control, 177-86

President's Commission on Higher Education, 3, 33

President's Committee on Civil Rights, 32, 33

President's Committee on Equality of Treatment and Opportunity in the Armed Services, 27

Primaries, Southern, 26, 58 ff., 82-89; *see also* Voting

Privileges and immunities clause, Court's rulings and interpretations, 40-45, 60, 75-77; when made inoperative: not yet revived, 75

Property, restrictive agreements re occupancy, 54, 89 f.

Property rights, raised to preferred position by Court, 37, 44, 45 ff., 60 f., 73

Psychologists, typologies of prejudice and discrimination, 177 ff.

Public, effectiveness of law dependent upon, 3 f.

Public accommodation, exclusion